D0429031

DUELING WITH KINGS

HIGH STAKES, KILLER SHARKS,
AND THE GET-RICH PROMISE OF
DAILY FANTASY SPORTS

DANIEL BARBARISI

TOUCHSTONE
NEW YORK   LONDON   TORONTO   SYDNEY   NEW DELHI

TOUCHSTONE

An Imprint of Simon & Schuster, Inc.
1230 Avenue of the Americas
New York, NY 10020

First Touchstone hardcover edition March 2017

TOUCHSTONE and colophon are registered
trademarks of Simon & Schuster, Inc.

For information about special discounts for bulk purchases,
please contact Simon & Schuster Special Sales at
1-866-506-1949 or business@simonandschuster.com.

The Simon & Schuster Speakers Bureau can bring authors to your live event. For
more information, or to book an event, contact the Simon & Schuster Speakers
Bureau at 866-248-3049 or visit our website at www.simonspeakers.com.

Interior design by Jill Putorti

Manufactured in the United States of America

10 9 8 7 6 5 4 3 2 1

Library of Congress Cataloging-in-Publication Data

Names: Barbarisi, Daniel, author.
Title: Dueling with kings : high stakes, killer sharks, and the get-rich
    promise of daily fantasy sports / Daniel Barbarisi.
Description: New York : Touchstone, 2017.
Identifiers: LCCN 2016052642 | ISBN 9781501146176 (hardback) | ISBN
    9781501146183 (paperback)
Subjects: LCSH: Fantasy sports. | BISAC: GAMES / Fantasy Sports. | BUSINESS &
    ECONOMICS / Entrepreneurship. | GAMES / Gambling / Sports.
Classification: LCC GV1202.F35 B37 2017 | DDC 793.93—dc23 LC record available at
    https://lccn.loc.gov/2016052642

ISBN 978-1-5011-4617-6
ISBN 978-1-5011-4619-0 (ebook)

For my dad, who would have found all of this funny

DUELING
WITH KINGS

PROLOGUE

The bass thumps so deeply that I can hardly hear Rob Gomes as he pours his heart out.

"They think I can't be a pro," he spits, rattling off the players who won him a million dollars. "I know the game, bro: Jonas Gray? Point-six percent owned. The Bucs D? That was because I know the game. I've played it all my life."

It's the day before the biggest day in the history of Daily Fantasy Sports—NFL kickoff, week one, 2015—and Gomes and I are standing by the pool, close enough that I'm getting splashed by the couples drunkenly staging chicken fights in the water. All around us, scenes straight out of MTV's old spring break specials are under way. This is Miami, after all, and at the posh Fontainebleau Hotel, pretty much anything goes.

Drinks are flowing, girls in barely there bikinis are gyrating, and chiseled guys with haircuts lifted from pro soccer stars are backflipping into the water to attract attention. Gomes, whose Twitter handle is "Big BoOTy Bob," fits right in with this crowd—hell, he owns it—but right now, he's only feeling what he lacks: the respect of the professional DFS players.

If you turned on a television set anytime in August or September of 2015, you'd recognize Rob Gomes. With his brother, Dave, he was one of the first men to win a million dollars playing Daily Fantasy Sports, carting away one of those giant cardboard checks for winning DraftKings' Fantasy Football Millionaire Maker competition in the fall of 2014. Their success was immortalized in a DraftKings commercial that aired over and over and over as the company sought to promote its brand.

Gomes answers all the obvious questions before they are even asked, with the practiced staccato of someone who has walked this conversational road before. Yes, his antics in the commercial are real—"That's not faked. That's raw emotion, bro. You can't fake that"—yes, the commercials get him recognized—"That's why I got the man-bun, so I can be incognito"—and yes, the commercials get him girls. "We won a million bucks, you know?" Gomes shrugs.

The Gomes brothers are something of a phenomenon at this pool party. For a pair of nobodies straight out of the Boston seen in Ben Affleck movies, this seems like the life. They're rich, they have women, they have D-list celebrity fame. DraftKings even chartered a private jet to fly the Gomes boys, some pals, a gaggle of pros, and a few lucky regular guys here to Miami for this celebration, a two-day blowout party to kick off the football season. The drinks flowed immediately, and the Gomes brothers camped out by the pool to work on their lineups and gaze at the ladies, soon settling in with a bachelorette party. They have achieved every bro's dream.

Yet Rob Gomes is restless. He wants what he doesn't have: to become a pro, to make a full-time life out of DFS.

Watching all this unfold, I can understand the feeling. I'm two months into my quest to join the ranks of Daily Fantasy's best players, known as "sharks," and so far, it's looking bleak. It seems like a blast to be one of the big names here, drinking and gawking, on the brink of a potential $2 million check—the top offering in the weekend's main $10 million tournament, the largest prize pool in the nascent industry's history. But right now I'm just another money-losing fish, and that doesn't look like it's going to change anytime soon.

Behind us, a DraftKings employee urges the pool partiers to be extra-raucous, making for better background scenes for the television show filming out on the pool deck. On the show, a crew of DFS experts are unveiling their top picks for the weekend, offering last-minute advice to legions waiting on the Internet for any money-winning wisdom. Usually, these shows are filmed in studios. All this flesh and frolic makes for a decidedly better backdrop.

"CAN-NON-BALL!" one heavily tattooed dude shouts, and it takes me a little too long to realize what that means. The plunging bro soaks my shorts and shirt, and I need to dry off. I head inside to DraftKings' watch room, the ballroom set up for viewing the weekend's football games. Once the games kick off on Sunday, the room is packed with hundreds of DFS players, nearly all male, sitting in groups on white couches, glancing from the massive screens back to their computers as their scores mount. If they get bored watching the games themselves, there's beer pong tables, video games, and free stuff arrayed as far as the eye can see, from high-end food and liquor to giveaways of DraftKings swag.

This is no Man Cave. It's a Man Cavern.

This entire September weekend is a coming-out party for DraftKings, the newer of the two Daily Fantasy giants. They spent years chasing FanDuel, the original DFS megasite, which controlled more than 80 percent of the market less than a year ago. Now the bitter rivals are neck and neck in size. Smelling blood, DraftKings waged a massive advertising campaign to push ahead—becoming the nation's top advertiser in early September—and the commercials blare constantly all around us on the huge, thirty-foot screens, promising big wins and massive payouts.

To pull off this ad blitz, they've spent lavishly, like someone had turned on a spigot of cash and no one believed the dollar bills would ever stop pouring out. DraftKings spent $24 million on TV commercials in the first week of September, putting them ahead of brands like Coca-Cola and Budweiser. That spend-first, worry-later ethos trickled down to this multiday party. There's so much money flying around that even the sharks don't seem to know what to do with it. So they do what comes naturally: they bet.

One picks up a football, and they start wagering—at $100 per toss—on whether they can throw it through a target. After a few throws, one says he owes the other $400. I can't tell if they actually plan on collecting, but they ask me if I want in on the action.

"No thanks, I messed up my shoulder in college," I say, a quarter-truth that hides the fact that $100 a throw is far, far too rich for my blood. Casual betting is everywhere. There are bets on who can run a faster forty-yard dash on the grass outside the hotel, bets on shooting a basketball, side bets on the NFL games themselves. Outside on the patio, a giant variant of beer pong has been erected, using basketballs and trash cans instead of Ping-Pong balls and cups. Two guys have been dominating all weekend, starting at $20 a game and then playing for increasingly higher stakes. Word is they've made $2,500.

Out by the pool, I'd met a lively, eccentric pro who goes by the user-name BeepImaJeep—"Beep" to all. He'd flown in on the private jet with all the other big wheels, and the Canadian is soaking up the Florida sun with aplomb. A math and game theory savant, this buoyant, high-energy twentysomething represents the flip side of the Rob Gomes part of DFS—the wonky brain to Gomes's tanned bro.

He's been guiding me around for much of the weekend, and as we stroll the watch room, Beep introduces me to another big-time player, a shark who goes by the name PetrGibbons. PetrGibbons, real name Matt Boccio, is a name I'd seen on the top-ten leaderboard for the day's main contest, the so-called Millionaire Maker. He entered 498 lineups in that contest, and the best of them has a real shot to win the $2 million first prize—but at the moment, he's bummed, because his receiver, Dez Bryant, has just gotten hurt.

"I'm in sixth in the 'milly maker' right now, but I have Dez, and he just got injured," he says.

We look at the screen as replays show the Cowboys star coming out of the game. It probably takes Boccio out of the running for first, though even holding sixth place would be worth $100,000.

He's having a good day regardless of what happens in the milly maker, turning his screen toward me to show that he has lineups all over the top ten of several other major contests, winning thousands upon thousands. Before he moves it away, I steal a glance at his account balance, there at the top of his screen. It's $143,000 and change, not including anything he'd wagered or might be winning today. As we walk away, I ask Beep if he's a full-time pro.

"Oh, no, he works for FanDuel," Beep says, as if working for the competition and yet being here to bet and win big on DraftKings is the most normal thing in the world. The relationship between the two companies—and their employees—continues to mystify me. Players are employees of one, and huge sharks on the other? There's no love lost between the two Daily Fantasy giants, and everyone knows it; for a time, early on in the day, whenever a FanDuel commercial came on the screens and played on the speakers, an awkward silence came over the room. But there were simply so many, drowned out by even more DraftKings commercials, that they all soon faded into so much background noise. I wonder if the companies could possibly be getting their money's worth out of it all.

The thought is lost as the room erupts around us, men leaping out of their seats, standing on couches, cheering. On every one of the enormous screens ringing the ballroom, I see Cowboys tight end Jason Witten celebrating a touchdown catch from his quarterback, Tony Romo. With both players picked by about 10 percent of fantasy teams, enough people have paired up that combo that the touchdown moves the needle. Money is flowing, changing hands, shifting electronically from one player to another, and the feeling in the room is electric. My lineups for the weekend are long dead, but it doesn't matter. Even though it gets me nothing, I can't help but follow the progress of DFS players I know, "sweating" it with them, as it's called.

Yet surprisingly few of the pros and high-level regulars are actually winning anything; on this day, the smart money is bombing hard, while unknown randoms are sucking up the cash. Beep is losing big this weekend, down $30,000 as the games unfold, but it doesn't seem to bother him, despite squandering more that day than I'd made in a year around his age.

Why would he care? He can make it back next week. There is so much money to be made, so many new players flooding the contests, that for the best of the best—those with a true edge—a big win is always just a week away. Over the three-week period from the end of August through that Sunday in Miami, DraftKings added 1.5 million new users, growing to 4.5 million accounts. These new arrivals would make a median deposit of $25. Most of them would lose it.

And most of the winnings would go to these few, the ones making television appearances, gorging themselves on the free spreads, and partying at the pool, everyone so certain it will only keep going up, up, up. The party at the Fontainebleau makes me think of stock traders in the 1980s before the market tanked—so much testosterone, so much abandon, so much certainty that the party will never stop—and more than anything, so much *money*.

The numbers change like magic, millions moving this way and that in an instant. It feels like none of these winnings, these losses, are even real. The cartoonish figures piling up, the people who might be losing it—hell, even this party, with its giant screens and white couches and shrimp and booze. Except it is real, all of it. Everyone here is on a high, so certain they've latched on to the next big thing, something that can't be stopped, something that's going to change sports as we know it.

But the thing about a high is, eventually, you have to come down.

01

FOUR MONTHS EARLIER . . .

Baseball is so boring.

It's deep in the seventh inning of yet another Yankees–Red Sox game at Fenway Park, and I'm crammed into my seat in the century-old press box high above the field, doing anything but watching tonight's game.

My reporter's notebook lies open in front of me, so I turn to a clean sheet and start doing a little math. I'm trying to calculate how many games I've covered over the seven years I've been paid to write about baseball, at two different newspapers. Seven years, multiplied by about 140 regular season games, plus about 25 spring training and 15 postseason games annually. That comes out to . . . around 1,260 games, give or take a few dozen. That's a lot of baseball.

After so many four-hour Yanks-Sox slogs, I've started to lose my love for it all. That wonder that drives fans to the park, that excitement I'd felt about baseball as a kid, before this was my job? It's gone. Fenway is no longer a lyric little bandbox to me—it's become a cage, one of thirty spread across the country. Call me spoiled. You'd be right. I can't help it.

The final pitch is thrown, the last out is made. I fire off an email containing my initial game story to my bosses at the *Wall Street Journal* and join the other Yankee beat writers in our daily ritual of sprinting down to the clubhouses to interview players and managers.

We fight our way through the mass of humanity clogging the Fenway concourse, then crowd into Yankee manager Joe Girardi's tiny office in the ancient, musty visitors' clubhouse, dank from one hundred years of champagne celebrations, sewage overflows, and sweaty uniforms. After we finish our interview and file out, I run into John Tomase, a former *Boston Herald* sportswriter and now radio reporter and host in the Boston area. In his early forties, chunky, with a big mop of curly hair, the fellow Tufts University grad is one of the brightest, and snarkiest, reporters in the Boston press corps, and the perfect guy for me to complain to. I break down my press box math for him, laying it on thick as I bitch about my so-called dream job.

"I've lost my taste for it. I honestly can't remember the last time I actually watched the whole game," I whine, expecting to be rewarded with the usual fraternal sympathy of another cranky scribe.

"I watched every pitch," he tells me instead, matter-of-factly. "I had half the Yankee lineup. Those guys just won me four hundred bucks."

Huh?

"You were betting on the game?" I ask. "Like, with a bookie?" That would be a big no-no in the baseball writer's world.

"A bookie? I wouldn't know where to find a bookie. It's Daily Fantasy Sports—on FanDuel. It's a website. You pick the players, build a lineup, and the better they do, the better you do," Tomase says.

"I do it at every game I cover now," he adds. Then he beats me to my next question before I can ask it. "It's totally legal."

Remember in old cartoons, when Donald Duck or Bugs Bunny would hear about some unbeatable moneymaking opportunity? Their eyes would roll up in their heads and turn into dollar signs, spinning like the wheels of a casino slot machine. I have to imagine that's what mine are doing as Tomase explains how he picks players for his lineups and then watches it all unfold.

"And you made how much?" I ask again.

Four hundred dollars. And that's nothing. He's soon telling me stories about friends who had won $10,000, $15,000, all on quick bets on the games I'm there watching every day. All of it perfectly legal, all of it at the click of a button.

To me, this sounds like old-fashioned sports betting, conjuring up images of bent-over, graying men hidden in smoky back rooms, taking calls and setting money lines—the Pittsburgh Pirates as 2–1 favorites, the Detroit Tigers as 6–1 underdogs. Oh, and the big meatheads standing behind them who break your knees when you don't pay up.

No, he explains again. This isn't sports betting. It's fantasy baseball.

I'd played fantasy sports—where you choose players from across the league to create a baseball or football team, competing against similar teams fielded by your friends—for years, enjoying it as a recreational activity with a few bucks at stake. In fantasy sports, at the beginning of a season, users stage a draft to choose real-life players for their fantasy teams, and over the course of the year, those teams compile points based on how well the players do in the actual games. At the end of the season, the best team wins. This, he explained, is the same basic idea—but with two massive differences.

"It's fantasy sports, but it's every day," he tells me, like a teacher instructing his none-too-bright student. "And it's for money. Lots and lots of money."

"There's no way this is really legal. None. It's totally sports betting," I say, certain this is too good to be true, and that some government SWAT team is about to storm into our conversation and arrest Tomase.

"There's some crazy legal loophole for fantasy, so they can do this," he insists. "There's two big companies, FanDuel and DraftKings. Even the sports leagues are behind it—look around, DraftKings ads are popping up in every stadium. I don't know how they did it, but it's all legit."

Seduced by the possibilities, the night after Tomase's introduction, I lie in bed dreaming on the chance of hitting it big on this crazy new thing. In the morning, I catch a flight to Toronto for our next series, Yankees–Blue Jays, and race to the press box in the Rogers Centre, home of the Jays. As fast as I can, I set up my computer and immediately go to

FanDuel's website. The home page is clean and attractive, white offset with green, the kind of green that makes me think of cash money. It asks me to create a username, and I put in "Pimpbotlove," my go-to when I need a random moniker that is guaranteed to be available.

On their ads, FanDuel trumpeted a deposit bonus, saying they'd match every dollar I put in up to $200. A good deal, right? So I put the maximum $200 on my credit card, and figure that means I instantly get $400 to play with.

Not so fast. My account balance says I have only $200 worth. Where's my $200 bonus? I didn't expect to be able to withdraw the extra money instantly or anything crazy, but I figured I could use it to enter more games. Where is it?

Poring over the fine print, I find some galling language. The deposit bonus pays out at a rate of 4 cents for every dollar in entry fees—meaning I'd have to bet $25 to get $1 back. It would take months of playing and winning just to get that $200. Whatever. Too late. I'm in regardless.

After the sign-in screen, the site takes me to a lobby where I can scroll down a list of available games, reminiscent of online poker sites I remembered from a decade ago, before those were banned. There are games at all levels, with entry fees ranging from 25 cents, all the way up to $10,000. I figure I should start just a wee bit under $10K, and buy into a $5 tournament. From what I can tell, only the best 1 percent to 5 percent of lineups make any real money in these top-heavy tournaments, but they win big. Then I try out a few so-called cash games—easier to win but with lower payouts. I put $10 into a "50/50," which is just what it sounds like—50 percent double their money, the other 50 percent lose it. Finally, I enter a $10 "double up," which looks like roughly the same thing as a 50/50, just with a slightly better payout and slightly inferior odds of cashing. Those seem pretty safe.

Now I need to choose my team. The players are arranged by position—catcher, first base, shortstop, etc.—and each one has a salary figure listed next to his name. The salaries are determined by the site itself, and seem to range from $2,000 for scrubs to $12,000 or so for a star pitcher. I've got about $35,000 in "salary" to play with, to build a nine-man team—one pitcher, eight hitters, just like a regular baseball lineup. I scroll through the pitchers first, settling on Houston Astros ace Dallas Keuchel. To start with, the lefty has a pretty sick beard; more important, he's darn good, and tonight he's facing the Texas Rangers, who have a lot of lefty hitters and strike out a lot. He costs me $8,500. Next I lock in my first baseman, Los Angeles Dodgers contact machine Adrian Gonzalez, who I remember being prickly and overly sensitive when I covered him with the Red Sox. He costs $4,300, which seems to be a lot for a hitter. Maybe they're afraid of pissing him off, too.

For the bargain price (I think?) of $3,000 I pick my catcher, Stephen Vogt, a power-hitting, late-blooming success story out of Oakland. I've even got enough cash left over to select Yankees outfielder Jacoby Ellsbury—who, conveniently, is playing in the game I'll be covering tonight. But it's three thirty now—clubhouse access time, time to start actually working. Grabbing my notebook, I head off to the visiting team clubhouse, more excited about a night of baseball than I've been in a long time.

As I stand around in the clubhouse, waiting for Brian McCann to stop by his locker, I can't stop thinking about this new world I've discovered. To me, it seems like it appeared overnight, but of course, it's been growing for some time. A little googling taught me that Daily Fantasy Sports traces its birth to 2006, and the law that banned online poker. Back then, the government was going after online gambling in a major way—but some feared that their push would imperil the small but growing fantasy sports industry, which was bringing eyeballs to sports and attracting younger viewers. So Congress wrote in a carve-out to the law that killed poker, one specifically protecting fantasy sports. There were some conditions put on the carve-out to make sure that fantasy was sufficiently differentiated from sports betting—players can't all be from the same team, there's got to be more than one game involved, skill has to play a part, some other junk—but effectively, fantasy sports were exempted from the antigambling laws.

Before long, some geniuses figured out that if they built a game to the exact standards defined by that law, they could basically pull off fantasy sports betting. Voila. Daily Fantasy Sports was born.

It took a while to get off the ground, but by about 2011 it had begun to grow in earnest, and by 2014 two big companies had come to dominate the scene: FanDuel, out of New York, and DraftKings, from Boston. They'd each raised approximately $100 million in venture capital and were in talks to raise a whole lot more. FanDuel offered the four major sports; DraftKings added some other ones, like soccer and golf. There are rumors of coming partnerships with ESPN and Disney. FanDuel had already partnered up with the NBA, DraftKings with MLB and the NHL, and about half of all NFL teams had individual deals with one site or another. Even after all those years of high-minded antigambling rhetoric, the leagues didn't seem to mind jumping into bed with an obvious sports betting enterprise when it meant more young eyeballs to their product. Pete Rose must be miffed.*

That night, as the Yankees take the field below me, my FanDuel team plays its own special game at ballparks around North America. Refreshing the mlb.com app like mad every time one of my players is at bat, I watch with glee as my pitcher, Keuchel, delivers a strong performance, and my catcher, Vogt, hits a grand slam, powering all my lineups into the money. I profit $24, on my initial $25 bet. This is easy! If I can just double my money every time, using the knowledge I already need to do my day job, pretty soon I'm going to be frickin' rich.

I start playing FanDuel every day, and after a week I've signed up for DraftKings, as well. In a greater miracle, I actually start watching baseball at home, activating the MLB TV package I got through work but nearly forgot I had. Soon I'm following four games at once on my big screen. Dodgers games. Mariners games. I need to find my players and

---

* A DraftKings employee told me Rose has an account, and Rose later partnered up with a fledgling DFS site, fanDaction.com.

see what they're doing in real time. It's an instant obsession, and man is it fun. I love baseball again. Love it.

Other Yankees beat writers see the fun I'm having, see me winning a little cash, and soon they're in, too. Mark Feinsand, the Yankee beat writer for the New York *Daily News,* falls for it hard and fast, and he and I start running a private, beat-writers-only DraftKings contest for the group each day, brilliantly titled the "beat-off." We spend afternoons in the clubhouse comparing potential lineups, every night talking about how our players are performing, how much we're winning, usually $10–$20 a day in those heady first few days. It doesn't take long before DraftKings feels more important than my real job; when we get the news that Yankees outfielder Slade Heathcott has been scratched in the final minutes before a game, my first instinct isn't to tweet the news or fire off a blog post. Instead Feinsand and I both scamper to our computers to get him out of our lineups. Then we write.

With my knowledge, and this level of commitment, I'm sure I'm going to hit a bigger win soon. Look at those bozos they show winning money on all the commercials—even their champions, the ones holding up those giant cardboard checks for hundreds of thousands of dollars, reek of being typical "bro" sports fans, fueled by testosterone and Coors Light, certainly no challenge. I'm a professional ballwriter! This is going to be easy.

———————

For a few more days, hubris, or confidence—or probably luck—carries me forward.

Then, everything starts coming down to earth. Betting about $50 a day, I begin hemorrhaging cash. Every night, I look at the screen, see the "current winnings" box reading "$0," and cringe. I'm taking a beating in 50/50s, in tournaments, and particularly in head-to-heads—one-on-one contests pitting my lineup against a single other user. In those, I'm getting crushed by the same usernames, smart players who eagerly pick up my $2 and $5 games as soon as I post them. At first, I figure I'm just experiencing a run of bad luck to correct my early good fortune. That would be fine. But after a few weeks of consistent, agonizing losing, I'm forced to acknowledge what's really going on: I'm in way over my head.

Look, despite my bravado, I always knew that this was going to be much harder than those first days suggested. I'd heard early on that there were cadres of pro players out there who spend all day at DFS, known in this world as sharks, and of course they're likely to beat me. But I thought I'd be better than this, a big-money loser already—what the industry calls a fish. When I started playing in the first week of May, I'd deposited that $200 in FanDuel and an additional $600 in DraftKings (gotta get that fully matched deposit bonus!). Three weeks later, I've lost nearly all of it.

I thought my insider baseball knowledge would give me a leg up— but in reality, it's next to useless. Maybe even worse than useless—it may be causing me to pay attention to narrative and small-sample-size events and not bigger data.

When I consider rostering Pittsburgh Pirates pitcher Francisco Liriano one day, for instance, I text his current catcher, the former Yankee and all-time good guy Chris Stewart, to ask if Liriano's improvement against right-handed hitters is for real. Stewart, who had no idea I was asking for gambling advice, responds that it is, because Liriano is being more aggressive pitching inside to righties. A perfect pregame sound bite, and it seems like useful info, no? Liriano goes out and gets rocked by the mediocre Minnesota Twins, savaged particularly badly by righty batters.

Honestly, I shouldn't be surprised. The truth is, beat writers aren't holding on to any good nuggets anymore. The old journalistic adage is that good reporters write a third of what they know. But the constant demands of Twitter—and the incredible competitiveness of most baseball beats—mean any scrap of information is now tossed into the public domain ASAP, right out there for the sharks to see. There are no media gatekeepers anymore: On a big beat, educated fans know just as much as we "insiders" do. And in a venture like this, it seems that easily available stats are far more important than "inside" info anyway.

To counter this, I've been reading up on Daily Fantasy strategy, and trying to study the lineups of the players who keep beating me; it's an expensive lesson, but I'm starting to learn who some of these top users are, both so I can emulate their picks and so I can stay the heck away from them in head-to-head contests—names like Birdwings, Assani, Ganondorf, Ehafner, Empiremaker. These guys are remarkably good—it seems like their picks all get three hits, hit a home run, or steal two bases every night. Their predictive abilities are astounding.

But there's one name I've seen more than all the rest over these painful few weeks. He's everywhere, and I mean everywhere: MaxDalury. He's in every three-man $10 contest, every big tournament, every 50/50, in head-to-heads at every level. He appears to be omnipresent. A new player basically can't avoid playing against him. And it seems like he always wins. I've started to check to make sure he isn't in my three- or five-man contests before I join, but it's virtually impossible. He seems to enter every one as soon as it appears—the guy must have ten hands. In the bigger tournaments, he enters scores of different lineups, all of them competing with my one. I can't imagine how he does it all.

But I'm willing to learn.

Tonight, there's a big $27 entry-fee tournament on DraftKings, with a $100,000 first prize and $900,000 in prizes for the other top finalists, called the $1 million Mega Payoff Pitch. I'm going to go hard at this one, or, at least, hard for me—I'm going to build three good lineups, and really make them count.

My afternoon is devoted to studying stats at baseball-reference.com and fangraphs.com, parsing out line-drive rates, hard-hit ball percentage, and batting average on balls in play; I'm looking for underpriced players who are hitting it hard but not getting the results they deserve. I focus on Blue Jays third baseman Josh Donaldson and a few others and build what I think are darn good lineups for this big tourney. I can feel a true confidence when I click to submit them, like I can see the future and it is mine, the way I'd felt in my first few days in DFS. I sit back in my chair and prepare to watch the money flow in.

By midnight, I am more than $100 poorer. Again.

Beaten and smarting, I scroll to the top of the leaderboard, to see what the winning score is, and who notched it. There I find the perfect salt to rub in my wounds. MaxDalury. Of course. He's in first, and in third, sixth, eighth, ninth—his entries just keep coming. There must be hundreds of them. Literally hundreds: his ninth-place lineup is listed as #529. It seems most lineups have pitchers Matt Shoemaker and Clayton Kershaw, Donaldson—who had a monster night—and a few other key building blocks in common. Other than that, they seem to be a vast rotation of combinations and permutations, many of them using four or five players from one single team or another with that foundational trio, a strategy apparently called "stacking." Some of these seemingly random combinations stunk. But some were very, very successful. More than some. A lot.

After a few minutes I stop scrolling down, having seen more than 500 MaxDalury lineups. Those are just the ones I can count—a quick scan shows that there are hundreds still to come. That's probably around $20,000 in entries, in this one contest alone—to say nothing of all the others I saw him in tonight. He must have put in $50,000, $100,000. Or more? Could it really be more? I had Donaldson, who was the star of the night. I still got creamed. What was I thinking? Three lineups versus 500?

I slump back into my plush leather office chair, defeated.

As I'm sitting there moping, my wife, Amalie, walks into the room. She's a sportswriter, too, at the *Boston Globe*—we first met on the infield of Fenway Park—though she's now moved from baseball to hockey. Spotting the DFS contests on my computer screen, she decides it's a good time to ask me how this DraftKings stuff is going.

"It's fine. I'm down a little, but not much," I say quickly, in a clear example of healthy, responsible, and honest gambling behavior.

The truth I'm hiding from my fiscally responsible wife is that I'm now down more than $700 in less than a month at this. If she knew the truth, she'd tell me to walk away from DFS, never think about it again. I wouldn't blame her.

But a bitterness is coursing through me. I don't have enough answers here. How are these guys so good? What do they know that I don't? How can they enter so many lineups? And who the hell is this MaxDalury guy, really? I need to know more.

Typing MaxDalury's name into Google brings up one interesting hit right away. It's a month-old Reddit post from another angry loser, just like me. It's titled "If MaxDalury is real he should be robbed for what he did tonight."

I click on it, expecting some drunken, misspelled rant. But reading through the post turns up some interesting information, and a few more links. Apparently MaxDalury had a huge night a month ago, winning hundreds of thousands. And he did it using something called "scripting."

Scripting appears to be the practice of using purpose-built computer programs to gain an edge over everyone else—in this case, manipulating the way your computer interacts with the websites themselves to allow instant changes across hundreds of lineups at the click of a button, when other users have to edit each individual entry by hand. There are numerous angry posts about it from users on multiple forums, accusing MaxDalury and other high-level players, calling them cheaters.

My antennae go up, and I start looking closer. It doesn't stop at building programs to change your lineups; reading through posts with titles like "How to stop this scripting B.S.," I learn that some top players, these sharks, build or buy specialized programs allowing them to identify, catalog, and subsequently target new schmucks—fish—in one-on-one matchups. Digging deeper, it seems that most of the top pros have developed complicated algorithms telling them who the best picks are each day, automating the process to a far greater degree than I'd ever realized. I'm fighting an army of machines—Daily Fantasy Skynet.

I read on, learning about syndicates of pros who play together, sharing lineups, information, and sometimes even fees and winnings. Others have staffers who help them collate information and react to late changes. It's not clear if any of this is illegal, per se, but it's certainly unnerving.

The more I think about it, the more it hits me that these aren't the first warning flags I've seen; I've experienced some odd stuff in DFS even in just these first weeks. There were a lot of strange little moments that bugged me—things that awoke the old news reporter in me, the one who had witnessed enough sketchy stuff when covering Providence City Hall to smell when something isn't right.

Like the time when three different users took my three FanDuel head-to-head games on the same day, and when I clicked their entries, I found that their lineups were exactly—and I mean exactly—the same. That could be a freak occurrence, or the lesser evil of a paid lineup generator spitting out the same optimal combo. Or it could be something sketchier, like one user with multiple accounts, or various users buying the same custom-built lineups from shady lineup dealers who prowl the Internet. Once I started following a few DFS-related sites on Twitter, I received a message from a lineup seller, offering me top lineups for a price. It seemed slimy and I ignored it, but not everyone does.

The more I google, the more weird stuff I find about DFS—including something that's hard to believe: some of the top players are actually employees of the DFS companies, working at FanDuel during the day and playing on DraftKings at night, or vice versa—and doing pretty well.

It seems that many users, burned by losing, took their complaints about these problems to the companies, and have seen little or nothing change; the companies are motivated to keep the top players happy because they provide so much revenue in the form of the rake charged on entry fees, or so the online arguments go. The multi-entry sharks keep the big contests filled and the prize pools high, those big-prize contests in turn attract more fish, and as long as DFS advertising brings new players signing up—new fish, like me, for the sharks to munch on—the whole system would continue working perfectly.

It's a lot to process. The entire DFS industry has grown so fast, and with so little control or oversight, that it truly is a situation where the inmates run the asylum. With so much money flowing in, it's like someone dropped a fully formed casino operation into the middle of a frat house and told the players that they could gamble to their heart's content—as long as they also managed the betting, ran security, kept the books, and made sure things never got too out of hand.

My mistake was failing to realize just how deep a rabbit hole I was going down, with an established subculture, lexicon, and most of all, a class of professional players, these sharks swimming in the waters just waiting to gobble up chum like us. Like poker pros in old Vegas looking to prey on tourists, they hang back and wait, quietly—and when you see that you're matched up against one of them, you've already lost. Yet because there are virtually no limits on how many contests these top players can enter, they run wild in a way poker pros never could. In online poker, even the best players could divide their attention among only ten, fifteen tables at once. In Daily Fantasy, a MaxDalury can be nearly everywhere if he wants to be, high-stakes, low-stakes, ubiquitous, and deadly.

At first I'm queasy at how naïve I've been, to think I could win with just baseball knowledge and a history as a strong fantasy player. These sharks hold every advantage: money, time, scripted programs, and a system that lets them leverage their edge to a massive extent through a largely unrestrained multiple-entry format.

Then something else hits me. Anger. This whole affair is ruinous to the little guy, who sees those commercials promising easy riches, signs up, and quickly becomes a snack, unable to avoid facing the best players in the world at absolutely all times. And no one is doing anything about it. This could have been something with the potential to change the way we all watch sports. Instead it's skewed, unbalanced, rife with problems. I should probably just quit.

But another feeling is welling up, from somewhere deep down inside.

It's that sensation of excitement, of something sparking, beginning to catch fire.

I have a plan.

"This is not going to be easy," Tomase says, taking a deep breath and pursing his lips. "I don't know."

Great. I've just started telling him the basics of my scheme, and he's already skeptical. Not an auspicious beginning.

We're sitting at the bar in one of my old haunts in Providence, Rhode Island, where I'd spent nearly a decade covering crime and politics before becoming a sportswriter. The bar, Local 121, used to be a brothel in Prohibition times, and has been restored to look like an idealized 1920s speakeasy, all dark mahogany and stained glass. Late at night it's crawling with hipsters and the largely insufferable. But in the midafternoon hours, it's a sane enough atmosphere for a pair of guys on the wrong side of thirty to play at hatching something big.

I've asked Tomase to meet me here so I can explain the plan I've been hashing out for weeks, ever since that night when I learned just how perilous Daily Fantasy really is.

"Take it from the beginning again," he offers, and I ready myself to give the full pitch, like a start-up geek wooing a new investor.

"I'm going to become a pro," I say, dropping my opening line with extra emphasis. "I'm going deep inside Daily Fantasy Sports, embedding myself in it, becoming part of it. I'm going to leave my job and spend a year as a professional DFS player, one of the sharks we hate so much."

He nods. I continue, starting to roll now, my hands flying this way and that. I'm a big gesticulator. It's an Italian thing.

"I'm going to test whether a regular guy can succeed, I mean truly succeed consistently, without these algorithms, without scripting, without a staff of people on my side, without a computer mass-entering five hundred different lineups to win," I say.

He seems to be buying it, so I continue, telling him about my plans to get in with these sharks, convince them to help me, and study under them—using their methods for my own ends. Once the baseball season's over, I explain, I'll ask for a leave of absence from the *Wall Street Journal* and begin training full-time to see if I can make the leap.

"If I can pull it off, if I can go from fish to shark, then maybe Daily Fantasy is on the level after all. If I can't, it's more evidence that this thing is unfair, and we can shine a light on it, maybe help clean it up. Make sure the average guy is protected," I say, nearly out of breath. I'm doing that thing where I get a little overexcited, and talk so fast that my words start to bump into one another.

Lucky for me, Tomase holds up a finger, giving me a chance to recover.

"You're forgetting something. You're not an average guy. You're a professional sportswriter, with knowledge, contacts, special access. These pros might help you because you're in with the Yankees or whatever, but they won't help a regular guy the same way."

He has a point. Fortunately, I've factored this in.

"I get that," I say, "so I'm not going to set average goals. I'm going for it all. I'm going to try to win one of their big, final championships—you know, the ones they show in the commercials, where the winner is holding up the giant check and wearing that goofy championship belt."

"That's impossible," he shoots back, looking skeptical.

"Maybe—maybe not." I shrug. "Okay, forget winning it all, for now. If I can even qualify for one of those finals, that'll be a massive success in itself."

Regardless, I tell him, my hope is to make enough money to cover what my newspaper salary for 2016 would have been, about $70,000.

"What if you lose that much?" Tomase interjects.

"If I lose it, I lose it," I say. "I've got to have as much on the line as anyone else in this thing."

And I'm going to do much more than just play, I explain. I'm going to document where all of this came from, tell the story of it. A bunch of bros managed to nationalize and legalize sports gambling via some loophole, and somehow it's getting virtually no national attention. Meanwhile there's hundreds of millions in capital flowing into it, the sports leagues are eagerly jumping on board, and thousands of new patsies are showing up to get crushed every single day, while the companies seem to turn a blind eye to any problems because they're so concerned with growth. Somebody needs to tell people what's happening here.

"You're so full of shit," Tomase cackles. "Okay, fine, you want to learn the truth, but be honest, you want to win a boatload of money, too."

He's not wrong.

"No harm in doing both, right? Look, maybe all these negative theories are wrong, or overblown. Maybe it's just a bunch of pissed-off losers like me, venting. But I want to know."

"Okay, fine," Tomase says again, waving his hand in front of my face and cutting me off. "Let's say this plan is going to work. Still, the best players guard their secrets like Smaug. Finding one willing to give up the goods is going to be harder than I think you're anticipating."

He has a point. But I know just the shark to start with.

MaxDalury.

———

The first step in my plan is to track down MaxDalury himself. I want to both probe him for information and see if he will agree to teach me—or at least point me in the direction of someone who will.

I've got a little bit of luck on my side here. When I found him on Facebook, his page featured pictures of an early-twenties kid playing sports in a Tufts uniform—my alma mater! And it didn't stop there—I'm far older than him, graduating in 2001. But my sister graduated in 2007, and Facebook suggested they had friends in common. Maybe they even knew each other a little bit. Now I just need to make the connection and use our mutual ties to set something up.

Max keeps a low profile in the DFS world, but finding a way to contact him is easy. There's a MaxDalury Twitter account, and while it doesn't post much, judging by the people (and DFS companies) he follows, it's the DFS player. His Twitter profile features a picture of the army of robots from the Will Smith movie *I, Robot*. Either Max is a big Isaac Asimov (or Will Smith) fan or he has a sense of humor about the whole perception that he's a computerized, robotic DFS killing machine.

I send him a private message on Twitter, introducing myself, explaining our mutual ties, and asking if I can speak to him for a project I'm working on.

His response is a little baffling.

"I am not actually the Max Dalury who went to Tufts. But we can still talk at some point next week if you want."

So much for my in. But at least he agreed to talk. A week later, he calls me. Not long before, he'd officially taken over the top spot as the number-one-ranked DFS player, unseating the longtime top player, Condia, and affirming what everyone in the Daily Fantasy world already knew: MaxDalury is the best DFS player alive. I congratulate him and make some small talk.

"So, my bad for getting you and the other Max Dalury mixed up—that's funny that you have the same name as the Tufts guy," I say, jovial and friendly.

Then things get weird.

"Um, yeah, my real name's not Max Dalury. I don't give out my real name," he says, sounding nervous.

So why the heck is he calling himself MaxDalury? Does he know the real Max? I ask what gives.

"I met him once, years ago. It wasn't someone I'd consider a friend, or even an acquaintance," he says.

Oh. So he simply took the other guy's name. That's weird. That's really, really weird. Great. I'm dealing with the DFS Don Draper. Uh, I mean Dick Whitman.

FakeMax says he had played squash against RealMax in both high school and in college. And for some reason had been inspired to use his old squash opponent's name when beginning his DFS career. This, of course, begs another question: why on earth did he take the name of someone he played squash against a few times?

"It was just random," FakeMax says, clearly embarrassed. "I don't even know what came over me. I never thought it would amount to anything, so I just thought it was a good way to stay anonymous. Put this out there, no one will ever know. And then here we are, years later, and I respond to it."

At first, prudence prompted him to protect his true identity. Later, fear became a factor, too.

"I've gotten threatening messages from some people," FakeMax said, sounding harried. "At first I wanted to keep it secret from my job, that this person is spending a lot of time doing this. At this point that's not a concern. I don't think I'd have as big a concern about putting my real identity out, but it's not something I want to do."

Seriously? Threats?

"There's definitely been people that have said some things," FakeMax says. "People I've beaten and people who, when I've been in tournaments, they've said, 'He's going to get what's coming to him. He should be robbed.'"

We chat some more about how he got into Daily Fantasy, and along the way, Max says that he went to Amherst College and grew up a Yankees fan in northern New Jersey; he also refers to himself as a "five-nine Indian kid." With those and a few other bread crumbs to follow, and knowing that he played squash against the real Max Dalury, it doesn't take long on the Internet to sleuth out that I'm talking to Saahil Sud, a 2010 grad of Amherst College. But I don't let on, not wanting to disrupt the vibe, as Max—Saahil?—is telling me why people hate him so much, why they would make threats against him.

"They're probably not very good. They're looking for reasons for why they're not winning. It's a very tough game, since DraftKings and FanDuel are taking out ten percent as rake. That leaves a very small, single-digit percentage of people who are making a profit, probably one percent are making sixty to seventy percent of the profits," he says.

One percent, I ask him? That sounds crazy. It's that bad?

"It's pretty extreme. Actually, there's probably a couple hundred people that make up close to eighty percent of the profit," he says.

Those numbers are outrageous, terrifying even. I ask Max how the top players are so dominant. Partially, it's because they're cyborgs.

Like many sharks, Max has built an algorithm, one he's customized over the years, one that does most of his number-crunching for him. He won't tell me more than that, but it's obvious that perfecting that algorithm is at the very root of his success. He's played virtually every single day of the year since quitting his job doing data analysis in the online advertising industry to become a full-time pro. He's made millions already in 2015, with the year only half over.

Max, who seems nice enough despite the creepy name situation, offers a few basic words of wisdom—don't play head-to-heads against the best players, make sure you're using the right types of players for tournaments versus cash games—but other than that, he guards his secrets zealously. This guy isn't going to be my Yoda—for starters, he won't even reveal his identity, and more than that, he's winning via a HAL 9000–style computer program. That's the opposite of how I'm trying to do this.

Which makes me wonder—is there any chance of success without doing it Max's way? Those poor saps signing up every week, would they ever win without algorithms, without years of experience, without staffs and assistants and collaborators, without doing it full-time? In short, I want Max's take on the most essential question here: unless lightning strikes, can a normal guy actually make money playing this? His answer makes all the hubris that had carried me since the bar meeting with Tomase evaporate in an instant.

"I think they're setting themselves up for disappointment," Max says. "I think you can have some success if you make sure you pick your spots,

you make sure you play small stakes, make sure you're not doing anything too stupid. You can maybe break even. But if people are really
playing for a profit, and you don't have this level of intelligence, and
time—it's just not going to happen."

Then, abruptly, he stops.

"I have to go," he says in a rush of words, and hangs up.

The dial tone echoes in my ear as I contemplate what the hell just
happened. Fake names? One percent winning all the cash? The average
guy having no chance to win?

What am I getting myself into?

02

I feel the sweat start to trickle down my back as I run along Central Park South, trying to find the perfect balance between moving-fast-enough and not-ruining-these-clothes. I am running late. This is, unfortunately, not altogether uncommon. My wife says that it's a function of poor organizational skills, but I don't think that's it at all. I think it's a subconscious desire to create excitement in even the most mundane situations, to pull victory from the jaws of defeat by leaving just enough room to get everything done.

This is probably a common characteristic among gamblers. The lousy ones, anyway.

I'm running because I'm late to join a bunch of lousy gamblers as a bunch of really good gamblers teach the lousy gamblers how to be a little less lousy. This is the first of this season's Daily Fantasy Boot Camps, held at the posh JW Marriott Essex House hotel off the south face of Central Park. It's a beautiful day, the first of August, right at that time when the monster that is the NFL starts to enter the consciousness of most casual football fans, and by extension most casual fantasy players as well. Training camps are under way, preseason games are only a week or two off, and the first broken fibulas and collarbones are just starting to trickle in. This Daily Fantasy Boot Camp is billed as a chance to survive, via a daylong session learning at the knee of a stable of big-name, money-winning professional players. For between $250 and $500 (depending on the package), one of the resident gurus of DFS—a man known to all as Al_Smizzle—will teach a group of seventy paying customers the basics of being a shark in one of a series of sold-out workshops held in cities from Chicago to Vegas, Atlanta to Los Angeles. MaxDalury, the feared pro, had suggested I check it out, and who am I to turn down advice from the best of the best? Tired of losing, I've taken a few days away from my *Wall Street Journal* day job to see how the other half lives—and to learn their secrets. But I'm here to do more than just soak up the wisdom of the sharks. This is my first time meeting pro DFS players in person, and I'm here to cozy up to them, learn how they think, talk, act—to join their world. Maybe, just maybe, I can get in good enough that I can call on them for advice, information, and tactics when needed.

My shirt starts to stick to my chest as I slow down to a brisk walk for the final steps up to the Essex House, a good fifteen minutes late now. The Essex House is one of those grand old New York hotels, steeped in lore and a bit player in everything from the Watergate conspiracy to the early history of *Saturday Night Live,* as the show's featured guests would stay there and raise hell until dawn. Construction started the day after the stock market crash of 1929, making it perhaps the perfect place to host a quasi-gambling conference. Padding into the lobby, I flag down a concierge to ask where I'm supposed to go.

"I'm trying to find the Daily Fantasy Boot Camp," I say, realizing for the first time how ridiculous that sounds.

She looks at me quizzically, then realizes what I'm talking about.

"Oh, the football thing. Yes, that's on the second floor," she says, pointing me toward the elevator bank.

I come off the elevator, straighten up as best I can, and turn the corner to where a murmur of activity can be heard. There's a check-in desk, and people are milling around. It doesn't seem like they've started yet. Victory, once again!

At the desk, I point out my name on the list, and am handed a lanyard and oversized name badge. Even though I can pretty well figure that the cool-kid thing to do is to not wear the badge, I write "Daniel" on it in blue Sharpie anyway. We're all friends here, right?

Grateful that I haven't missed anything, I slip into the main hall, a long, rectangular conference room with what look to be eight circular tables, with about eight or nine seats at each. Each one is mostly filled already with men zealously hoarding their space, a few talking to the guys next to them, the others playing with their phones and darting their eyes around the room.

If this whole event didn't have a first-day-of-school vibe before, I certainly feel it now, looking around for a place to throw my stuff down. I squeeze past the placards proclaiming Uber and AT&T as the primary corporate sponsors, and finally spot an open seat in the middle of the room, next to an Indian man in his late thirties with a name tag that reads "Jagan." He gestures at me to take the spot.

The table's other inhabitants give me a once-over as I sit down, then return their eyes to their phones. There's Jagan, and to his left an early-twenties man whose name tag says "Mike"; probably a low-level finance type or a law student. Next to him is a translucently pale kid around twenty wearing a black DraftKings polo, who I assume must work for the company. Smizzle is partnered up with DraftKings, which has proven to be the far more aggressive of the two main DFS companies in courting players and interacting with fans. FanDuel, with its traditionally larger market share, puts the product out there and lets the users come in. As with all second-bests, DraftKings tries harder.

Rounding out the group is a squat, early-thirties man in a black hat and golf shirt who introduces himself as Jamison, and a pair of gents in their late forties, Mediterranean-looking and deeply tanned, with slicked black hair, who clearly know one another.

We all sit, quiet, as my few fellow stragglers find their seats in the packed room. With nothing happening, and being the newest guy, I venture something, turning to Casper the Friendly Ghost in his DraftKings shirt.

"Do you work for DraftKings?" I ask in a pleasant tone, trying to break a little ice and maybe see how involved DraftKings is here.

As it turns out, he just likes the shirt, and seems embarrassed that I pointed it out—the old "wearing the shirt of the band at said band's concert" thing. I immediately feel bad for drawing attention to him, smile, and our table returns to its blissfully uncomfortable silence.

Fortunately, right around then, four men and one woman stride into the room, their arrival instantly quieting the crowd. The group assembles at one end of the long hall, congregating around a podium, and four of them drop back as one man, clearly the boss, steps to the fore, commanding the microphone.

"I'm Al_Smizzle," he introduces himself, to a crowd that knows exactly who he is. In the DFS world, the big players are like fighter pilots—known not by their real names, but by their call signs.

Lucky for me, I already know him by another name.

––––––––

Alvin Zeidenfeld and I sat at a table in a crowded restaurant in the posh Time Warner Center on Columbus Circle—basically New York City's version of a high-end mall—dining on steak salad and salmon. My treat, of course. I'd managed to finagle Zeidenfeld—more commonly known as "Smizzle"—into meeting me the day before the Daily Fantasy Boot Camp to talk about the evolution of Daily Fantasy Sports, and his path through it.

He reached back into his past, when he wasn't Al_Smizzle, the celebrated and wealthy fantasy sports pro, radio, and television host. He was simply Zeidenfeld, a ninth-grade girls' basketball coach, who got his kicks outsmarting his opponents by using their own plans against them.

The restaurant table where we were dining was quickly pressed into service as a basketball court as Smizzle delved into that former life, grabbing a salt shaker and four packets of sugar to diagram basketball plays for my benefit. Meaty hands arranged them into a formation—the salt shaker at the center, the sugar packets in its orbit—as he explained his tactics.

When it came to high school basketball, he realized, the players have a hard enough time just following basic coaching instructions—and young players deviate from those at their peril.

"They're taught to think a certain way, and they have to do it that way, or the coach yells at them," Zeidenfeld explained. "So I let them do what their coach tells them to do, and then I'd take advantage of it."

I can't pretend to say that I exactly followed just how the sugar packets were moving around, but I think I got the most important thing—why this fast-talking, supremely confident forty-two-year-old succeeded as a basketball coach, then as a poker pro, and now as a Daily Fantasy Sports player, where he's shown a knack for picking undervalued, unheralded players who will win him money. It all takes the same kind of mind— one that anticipates what your opponent is planning to do, and then uses that knowledge to pull the rug out from under him.

"My big thing was always to mix people up," he said. "It's the same thing in poker, the same thing in coaching. I can manipulate it. I know what they're going to do, and I use it against them."

Relaxed now in a blue T-shirt and gray shorts, Zeidenfeld said that when he was a kid, people would say he looked like Fred Savage. I used to get the Fred Savage comparisons, too, and somewhere along the Savage genetic road, Zeidenfeld and I veered in vastly different directions. If I got the goofy, aquiline, Jason Biggs look, Zeidenfeld seems like he'd be more at home in a velour tracksuit, playing a two-bit mob heavy in a later season of *The Sopranos*. Standing at what I'd judge to be six two, his big, round face framed by a thin beard, Zeidenfeld talks fast, firing out his ideas in clipped, quick sentences. At this point, he had moved on from basketball and was holding forth on how Daily Fantasy Sports is perhaps a month from a true explosion. DraftKings has just announced a $300 million Series D funding round led by Fox Sports. FanDuel raised a $275 million Series E round to counter, each company preparing for an ad war.

"Things are about to totally change. As a result of the marketing deals with ESPN and Fox . . . this is the year that it really blows up," Zeidenfeld said, pointing his index finger into the table for emphasis. "Insane growth, insane growth, insane growth, but it'll plateau eventually. There's only so much insane growth you can get. You can't go four-five-times growth every year forever. But for now, insane growth.

"If this goes the way I think it's going to go, I'm going to be famous," he continued, ramping up. "Nobody listens to me now. Nobody knows me. I don't move the needle; I'm in front of a few thousand people a day. But if this happens how it's supposed to happen . . ."

"You're going to have a bullhorn," I ventured.

"Well"—he raised an eyebrow—"I might have a satellite dish." *

I'd sought out Zeidenfeld because I needed him. Many of the top professional players are reclusive, like the first great pro, Condia, or the secretive MaxDalury. These men rarely show their faces, and few know their real names. They look at what they do as a solitary pastime, and at social connections as dangerous—a chance for pretenders to either steal their secrets, or, in the case of MaxDalury, physically harm him for some of the unpopular methods he uses to win.

In DFS, Zeidenfeld is one of the closest things to an old wise man that there is, though he might be better described as a fraternity president. If there's a dominant clique among DFS players, then Zeidenfeld is one of its leaders, with several of the top players in his orbit. They joke with one another on Twitter, attend events as a pack, and now, with their Daily Fantasy Boot Camps, are banding together to teach their methods to the masses—for a price.

He isn't promising to turn me, or any of the rest, from chumps to champs in a one-day session. But he seems to genuinely want to help, enjoying the role of elder sage in a field where so many of the stars are

---

* A month later, Zeidenfeld would begin serving as a DFS expert on ESPN, touting picks across multiple ESPN platforms.

under thirty. And even if he isn't offering instant success, he's giving out something else.

"It's access," said Zeidenfeld, who of course knows what my day job is. "If you have a baseball question, you can go ask Alex Rodriguez why he did what he did. Well, if most DFS players have a question, they can't ask the best and brightest why they made a particular move except maybe tweeting a hundred and forty characters at them and hoping for a response. That's what I'm offering them—a chance to sit down and pick the brains of the smartest people in DFS."

I've quickly come to trust Zeidenfeld, because unlike most of the other pros I've met, Zeidenfeld didn't come into DFS needing to take my money—he's one of the very few who arrived already wealthy. That per-haps explains why he seems so much more interested in the fame part of this than the fortune. Born and raised in the Los Angeles area, Zeidenfeld decamped for Syracuse University and its media program in the early 1990s, hoping to become a sportscaster. But he didn't get the cardinal rule of getting into media: you need to start young, and be single-mindedly committed—just going to a journalism school usually isn't enough.

Tired of the Upstate New York winters and unsure what to do next, Zeidenfeld moved back to Southern California after college. While working at his family's stainless steel piping company Zeidenfeld read up on investing, wading into the stock market at just the right time, rid-ing the mid-1990s dot-com bubble up. He won't say exactly how much he made, but he doesn't mind letting you know that it's a lot.

"I didn't have to worry about money from the time I was twenty-seven," Zeidenfeld said with a shrug. "I could do whatever I wanted with the rest of my life." *

---

* Because he doesn't need the money and hence didn't play DFS or poker as his pri-mary means of making cash, Zeidenfeld doesn't describe himself as a pro—but for all practical purposes, he is one. You see this a lot: many serious players are hesitant to call themselves pros, often because of a perceived stigma. The definition is further muddied by the fact that few in DFS can agree on what exactly makes one a pro to begin with.

Still in search of a next move, Zeidenfeld dove into basketball coaching. He had to start at the bottom, of course, so he found himself drawing up plays for a bunch of ninth-grade girls, trying to teach them about post moves and under-the-basket finishers.

The thing is, his plays worked. Those strategies with the salt shakers and sugar packets? They led him up the high school ladder, and eventually to a state championship and a nationally ranked squad, and then into low-level college coaching—but from there it seems either his coaching fire, or his prospects, petered out. Zeidenfeld was in his early thirties, still wealthy, still looking for the next wave to ride.

He found it, in poker.

One of the first things I learned when I started asking DFS pros about themselves is that a tremendous number of them, if they were old enough, played poker before finding Daily Fantasy. A few of them are old enough to have been playing in casinos before the poker boom really hit, but most of them found the game when everyone else did, around 2003. That's when Chris Moneymaker—I still can't believe that's the guy's real name—won the World Series of Poker, and its $2.5 million grand prize at no-limit Texas hold 'em. Moneymaker was a regular guy who won his way into the World Series via a $39 satellite tournament, playing online—and in a dramatic final, nationally televised on ESPN, beat the biggest names in the game, legends like Johnny Chan, Phil Ivey, and Sam Farha. He proved that the poker schlub's fantasy was real—that by playing online, the players in their local Tuesday night game could challenge the top players in the world and win gobs of money.

I had a regular Tuesday night game around that time with a bunch of political reporters at the *Providence Journal,* but we all liked one another too much to be any good. We'd just pass chips around, never wanting to be the dickhead who raised the pot too high, and then we'd go get beers afterward, with the night's winner buying a few rounds. It was a gentlemanly system.

For the pros, people like us were suckers. There was real money to be made in online poker, and a class of young, smart, math-oriented online players sprang up almost immediately. With ESPN televising poker matches to fill space created by the lockout that canceled the 2004–2005 NHL season, and the Matt Damon/Ed Norton movie *Rounders* giving everyone an easy cheat sheet for learning terms like *whale, river,* and *fifth street,* poker was suddenly everywhere.

Zeidenfeld became one of these poker savants, good enough to beat the average players easily, and to at least hang with the famous pros. Through the boom, Zeidenfeld would have more than a dozen windows up on his computer regularly, playing games on each, and then head to casinos for real tournaments.

"The three levels of poker player are very basic. The level one poker player plays the cards in his hand," Zeidenfeld explained, mimicking holding a hand of cards in front of his face.

"The next level of poker player is playing the cards in his opponent's hand. The black belt, the third level of poker player, is not playing his own hand, and he's not playing your hand. He's playing a different game—what can I make you think I have in my hand?"

The poker industry died two major deaths that eventually made Zeidenfeld's pastime untenable. In 2006, when President George W. Bush signed the Unlawful Internet Gambling Enforcement Act (UIGEA)— the bill whose carve-out would eventually create Daily Fantasy—into law, several of the main poker sites shut their U.S. operations. A few continued to operate in defiance of federal law, but the government doesn't tend to let that last forever. In 2011, on a day now known as Black Friday, the FBI dropped the hammer on the remaining major sites—Full Tilt Poker, PokerStars, and Absolute Poker, shutting them down, seizing their bank accounts, and bringing their founders in on a variety of federal charges ranging from money laundering to bank fraud.

That, effectively, was the end of the online poker industry in the United States. It still limped along, but the days of players like Zeidenfeld popping up and spending the majority of their time playing online were over.

Right around that time, however, the early Daily Fantasy sites started to reach maturity, and they were a lifeline for this community of gamblers. For the mathematically minded, DFS wasn't just a substitute for online poker—it was an improvement, a revelatory one. Most of the poker crowd were sports fans anyway. Now this allowed them to marry their love of sports with the math that helps one win at poker—and to win real money, of course.

"People always want to say that DFS is like poker," Zeidenfeld said. "And it is—but it's not perfect. It's a Venn diagram. There's overlap. It's like twenty percent. It's not huge. But that twenty percent is really, really close."

Zeidenfeld had always loved season-long fantasy sports—from what I can tell, he was that guy in your fantasy league who always took it way, way too seriously. I usually played fantasy by forgetting everything I had learned the year before, cramming on primers and rankings two days before the draft, printing out a couple of cheat sheets, paying attention and mildly boozing for the first ten draft rounds, and then letting the rest of it spool out while getting drunk and having dinner. For the record, this strategy works like a charm—in three years in the Boston Baseball Writers League, aptly named "Fellowship of the Miserable," I've finished third, first, and second.

But there are always those guys who start their preparation months early. They have their intricate strategies mapped out, breakout stars targeted, complicated formulas in hand for assessing value and appropriate prices for players. They do mock drafts. These people often pepper me on Twitter and on email demanding insight on the Yankees. Generally speaking, I do not like them.

While listening to his normal pack of fantasy experts, Zeidenfeld heard the early promos for DFS and quickly fell in love with the concept. It was fantasy baseball married with poker married with traditional sports betting, and for someone like him, it was perfect. But he was soon surprised to find that the traditional fantasy baseball experts he worshipped weren't playing DFS at all—were scared off of it, to some extent.

"It's a different skill set," he said. "Micro versus macro. In season-long, if you draft player X, you're saying they're going to have between twenty-two and twenty-seven home runs this year. You don't care what games they come in, as long as they end up in this range. In Daily Fantasy, I've gotta have the guy the day he hits the home run. So how do you figure out what day he's going to hit the home run? And can you handle the variance?"

Most fantasy baseball players just aren't used to throwing $50, $100 a day behind their players. They put in $50 for the season, maybe, and at the end of the year, if all their decisions add up, they claim a couple hundred dollars in prize money. Daily Fantasy was terrifying to much of that group. It smelled like gambling, for a host of reasons, no matter how much the early ads portrayed it as simply an offshoot of fantasy baseball.

But the poker crowd? They could handle those wild swings, and assume that risk, no problem. And they didn't care about being seen as gamblers—they were already gamblers. They were a perfect target audience.

Once the prize pools got big enough, around 2013, poker players started arriving in larger numbers—and mostly to DraftKings, which advertised directly at them.

Zeidenfeld did well in his first year in DFS but was still a casual player. Then, in February 2012, he qualified for a live final in a major basketball tournament. The main prize was $50,000—as big a pot as players saw in those early days. He picked a team. He won. He was all in.

He parlayed his win, his Syracuse sports background, and his com-mentating dreams into regular podcast spots discussing DFS. Over time, he became well known throughout the industry. The more he won, and the more his advice helped others win, the more they flocked to him. There was so much money at stake, yet the community remained tiny, with few places to go for people who wanted to get better. So Daily Fantasy Boot Camp was born, offering a way in for us, and a way up into the limelight for him.

"It's access. It's the ability to pick the brains of the best," he said, clearly proud to be one of that number.

———————

That access is now mine. At yesterday's lunch, I offered Zeidenfeld some tips on the best Yankees to roster—on pitcher Nathan Eovaldi's developing splitter, to be exact—for his wisdom in how to build better DFS tournament lineups.*

Now, leading the Boot Camp, Zeidenfeld is in his Al_Smizzle persona, commanding the room, surrounded by his fellow pros. He's ditched the casual shirt and shorts of Friday's lunch, and is now outfitted in slacks and his own custom-made Daily Fantasy Boot Camp polo. He gives an overview for the crowd, identifying the presenters one by one—by their usernames, of course: Levitan, Draftcheat, ReneeMiller01.

Finally, he introduces the star of the show, the man whom all these people are here to see.

"When I have lineup questions, I don't look online to see what the so-called experts are saying," Smizzle says. "I call this guy. Everyone, meet perhaps the best DFS player in the world: CSURAM88."

As everyone applauds, I realize that until that moment, I hadn't known that CSURAM isn't actually pronounced "C-Suram," and that it's instead spelled out as "C-S-U Ram eighty-eight." That suddenly makes a lot of sense—he's not a guy with an Indian last name, he's a former Colorado State University Ram, born in 1988.

Even though I didn't know how to pronounce his name, I know who CSURAM is. If there's one crossover star in the industry, it's this guy. A former stockbroker at Charles Schwab, CSURAM—real name Peter Jennings—embodies the gambling dude's fantasy. In some ways he's their apotheosis. Every twenty-four-year-old finance geek stuck in the low levels of Morgan Stanley, taking his (twenty-nine-year-old) boss's

———————

* He'd later tell me that Eovaldi made him some money over the rest of August.

shit and getting blackout drunk at Dorrian's or Cipriani after work, dreams of using his market savvy, innate knowledge, Penn State degree, and natural charm to get around climbing Wall Street's ladder. In the 1980s, it was becoming a junk bond investor. In the 1990s, founding a tech start-up. In the late first decade of the 2000s, creating an app. Now CSURAM has found an even better wormhole to leap through: fantasy sports betting.

CSURAM is a god to these men because he is so clearly one of them, made good. He long ago quit his finance job to become a full-time pro, one of the first to prove it could be done. He doesn't talk about how much he has—that would be gauche—but others are happy to tell you he's won millions. In 2014, he placed first in the Fantasy Baseball World Championship, taking home $1 million in a live final at the Atlantis Casino. He too will soon have a role on ESPN, breaking down picks before football games. His "brand," which he speaks about incessantly, is blowing up, becoming more important to him than the money.

Yet brand focused or not, he is still comfortable among his peers, knowing their customs and speaking their language with perfect fluency. And in this group, the perfect openers? Make fun of yourself, your friends, and Johnny Manziel.

On the screen next to the podium, a picture flashes up of the scandal-prone young Cleveland quarterback, the butt of so many jokes. CSURAM had been in a major football final, with massive money at stake. He knew that most of the players would go for the big names. So he got cute. He tried to outsmart everyone else, and ended up outsmarting himself.

"I somehow played that idiot up there," he says, nodding at Manziel's picture.

Of course, he lost badly. You can't get away with that kind of decision making, he stresses, pausing a beat and looking at Smizzle, "unless, of course, you have a horseshoe jammed up there like our friend over there."

The room cracks up, and the show is on. Over the next hour,

CSURAM goes on to drop one tidbit of gambling wisdom after another. Pearls like the best times to post NFL head-to-head matchups: 2 a.m. on Saturday, when people are just getting out of the bars. They'll be drunk, come home, and start drafting lineups in anticipation of the next day's games.

Almost as good? Sniping head-to-head games in the twenty minutes before NFL or college kickoff.

"The best time by far is right before lock on NFL Sunday," CSURAM says. "The fishiest players by far are those guys waking up on Sunday morning like, oh, I'm gonna fire into this—or playing on their phone, at the game. You'll find so many fish just before lock."

CSURAM's advice seems engineered to make him as relatable as possible—his possibilities are your possibilities, his problems your problems. Case in point: his advice about conquering the live final. Live finals are the signature events of the DFS world, an industry conference, reality television show, and frat party all rolled into one. Players qualify in through a series of satellite tournaments, and there is usually one massive prize at stake—$100,000, $500,000, a million dollars. The fifty or so finalists are sent, all expenses paid, to destinations like Las Vegas, the Bahamas, New Orleans—all locales well suited for a bachelor party. In true bachelor party form, they spend the first few days meeting and greeting, riding ATVs in the desert, having pool parties with models, visiting a batting cage with Bo Jackson—before drafting lineups on the final day, with the winners decided on that night's games. FanDuel or DraftKings set the contestants up in massive ballrooms and film the events, complete with emcees, giant scoreboards to chart players' progress, and the equivalent of boxing's ring girls to help make it less of a sausage-fest. At the end of the night, one player holds up a giant cardboard check with a lot of digits on it. CSURAM has been that guy, and it's helped make his legend, his brand. Really, it's why all of us are here. We want the giant cardboard check, too.

His battle-tested advice for surviving a live final? "No hard liquor," he says, fully serious.

Everyone's having fun, he explains, finally meeting the faces behind the usernames, drinking for free, eating on FanDuel's or DraftKings' dime. Yet players who get too drunk can't get up early on the final day to start researching lineups.

"They ended up really hurting themselves by being hungover before a big championship," CSURAM says, before pointing out his fellow pro, Draftcheat, across the room, and telling the story of the time Draftcheat got so drunk at a live final that he lost his computer. Reeking of booze, Draftcheat had to find another one to work on the day of the final—and predictably, he got crushed.

So CSURAM now sticks to beer only at these live finals, a revelation that garners murmurs and nods of agreement from the attendees. I have to give the guy credit—he knows his audience, and how to speak to it. He makes the pro's world seem attainable, a new life only one big live final win away—as long as you steer clear of the hard liquor.

Lunch break. I wander out into the hall to grab a bite, returning with a surprisingly healthful quinoa salad and a Pepsi. Most of the sharps are in the back, keeping to themselves. CSURAM, on the other hand, is holding court, surrounded by a pack of five would-be protégés, hearing tales of their successes and failures and seemingly eating it up. Mike, the finance type from my table, is among them, hanging on the pro's every word every time CSURAM interjects to drop some knowledge.

Between bites of quinoa, our table grinds into gear on some low-level small talk about how often we play. Jamison, a warehouse worker from far out on Long Island, is a three-sport player: baseball, football, basketball. In season, he plays pretty much every day. The man next to me, a well-tanned one whose name I never quite get, says if he takes a day off from baseball or basketball, he feels like he's fallen way behind—so much can change in a day. Casper in the DraftKings shirt, real name Chris, says he never misses a day, and goes on to prove it. It's his first trip to New York, and we're sitting right off Central Park, but instead of venturing outside, he spends the rest of lunch hunkered down with his computer, drafting lineups for that night's baseball games.

I'd assumed that despite the high entry fees, most of the Boot Camp attendees were recreational players, hoping to maybe cash in a big score or two and buy a sports car. It begins to hit me, however, that everyone's dreams run a little grander than that.

"If you guys could, would you turn pro?" I ask them. "Do this full-time?"

"Absolutely," says Jamison the warehouse man.

"In a heartbeat," says well-tanned medical guy.

"I don't want a nine-to-five job," says Casper.

Finance Mike returns to our table from his session at CSURAM's knee just as lunch is winding down, and he won't shut up about what a great guy "Ram" is.

"He's totally normal, down-to-earth," Mike says, relating how he peppered the pro with one technical question after another and his new buddy "Ram" was only too happy to offer insight.

"He even gave me his number," Finance Mike boasts, beaming like he just asked the prettiest girl in school to go to prom. Actually, that's exactly what just happened, I realize with a sudden pang of jealously. If I'm going to turn pro, I can't be letting Mike et al drink at the fountain of professional wisdom ahead of me.

I need those digits.

On the first advertisement I saw touting Al_Smizzle's Boot Camp, the pro and his group laid out two levels to the experience. For $250, players could attend the daylong conference, with its presentations, opportunities for questions, tiny bit of chummy time with the pros, and quinoa salad. But for a cool $500, players could opt for the VIP experience, which included Boot Camp, plus more: a ticket to that night's New York Mets–Washington Nationals game, in a luxury suite behind home plate. All the sharks would be there, drinking and mingling and hopefully giving up the goods.

There, I'd have the advantage. A baseball stadium is my turf, my dirt-and-grass office. My plan is to trade a little of my knowledge—insider access and stories—for a little of theirs, a sort of informal bargain struck over Shake Shack fries.

Brandishing my all-important Baseball Writers' Association of America card, I talk Smizzle into letting me come to the VIP portion for free, since they wouldn't need to buy me a ticket anyway. I've often said the BBWAA card is the most valuable thing I own; it offers entry into any park, anytime, anywhere, and no security guard ever looks at the tiny, grainy, fifteen-year-old picture on the front. For anyone who wants to mug me, forget the wallet, go for the writer's card.

(Please don't mug me.)

Even among players who are willing to wager $100, $200, $500 in a day on DFS, throwing $250 toward a baseball game—with no chance of winning more—feels like spending a lot of money. So it's a minor surprise that the VIP experience is almost totally sold out, with Finance Mike from my table snagging the final available ticket at the last minute.

Our Uber-sponsored van pulls up outside Citi Field, a stadium dropped in between a residential neighborhood, an airport, and a wasteland of auto parts and repair shops. We bypass all that quickly; Al_Smizzle and his group are connected to DraftKings, and DraftKings is connected to MLB, and MLB is of course connected to the Mets, and that leads to some pretty sweet perks. Every day DraftKings runs contests where the prizes are suite experiences, or watching batting practice from the field, and it looks like some relative of that connection is at play here—the Boot Camp suite is massive and directly behind home plate on the first level, a far better view than what I'd get in any press box. (Except the former Los Angeles Angels box, destroyed in a fit of anti-press pique by Angels owner Arte Moreno; RIP, awesome press box.)

The VIP attendees file in, probably thirty-five in all, milling about and killing time, ordering food as the minutes tick away until the game starts. There are eight seats at the front of the box, facing the field, and behind them, clusters of circular high-top tables. Very quickly, a sort of informal social order breaks out. The pros take the seats facing the field, their backs to the rest of the group, chatting among themselves.

Before long, I find myself in a clutch that reminds me of the famously awkward couch from the frat rush scene in *Animal House*—there's Jagan, Casper the DraftKings ghost, Finance Mike, and some strange older man who doesn't speak and just stands around us. Watching the pros wall themselves off, I'm a little annoyed—my own ambitions aside, these VIP attendees shelled out significant dollars to hobnob with the professionals, and now they're being ignored, shoved into the back area like second-class citizens.

Then, an interesting thing happens. Draftcheat pulls out his computer, CSURAM as well. And I realize these pros aren't socializing—they are working, researching, conferring, figuring out who the best plays are that night. The dusky stadium fills up around them with forty thousand buzzing fans, all swilling beers and talking about the game about to unfold. But for these professional bettors, it's crunch time, and they sit intently staring at their computers, inputting real players to create their fake teams.

Finance Mike notices the display around the same time I do, and we quietly watch them work as the anthem singer steps up to the microphone.

"The Star-Spangled Banner" begins, enough to disrupt their work, briefly. CSURAM simply stands up, his laptop open atop his palm, and continues working between verses, the bombs bursting everywhere but over his seat.

Mike leans over to me as the anthem concludes.

"He's putting in fifty thousand dollars' worth of action right now," he whispers.

I realize that's probably underselling it.

Anthem complete, the game gets under way, and our box settles into a quiet attentiveness as the first innings unfold. This group is watching this baseball game, yes, but in its own way; most of the attendees have picked the Mets' starting pitcher, Jacob deGrom, for their DFS teams. As he struggles in the early going, groans come from throughout our box, the sort of "I knew this was going to happen!" second-guessing that comes with any early failure.

Even with their lineups set, the pros are still a group apart, sitting in their choice front seats and joking with one another. From time to time, a VIP attendee leans over one of their seats, introduces himself, and an awkward five-minute conversation ensues. That's not what I'm looking for, so I make small talk with another early-twenties finance-type, also named Mike, who says he started playing online poker with his parents' credit cards when he was twelve years old, becoming every senator's case study for why online poker needed to be banned. He racked up a $30,000 profit before his parents realized what was afoot, he claims; the money went into his college fund.

Interesting tales, but as the innings slip away, I feel my mission starting to crumble. The day is mostly over, and with the exception of Al_Smizzle, I haven't talked to any of the sharks.

Finally, the first of the VIPs, Adam Levitan—username Levitan—a writer for the fantasy sports site Rotoworld and expert in the NFL and gambling lines, breaks ranks, milling about to eat some of the Shake Shack grub arriving from the main (and perpetually crowded) restaurant in center field. I've got an easy in with him because he used to be a beat writer for a small paper outside Philadelphia, covering the 76ers—and he knows what a trying life it can be, even if all your friends think you have the world's greatest job.

I stop him, we talk the woes of the traveling beat writer, and soon we are discussing something I don't even claim to halfway understand—the gambling monster that is Las Vegas, and how it can teach us. Levitan is an expert on Vegas—stressing that there's no need to reinvent the wheel for DFS; there's already an entire industry expertly betting on these games, and DFS players simply need to access, leverage, and understand their picks. He's so tuned in to Vegas, his fellow pros call him Ace Rothstein.

"I don't look at the line and say, 'Patriots are favored by seven, all week, cool I'm done for the week,'" Levitan says. "Instead, I'm tracking that line as it moves all week, because I want to know who the sharp people are on, and who the fish are on."

I nod like I am not, clearly, a fish.

"I want to know what the sharpest point-five percent of sports bettors in the world are doing. They have better algorithms than CSURAM. They have better algorithms than anybody. When they make a big bet—a ten-, twenty-, fifty-thousand-dollar bet—the line moves in that direction, no matter how much money is coming in on the other side."

Wiser and emboldened, I look around and spot one of the other VIPs, Renee Miller—username ReneeMiller01—seemingly toward the back end of a conversation with a Boot Camp attendee who appears to be trying to persuade her to get another beer.

Miller was one of two women at the conference—outnumbered roughly 80 to 2. The only other female was a Boot Camp assistant who brought the microphone to questioners; I watched as various morons in football jerseys eyeballed her ass as she passed the mic. While it wouldn't be at all fair to say it's a hostile environment for women, it's certainly an odd one, and Miller obviously stands out, on multiple levels. In a room full of men who are gamblers first or hoping to be, she is an exception— her DFS work is secondary to her real job, as a lecturer in brain and cognitive sciences at the University of Rochester. The PhD in neuroscience has managed to merge her two worlds, authoring the book *Cognitive Biases in Fantasy Sports*. It's why her presentation at Essex House was perhaps the most fascinating to me—it was about the traps your brain can fall into, tricking yourself without even knowing it.

"Let's say," she explained, "that we're trying to ward ourselves against two easy traps: primacy and recency bias."* The human mind is naturally going to weigh certain information more than certain other

---

* Primacy bias is prioritizing the first information we receive too heavily, while recency bias is prioritizing the most recent information in the same way.

information—and this ruins too many DFS players, who have shown a clear bias toward players who jump out to hot starts, and those who are riding unsustainable hot streaks.

"If it's week twelve, why should what a running back or receiver did in week one, or week eleven, be the information that we're going to weigh heaviest when making our decision?" Miller asked during her presentation. "Why isn't what he did in weeks four and five just as important? There's no good reason."

A shelf of advanced degrees, however, is no shield against the macho set, who couldn't quite figure out what to make of her. One, for instance, called for the mic and asked a question clearly meant to endear him to the other bros in the room.

"Is there any studies done on the amount of time I spend on DFS and how pissed my girlfriend is?" He craned his head around to see if he'd gotten any laughs, but it mostly fell flat.

Miller had an easy answer queued up: "Teach your girlfriend how to play." She smiled before moving on, but not before another bro chimed in, "Or just win a lot of money; she'll let you do whatever you want."

Now, with everyone a few drinks in, and as an attractive woman with no visible wedding ring on her finger, Miller has become a popular figure in the luxury box. A rotation of the Boot Camp participants come in to schmooze, ask her if she needs another drink, try a joke about the action on field or Jacob deGrom's hair.

I wait for a lull, and then strike, telling her how much I enjoyed her presentation, and explaining who I am in real life. Once I find a way to drop in a mention of my sportswriter wife and it's clear I'm not hitting on her, we're fast friends. Miller wants my Yankees insight—especially now. For her two DraftKings pitchers* that night, Miller picked all-world Mets pitcher deGrom, and Yankee fill-in starter Bryan Mitchell,

---

* Users select two pitchers on DraftKings, versus only one on FanDuel—one of the many small but important differences between the games on the two sites.

just up from the minors. Now, perhaps with buyer's remorse, she wants my take on Mitchell, who's pitching against the Chicago White Sox, and surviving through the early innings with a 1–0 lead.

"Mid-nineties fastball, touches ninety-seven, curveball, changeup, good control," I tell her. "A little more than just a guy, but probably not a building-block piece, either. Also, he has an amazing back tattoo, his name written all the way across his upper back like it would be on a jersey. Makes him look like an idiot."

Mitchell is only making this Saturday night start because the Yankees' burly ex-ace, CC Sabathia, had his outing against the Texas Rangers moved up when fellow starter Michael Pineda went on the disabled list.

My first thought was not, of course, about the story I'd need to write about Pineda's injury. That thought instead? The struggling Sabathia, off schedule, in boiling Texas was gambler's manna from heaven, a perfect pitcher to bet against, and bet big.

Now, I say this feeling both that Sabathia is a supernice guy, and that he'd fully understand my acting this way—heck, he'd maybe even draft against himself if he could. Sabathia is one of the few major leaguers who openly and actively play DFS. In fact, he's so into it that he's partnered up with FanDuel, and he has his own sponsored leagues. In theory, when you're joining "CC Sabathia's Fantasy Baseball League," there's some suggestion that you're playing against CC himself, or even winning some of his mountains of cash.

In reality, he says, he doesn't play the baseball portion; he just lends his name to the contest—the commissioner's office has warned baseball players against participating in DFS baseball. But he's all over DFS basketball, and got much of the Yankee bullpen into it. I sidled up to him one day a few weeks before the Boot Camp and let him know I'd started playing, and CC was thrilled at having someone else to commiserate with over losses.

"It's hard as hell," he guffawed, breaking into his signature wide grin. "I play with my cousins, and with Dellin [Betances], a few other guys in here."

"I've only played baseball so far," I told him, "and that's hard as hell, too."

Sabathia played during the NBA playoffs, did well sometimes, got smoked at others.

"I don't want to sound like a dick," I prefaced, certain to thusly sound like a dick, "but you know, you've got a ton of money already. Are you betting big?"

"No, no way," CC said. "I just like to play it, you know? So I've got something on the game when I'm watching. I bet like five bucks, ten bucks. I just like to beat my cousin."

CC may not need the money, but I do. So his spot start was license to put every Texas Rangers right-handed hitter in the lineup. CC is a former Cy Young winner, but with a bum knee and high-mileage arm, he's getting crushed by righties at this point in his career.

We were in the Yankee clubhouse when the CC spot-start news came down, and my fellow reporters and I immediately pulled out our phones and started reengineering our lineups to put in all the Texas hitters we could.

"Who is Adam Rosales?" one asked me.

"I don't know, but he only costs two thousand dollars, so he's in!" I said with glee.

Just then, a massive figure loomed over us, and I realized we were standing directly in front of the locker of the man whose corpse I was dancing on, Sabathia himself.

"Excuse me, guys," CC said.

"Oh, uh, sorry, CC," I stammered as we quickly skittered off, hoping he hadn't heard quite how eager we were to witness his demise.

For the record, that Thursday night CC gave up five runs in five innings, before leaving the mound due to heat exhaustion and being rushed to the medical center at Arlington for treatment. And before I'm called completely heartless, he was fine! He just needed some fluids.

Anyway, by Saturday night at the Mets game, Thursday's plays are long forgotten. And to Miller's consternation, suddenly Sabathia's teammate Mitchell isn't doing much better—the scoreboard at Citi Field changes to show that Mitchell has given up four runs.

Miller lowers her head in mock anger, and gives me some ribbing about my positive scouting report on Mitchell.

"I guess maybe he is 'just a guy.'" I shrug.

We exchange numbers and emails, and follow one another on Twitter, the surest modern sign that two people are now inextricably linked.

I spot CSURAM across the box, but he's still surrounded by people, a group conversation that allows for no one-on-one time.

I reset my focus to Draftcheat, real name Peter Christensen, the pro who had gotten too drunk and lost his computer at the live final. Draftcheat is a big, strapping, bearded Minnesotan, one of those quiet-on-the-surface-but-loud-in-the-bar types that the Twin Cities seem to produce so well. We hit it off pretty quickly—he wants to know who the biggest assholes on the Yankees are, a topic that comes up frequently—and I want to know what other sports to expand into. He explains that soccer is the promised land: the DFS players are mostly homers who pick their favorite players regardless of the best matchups.

"Just a bunch of English donkeys," he says.

Unlike baseball, soccer stats are in their infancy, so understanding what will score points requires watching much more game film than most other sports. But Draftcheat is fine with that; as a former collegiate soccer player at Luther College and an Arsenal supporter, he's a legitimate fan.

We make an agreement to discuss soccer stats going forward, and he gives me the link for what he claims is the best soccer site to play on, Mondogoal. I tell him I'll give him the referral so he gets a kickback every time I play. We exchange email addresses, jointly cheer as Nationals pitcher Joe Ross notches a strikeout for both our DFS squads, and then part as I go for my first beer of the night.

A Shock Top in hand, I settle in to actually watch a little of the game while I stalk my true target. The alcohol is beginning to take its toll on everyone; the stratification that existed early in the game is long gone. There are clumps of VIPs strewn throughout the box, and one-on-one conversations are a distant memory. Everyone is butting into everyone else's space, and all are fine with it.

In this context, I've got to time it right, and the time isn't right just yet. So I wait. It's odd to be watching a baseball game without any intention of writing something about it—you notice things you wouldn't otherwise. Freed from the hermetically sealed and culturally silent press box, and so close to the action, the stadium just feels so alive—especially when the Mets stage a big comeback against their division rival.

But the announcer is soon calling the seventh-inning stretch, which to me means there's little time to waste as I see CSURAM head to the bathroom. I situate myself alongside a metal girder near the suite's entrance, my head swiveling between his likely return path and the action on the field as the Mets' Lucas Duda crushes a long home run over the Citi Field wall. I can't say I'm like a lion tracking his prey—I'm much more hyena, lurking in the shadows for someone who hopefully washed his hands when he finished in the bathroom. Pride officially swallowed, I see CSURAM coming out of the men's room and virtually leap out from behind the girder to make sure no one else can get to him before I do. I stick out my hand, make the briefest introduction, and assume that millions in DFS winnings will now soon be mine.

"Let's get a beer," he says, beckoning me over to the waitress doing the game's last call. A man with his priorities in order, I can respect that.

Whatever part of his brain is devoted to building the CSURAM brand goes into overdrive the minute he hears "*Wall Street Journal*," and soon we're buddy-buddy, deep in conversation about the future of DFS and how it might grow. I entered this conversation as the supplicant, looking to gain his favor. Within minutes, it feels like the other way around. When Al_Smizzle and I discussed CSURAM a day ago, Smizzle said that CSURAM's superpower was his ability to network. I don't totally agree; I think it's the ability to make it seem like—without being desperate—he wants to be your friend more than you want to be his. And it isn't just with me; he'd been like this all night long, with most of the attendees.

Before long, CSURAM whips out his phone and takes me on a tour of cool things he's done and seen as a result of DFS. There's him with Tiger Woods, him playing poker with Mark Cuban, then, even more interesting—a picture he took of the elusive Condia, the first great DFS pro, with Condia's Ferrari.

"There's maybe ten people in all of DFS who have ever even seen what Condia looks like," he crows.

Just then, one of the attendees, one who had been monopolizing CSURAM's time earlier, dive-bombs our conversation. This dude, wearing a loose plaid button-down and a backward cap, hails from Ottawa, and is openly defying the public address system announcements that fans should consume alcohol responsibly. He plants a hand on CSURAM'S shoulder and asks about the coolest thing "Ram" has ever gotten to do in DFS.

CSURAM immediately launches into a tale of how, in his days working for since-swallowed early-era DFS site StarStreet, he helped organize DFS-related parties at the Playboy Mansion, back in the true Wild West days of the industry. Did we know, CSURAM asks rhetorically, that there are four tiers of women who can be hired for each Mansion event?

At the top, of course, are the actual Playmates themselves, and they cost enormous amounts just to rub elbows with. Then there are models who have done legitimate photo shoots in major magazines—*FHM*, *Maxim*—and they're almost as exclusive and pricey.

"And they cost more if you want to fuck," our Canadian interloper shoots in, his tone clear that he's waiting for the verbal equivalent of a fist bump.

"They aren't banging anybody," CSURAM says with authority. "They're there as professionals—this is what they do."

Below that is a middle tier of porn stars, he explains, who might be recognizable if they walked by at the mansion—maybe they'd been in a video by one of the major companies, or done some crossover acting work. They have name value, at least of some sort.

Then, CSURAM says, there are the "cam girls"—those who are plucked away from doing video-chat porn and bused in. They're mostly Eastern European immigrants, and chances are they will stay long, long after the Playmates have left.

"You don't want to go near those girls," CSURAM states, definitively.

The Ottawa drunk is sufficiently sated with tales of debauchery that he heads off to watch the final inning of the game, the Mets clinging to a 3–2 lead. This is my chance. I lean in and make my pitch: that I'm serious about joining his world, that I think my baseball knowledge and connections can maybe give me a leg up, that I need guides to help me along the way. I ask him if he'll help me learn what it takes to be a pro.

CSURAM smiles broadly and holds up his hand, awaiting a high five.

"Dude, another one of us! I'm so in. Let me get your number," he says, as we execute a perfectly resonant high five—good palm contact, loud clap, a direct hit of awesome.

With that sealed, we turn to the field, where the Mets have two outs to go with closer Jeurys Familia on the mound. I think my lineup is a slight loser, and that I've shed a little more cash on the night. CSURAM seems to feel the same, even if "a little money" for him is, say, $40K. Neither of us is a Mets fan, and neither of us has what we consider significant money riding on this game. But for just a minute, we are swept up in the moment, cheering and clapping along as Familia goes for, and gets, the final out, pumping his fists wildly as his teammates crowd around to celebrate.

Maybe baseball isn't so boring after all.

03

In March 2015, a sixty-second television advertisement featuring brothers Dave and Rob Gomes aired for the first time. The DraftKings ad, titled "Real People, Real Winnings," showed the Gomes brothers in sports jerseys, gnawing on their fingernails as they watched their fantasy players perform on a Monday night in November 2014. They were in their mother's Italian restaurant, Antico Forno, in Boston's scenic North End, surrounded by friends. Then something happened on an unseen television screen, and soon the brothers Gomes were leaping around, throwing their hands in the air, bro-hugging in more ways than one.

"This is what it looks like when real people win a million dollars playing fantasy football," a voice intoned.

The camera cut to the Gomes boys holding a giant check with many zeroes, as champagne sprayed all around.

"Just pick your sport, pick your players, and pick up your cash," the voice-over promised.

A line flashed across the screen, tantalizing viewers with an astounding figure: "The average user's winnings over the last 12 months: $1,263."

"It's the simplest way to win life-changing piles of cash every week," the voice offered.

In case you didn't get the message, you'd have to wait only a few minutes to see it again. As football season neared in 2015, DraftKings would spend enough to make the advertisement into the most frequently seen spot on TV. According to estimates by television ad tracker iSpot.tv, DraftKings spent $32,578,055 airing the advertisement a whopping 15,108 times. When I'd met Rob Gomes out by the pool at the Fontaine-bleau in early September, he said even he'd gotten tired of seeing it by then.

But it kept airing, and airing, along with many ads just like it. There were 57 million fantasy players in North America in 2015, according to the Fantasy Sports Trade Association, but nearly all of them played season-long fantasy sports, with somewhere under 10 percent of that population actively playing Daily Fantasy.

DraftKings, flush with venture capital and valued at more than $1 billion, believed it could use this ad blitz to attract those season-long players, unseat its bitter rival FanDuel, and take over the top spot as the biggest DFS company of all.

It wasn't just a business move. It was personal. There was no love lost between the CEOs of the two companies—FanDuel's Nigel Eccles and DraftKings' Jason Robins. Eccles, viewed by many as the father of the industry, saw DraftKings as a dangerous upstart, too aggressive and loose with the rules. Robins, conversely, viewed Eccles as condescending and dismissive of DraftKings and what it had built, according to people close to the DraftKings CEO. The DraftKings advertising campaign would be the great equalizer between the two companies, allowing DraftKings to bridge the gap in both prestige and customer base.

At FanDuel's board meetings that summer, members blanched when they saw DraftKings ads airing over and over. Paul Martino of Bullpen Capital, one of FanDuel's first investors and a four-year board member, recalled the moment when they grasped just how much DraftKings was willing to spend on advertising—and recognized it meant they'd need to respond with an ad blitz of their own.

"I remember those board meetings—we're saying, oh my God, are they really outspending GEICO?" Martino said. "They're outspending GEICO this week. Oh my God! As much as we were part of the ad war, man oh man, I'll tell you who I think started it."

Still, he said, what choice did they have but to fight back?

"This is a game-theory problem," Martino said. "When you had an opponent willing to spend like DraftKings did—a level three to five times what we thought they ever would have—you have a set of very bad choices in front of you. What do you do? I'm not going to spend? I'm going to cede the market? I'm going to quit?"

FanDuel waded into the fray, and the arms race propelled both companies into the advertising stratosphere, ranking alongside giants like AT&T, Warner Bros., and the U.S. Army. DraftKings spent more than $150 million on television advertising in 2015 and was the nation's top advertiser through parts of August and September. FanDuel was close behind with top-ten advertiser status, as each company tried to bring in new users and outflank the other. A Daily Fantasy ad aired every 1.5 minutes across all TV platforms nationwide at the peak of the onslaught, and sources said the companies spent roughly $750 million on advertising across all platforms on the year.

It worked. In August and September, the DFS giants attracted huge numbers of new users. DraftKings went from a half-million real-money active players to roughly 2.5 million in a matter of months, according to a company official.

Their ad war also alienated pretty much everyone who didn't sign up, and some who did. The backlash, which began with scores of anti-DFS postings on social media and forums like Reddit early in the month, reached a fever pitch by late September.

At the same time, other worrying issues were quietly building. People were starting to realize what I already knew—how badly lopsided the ecosystem was. When MaxDalury explained that 1 percent of the players were winning 60–70 percent of the cash, I figured it had to be an exaggeration. It turned out he was underestimating. Before the NFL season, McKinsey & Company released a study based on the first half of the 2015 baseball season, showing that 1.3 percent of players took in a whopping 91 percent of the winnings. Unlike online poker, where top players have a much harder time dominating, the basic structure of DFS and the few limits set by the companies allowed the best players to be everywhere at once. Omnipresent and lethal, they were destroying the little guys, according to study coauthors Ed Miller and Daniel Singer.

"DFS offers no protection for novices," they wrote. "In poker, there is a large skill gap between the best players and the typical recreational players. But fortunately for the recreational players, the best players won't be found at their tables. The sharks focus their energies on the tables with $5,000 buy-ins and higher. You can sit at a $50 buy-in table and be safely insulated from the best of the best, because it's not worth their time to try to take your money.

"In DFS, the top players can enter every contest. One player, who goes by the handle Maxdalury on DraftKings, every day enters nearly every MLB contest on the site, from the $10,600 buy-in contests to the $1 buy-in tournaments. Indeed, sharp players often enter each small buy-in tournament dozens or even hundreds of times. The novice player is like Neo in *The Matrix Reloaded*, fighting hundreds of Agent Smiths simultaneously."

The companies responded that baseball is a particularly shark-heavy version of DFS* and that this represented a worst-case scenario in an insufficient sample size, but they didn't deny the overarching thesis that the top players were dominant to an almost comical degree—none of which was reflected in the get-rich-quick ads, of course. The study was widely circulated, and educated players and observers started to understand just how formidable the top players really were.

Overwhelming ads and an unfair playing field might have been enough. But a third issue nagged at the American public, tipping the scales for many from annoyance to mistrust.

---

* Which I believe is probably true. For shark dominance in the major sports, I'd say it goes NBA-MLB-NFL-NHL.

As mainstream media took an interest in Daily Fantasy as a result of the commercial ad binge, questions were posed about the legality of it all, and the response from the company founders was curious. The UIGEA loophole was always referenced, but they often took it a step further—saying not only that they were perfectly legal, but that they weren't a gambling product at all, because theirs is a skill game. They aggressively promoted this idea—going so far as to demand that advertisers or affiliates scrub any gambling-related language from their sites.

Sometimes it worked. SuperLobby.com, an affiliate site that tracks DFS traffic, got a letter from the Fantasy Sports Trade Association instructing it to change the gambling-related word *rake* to *margin*. The site complied, site founder David Copeland told me. Other times, it didn't go so well. In July, DraftKings requested that comedian Bill Burr stop referring to them as a gambling company on his DraftKings-sponsored podcast. It backfired when Burr took their complaints on the air.

"Fucking DraftKings has been breaking my balls—breaking my fucking balls," Burr said. "I love DraftKings. I don't know what their— they don't like that I'm making a joke that they're a fucking gambling website. They don't like it. I get a text, 'we love the reads, just don't say we're a gambling website, it's more of a skill-based thing.'

"What are you talking about?" Burr continued. "You're gambling. You've combined fantasy baseball or fantasy football with a Vegas sportsbook. We're all adults. I don't have a problem with it. Why can't you just be who you are, DraftKings?"

It all rankled.*

"I believe strongly that there's an underlying belief that the industry is not being sincere, or genuine, when they say that they're not anything

---

* At the Fantasy Sports Trade Association conference in January 2016, two researchers, Brody Ruihley from the University of Cincinnati and Andrew Billings from the University of Alabama, delivered a presentation detailing survey data from five hundred FSTA-associated fantasy players and fantasy industry members. Fully 70 percent of respondents said that, when money is involved, fantasy sports is a kind of gambling. These are the people who know best. If they didn't buy the companies' line, why would the general public?

close to gambling," ESPN gambling reporter David Payne Purdum said. "When you hear them say that, colloquially, the general public just says, 'This guy is sitting here BSing me.'"

The ads, the not-gambling talk, the uneven playing field—the resentment stewed and burbled across those forums and social media outlets, the disaffected mob waiting for the companies to stumble.

One of the few who realized this was Jeremy Levine, who had founded the early DFS site StarStreet. It was later sold to DraftKings as he pursued a new DFS venture, Draft. He understood quickly as DraftKings and FanDuel commercials filled the airwaves that this ad war was going to have repercussions. The companies got the growth they wanted, sure. They also put targets on the backs of everyone in DFS.

"They shot steroids into the industry," Levine said. "That kind of growth got the industry where it was, and also got it where it is. It gets you what you want, but also has side effects."

"Real People, Real Winnings" last aired just after midnight on Monday, September 28, 2015, during a V8 Supercars race. The ad's final airing signaled the end of one period in Daily Fantasy's rise. Earlier that same night, another event took place that would take the industry in a wholly different, and far darker, direction: DraftKings employee Ethan Haskell won $350,000 playing on FanDuel.

———————

Chris Mazzone got into Daily Fantasy early, joining the beloved DFS site DraftStreet in May 2013. When the site was acquired by DraftKings in 2014, he stayed on as DraftKings' director of affiliate marketing. He saw the potential in Daily Fantasy Sports early on, and loved everything about it—working in it, talking about it, and playing it on competitor sites in both his DraftStreet and his DraftKings days.

For him, playing on other DFS sites was simply part of the job. It was part of what DFS employees did, part of the fun of living and working in the Daily Fantasy world.

Sometimes, before games began, he and his fellow employees would look at the ownership percentages for players on their site—Peyton Manning owned by 20 percent of teams, Tom Brady owned by only 10 percent, for instance—and marvel at whom their users were picking that day.

"I was doing it with other DraftStreet friends when we worked at DraftStreet," Mazzone said. "We all saw ownership percentages, and we'd talk to our buddies, saying, whoa, I can't believe this guy is so high-owned today.

"We didn't think we were doing anything wrong. We weren't saying, hey, here are the ownership percentages, use them to win. We were just talking."

Mazzone paused.

"But some people were smart enough to use them for their own ends."

As Daily Fantasy sites grew, DFS employees were encouraged to play on competitor sites, as a means of learning about the competition and improving their own product. Nobody saw anything wrong with it, at first. Most thought the positives outweighed potential negatives.

"When we were a small industry, a couple hundred thousand people playing, it was commonly known that our employees would try out and play on other sites, and it wasn't a big issue," FanDuel founder Nigel Eccles said. "They saw it as similar to Yahoo! season-long fantasy employees playing on ESPN's site, striving to build a better product, a better fantasy experience."

Clearly, an intimate familiarity with a DFS site is likely to help a person become a better player. But there was always a line there, between employees' having a general, if inside, knowledge of how the sites worked and actually using information about that day's lineups or opponents to gain an advantage. Yet no one was policing that line; because the industry lacked any regulatory oversight, the DFS public simply had to trust that adequate controls were in place to prevent malfeasance.

Eventually, some DFS employees—like FanDuel's Matt Boccio/PetrGibbons, whom I'd met in Miami—became elite, high-level sharks.

One of these was Ethan Haskell, a midlevel DraftKings employee who played heavily on FanDuel, under the username Haskele.

Haskell, a 2012 Allegheny College alum, joined DraftKings as a content manager in 2014, after two years as an editor at RotoGrinders, the leading Daily Fantasy support, advice, and news site. By the summer of 2015, he was well known and well liked in the DFS community, considered both a good player and a good writer. So when the DraftKings employee went on a scorching hot streak on FanDuel that August, most cheered him as his DFS side gig became far more lucrative than his day job.

Still, he couldn't ignore his work at DraftKings, and one of Haskell's jobs on NFL Sundays was to write up a blog post listing the ownership percentages for big-name players across the site—that is, what percentage of DraftKings users had picked Manning on their teams this week, what percentage went with Brady instead. The article would normally be published after all the games on the slate had kicked off. But in the process of writing his piece on September 27, about forty-five minutes after the first NFL games started, Haskell made a mistake. He inadvertently tweeted out a link to the ownership data—before the rest of the games on the DraftKings slate had actually begun.

I've seen the miscue compared to mistakenly hitting "Reply all" on an email that you meant to send back to one person. I think the mechanics of that are apt. It was the "Reply all" that would change Daily Fantasy forever.

Ownership data is more than just interesting information in the DFS world, and one of the most fundamental differences between traditional, season-long fantasy and its Daily Fantasy variant concerns player ownership. In season-long fantasy drafts, once I pick a player—drafting Tom Brady with my first pick, for instance—no one else can have him. That handsome devil is mine and mine alone.

But in DFS, everyone can draft all the same players—Brady could be on half the teams in any given contest. Or, theoretically, on all of them.

Part of the skill of the game, then, comes in forecasting just how many other users are going to select Brady that day—predicting player ownership.

Predicting ownership levels can be vitally important when competing in big tournaments, known as "GPPs" (Guaranteed Prize Pool contests), and if one can do it right, it offers an edge. That's because one of the smartest ways to win in a big tournament is to play a contrarian strategy, one of actively trying to avoid the players who are the clear best picks—the obvious choices, the ones everyone is likely to make.

That may sound counterintuitive, but the herd gravitates to these most obvious picks in a massive way. So what if the consensus picks fail? And what if you have instead chosen from a second tier of really good, but not great, players? That's where a contrarian player can pull away from the pack.

Suppose, for instance, you believe 45 percent of users will pick Manning to be their quarterback, because he has the best matchup that week—but you believe Brady, nearly as good, will be picked by only 5 percent of users. Wouldn't it be smarter to pick Brady?

Most top DFS minds think so. Most of the time, Peyton will do well, and the 45 percent of users who picked him will do equally well. But when Peyton bombs? All those users who picked him are wiped out. And suddenly the 5 percent of teams that owned Brady will leap ahead, competing with a far smaller group of users for the monstrous prizes at the top of big tournaments, where one of those wins can outweigh weeks of losing.

That's playing contrarian.

The problem is, a contrarian strategy is notoriously hard to pull off, because no one can know exactly how many users are picking which top players. Player ownership can't be predicted exactly.

Or can it?

The sites, of course, know the ownership percentages, the data constantly updating as new lineups are entered, up until lineups lock when the games begin. Because player ownership data could be valuable, many in the DFS community always assumed that no employee placing bets on any site had access to his own site's ownership information until absolutely every game had begun, when all lineups across all sites were set in stone.

When Haskell tweeted the lineup data, it proved that assumption false. Clearly even a midlevel employee had access to internal ownership data while some games on his own site were yet to start.

The inadvertent leak was first noted by user Colin Drew on the forums at RotoGrinders, Haskell's former employer. Drew was upset that an analyst like Haskell had the information at all. What made it worse was that no one knew exactly how early in the day he had acquired it.

"This is a big leak and should never happen," Drew wrote. "It also seems like something that your average analyst should probably not have access too [sic], and able to tell his buddies who is owned and who the best players have. . . . Given that they can access the macro results it seems probable they can access specific users during and/or before contests start."

Haskell himself quickly responded to the concerns, stressing that having the data wouldn't do him any good regarding DraftKings' late-swap contests, as DraftKings employees are barred from playing games at the site.

"This was published in error originally by myself," Haskell wrote in response to Drew's post. "I've fixed the error and we'll be putting checks in place to make sure it doesn't happen again. . . . I was the only person with this data, and as a DK employee, am not allowed to play on site. 100% my fault and I apologize for any issues."

That's right. He wasn't allowed to play on DraftKings. No one said anything about FanDuel.

As Drew noted, if a DraftKings employee like Haskell had access to supposedly privileged ownership information a little before 2 p.m., when DraftKings lineups could still be partially changed, then who's to say he couldn't access it an hour earlier? And if he did, then that employee could tailor his FanDuel lineups to account for that knowledge before FanDuel's games locked at 1 p.m. The ownership percentages from one site wouldn't match up exactly with the other, but would it be an edge? Absolutely; in this difficult game, every new bit of information helps.

That's where the Haskell story got interesting. Haskell could, and did, play on FanDuel, where as Haskele he was a deadly shark, in the middle of an impressive two-month winning streak. On September 27, the very day he released the lineup info early, Haskell hit the biggest score of his life—placing second out of 229,885 lineups in FanDuel's main NFL tournament. He won $350,000.

When users on the RotoGrinders forum made the connection between the data leak and Haskell's big win, there was a sudden and significant uproar, even among a user population that was used to living in this anything-goes world. Users demanded to know when exactly Haskell got the DraftKings ownership data, and if it helped him build his FanDuel lineup.

The complaints reached industry media, where a site called DFSReport published a basic accounting of the details. From there, another site, Legal Sports Report (LSR), followed up with its own story.

While DFS Report had the nuts and bolts, LSR, which acts as one of the few truly independent media outlets in the DFS space, tried to shake out what Haskell knew, when he knew it, and what DraftKings was doing about it. LSR reporter Dustin Gouker and site founder Chris Grove interviewed several of the principals and wrote a fairly comprehensive account of the issue, trying to weigh the clear appearance of impropriety with a situation where they had no evidence that Haskell had actually done anything wrong—only that he had accidentally leaked ownership data, and that he had won big the same day. They had no idea when Haskell had actually acquired the lineup data, and if it could have been used to build his winning FanDuel lineup.

"We agonized over the story," Gouker said. "We tried to make it clear that there's no evidence Ethan cheated. To this day, do we really know for sure if Ethan cheated? No. But it certainly laid out a situation where that kind of thing could happen."

They tried to find out what had happened from DraftKings, contacting company PR head Sabrina Macias, who was in the United Kingdom with CEO Jason Robins, but the company was not responsive.

"It was a Saturday night," Gouker said. "We emailed DraftKings, asked if they want to comment. She called us that morning from the U.K. and said you can't do this story without comment from us. She says wait ten minutes. They never call back. Which is what DraftKings does, they delay, delay, delay, until they can give it to someone they'd rather have write it."

That left others to try to fill in the gaps for LSR, including a loquacious lawyer from South Florida named Daniel Wallach, who had a small, gaming-related practice and a big interest in making a name for himself. His primary goal every time he got in the newspaper was to snag more gaming clients. But his secret ambition? To become a media personality, the number-one commentator in the sports law world— he proudly touts that he's appeared on Maria Bartiromo's Fox Business show, among others.

LSR quoted Wallach, who laid out the conceptual dangers of using insider information well for the LSR audience. After the LSR piece published on October 4, bigger media outlets pushed the story further.

At the *New York Times,* there was already a clear skepticism regarding Daily Fantasy. The morning of October 5, the *Times* ran an editorial titled "Rein in Online Fantasy Sports Gambling." The piece, however, was highly generalized, largely just airing concerns about the unbridled growth of DFS.

Thanks to Haskell, they suddenly had something a lot more specific to write about.

Veteran reporter Joe Drape was working the Haskell story for the *Times* and soon Wallach got what he pined for—an interview in that paper. In the original LSR piece, Gouker and Grove had fretted over stressing the insider element, nervous to connect the dots between Haskell making an honest mistake and any potential cheating.

Wallach had no such compunction, and he made the "insider trading" connection plain and simple regarding Haskell's win.

"It is absolutely akin to insider trading," Wallach said to the *Times*. "It gives that person a distinct edge in a contest."

It was the first time the words *insider trading* were used in the national media in regard to the Haskell incident. It wouldn't be the last. Armed with Wallach's quote, the *Times* sent out an email blast promoting the DFS story as a major scoop and tagged it with the headline "Fantasy Sports Employees Bet at Rival Sites Using Inside Information."

"The insider trading quote led to the headline, and that really snowballed everything," said ESPN gambling reporter Purdum.

It quickly resonated. At LSR, Gouker cringed when he saw how the *Times* had played the news.

"The *Times* writes this story, with its ridiculous headline. Max two hours it was up before they took it down," Gouker said.

In an unusual move, the *Times* soon softened the headline, to "Scandal Erupts in Unregulated World of Fantasy Sports," but it hardly mattered. The idea of a Daily Fantasy Sports scandal was juicy, and fresh off the advertising binge, the world was ready for it. The Daily Fantasy bubble was about to burst.

Before the *New York Times* story broke, FanDuel CEO Eccles had been tracking the Haskell incident through its early stages. He recognized there was a problem, and that some were angry, but as the player pricing—and hence, player ownership—was different on DraftKings and FanDuel, he didn't see it as a major issue, not something likely to spiral out of control.

"I didn't think it was a big story," Eccles said. "The information mistakenly shared was maybe of some use to players on DraftKings for the late games. And that's bad, and that's why it was a problem. But it was of no use, as far as I could see, on FanDuel. So, to get information from DraftKings, which has got a different pricing system, it just didn't make any sense to me that anybody would draw this line and think, there's a connection there. So I didn't think it was a big issue." *

But as the *Times* story and its insider trading suggestion spread virally, Eccles was soon forced to recognize the new reality: this storm was beyond anything DFS had seen before.

"Really, when the *New York Times* decided to create this story, of insider trading, that's when it suddenly became a crisis. . . . My initial reaction was that it's a category seven," Eccles said. "And so, once we moved further into that wake, it was a category ten."

DraftKings CEO Robins, off in Europe working on DraftKings UK, soon realized the same, and flew home to do damage control.

He was right to do so. Because within twenty-four hours, the entire landscape had shifted under both companies' feet. Numerous outlets piled on to do their own pieces following the *Times'*. Overnight, DFS became one of the biggest topics in America.

Everyone wanted a piece of this story, from major news programs to late-night hosts, a chance to finally take this rich, aggressive bro culture down a peg. The merrily snarky website Deadspin, for instance, created a "GriftKings & ScamDuel" graphic that accompanied its stories about the suddenly reeling DFS giants.

Even author Stephen King weighed in.

"FanDuel and DraftKings: Skeevy from the jump," he tweeted.

---

* I disagree completely—and I think he's understating the impact of knowing ownership percentages on one site versus the other. For instance, DFSReport noted that the players in Haskell's $350,000 winning lineup had remarkably similar ownership percentages on FanDuel and DraftKings. His quarterback, Andy Dalton, was owned by 2.3 percent of FanDuel users in Haskell's contest; Dalton was owned by 2.5 percent of DraftKings users in that site's equivalent contest. His running back, Devonta Freeman, was owned by 6.7 percent of FanDuel users; he was owned by 8 percent of DraftKings users. No individual offensive player Haskell rostered had more than a 4 percent ownership difference between the two sites. It's legitimately debatable how much of an edge knowing ownership data offers—I'd argue it's small, but it's there—but Eccles's claim that one site's data has no bearing on the other's doesn't seem to fly.

DFS allies and corporate partners frowned at the developing storm. Over at Major League Baseball, DraftKings' most important partner, MLB execs expressed surprise that DraftKings employees were allowed to play on competitor sites at all. ESPN, which had consummated a $250 million, two-year exclusive branding and promotions deal with DraftKings months earlier, briefly pulled all DraftKings-branded content, like fantasy segments sponsored by the company, as it sought to cover the news of the story—though it continued to run DFS commercials.

Worrisome as these developments were, they were the misgivings of parties with a financial stake in DraftKings' and FanDuel's continued existence. The watchful eye of government officials represented a much more serious threat.

At the office of New York attorney general Eric T. Schneiderman, the *Times* story resonated. The attorneys hadn't paid much attention to Daily Fantasy before, but they were like anyone else—unable to avoid the commercial onslaught, with its promise of instant, easy riches. With the insider trading possibility now on the table, they knew they wanted to explore the industry further. But initially, they had little idea what Daily Fantasy even was—how big the companies were, how it worked, who was winning, whether people actually were getting rich quick. The day after the *Times* story ran, attorneys from various divisions met to figure out just what they were dealing with. At the meeting, Schneiderman's Internet bureau chief, Kathleen McGee, wrote three words on a whiteboard: "Fraud," "Deception," and "Criminal." Those themes would guide their work going forward. Initially, they focused on the insider trading allegations and the Haskell incident. But they quickly started going down other avenues, shifting their focus to issues of false and deceptive advertising,* and larger questions of fraud. They were overwhelmed by the breadth and scope of what they found, McGee said.

---

* Remember that claim from the Gomes brothers ad that an average user's annual winnings were $1,263? Yeah, about that: "The way they calculated average winnings was to

"Because this was an industry that had really run wild, anywhere you turned there were issues. I cannot put enough emphasis on this," she said.

Within a few days, however, they started asking a different question: whether the entire operation was illegal gambling, and thus barred in the state of New York. Once they looked at New York state law and believed they were dealing with a wholly illegal enterprise, they shifted their focus to that front.

"Once you come to the irrefutable conclusion that it's gambling, as defined under our law at the time, everything else just falls by the wayside," McGee said. "If it's illegal, you simply have to deal with that."

Three days after the *Times* story ran, Schneiderman sent letters to Robins and Eccles, formally beginning the inquiry into DraftKings and FanDuel.

Even though investigators had quickly and quietly moved past the Haskell question, the companies themselves were still fighting the insider trading claims hard in the court of public opinion, even taking the rare step of working together to prove Haskell's innocence. Eccles and Robins made one public appearance after another, trying to restore trust in their companies as the media and the public railed against the commercials, the unfair playing field, and the potential for shenanigans. DraftKings conducted an internal inquiry, releasing data that it argued showed Haskell could not possibly have done anything wrong.

"The evidence clearly shows that the employee in question did not receive the data on player utilization until 1:40 p.m. ET on Sunday, September 27. Lineups on FanDuel locked at 1:00 p.m. that day, at which point this employee (along with every other person playing in a FanDuel contest) could no longer edit his player selections. This clearly demonstrates that this employee could not possibly have used the information in question to make decisions about his FanDuel lineup," they wrote in a release.

---

exclude all the losers. That's a very creative way to do math," said New York assistant attorney general Justin Wagner.

They later engaged the heralded firm of Greenberg Traurig, and former U.S. attorney John Pappalardo, to further investigate the Haskell incident, eventually releasing a summary of a report that showed the exact time Haskell submitted his FanDuel lineup, the details bolstering their initial claims that there was no wrongdoing.

"A fantasy lineup identified as S227527336 was submitted in the FanDuel.com $5M NFL Sunday Million at 3:28 a.m. on Sunday, September 27, 2015. The lineup was submitted under an account registered to DraftKings employee Ethan Haskell," the summary read.

Their arguments started to gain traction, but it hardly mattered; already, Haskell himself wasn't the real issue. The problem instead had metastasized into a much larger question: did the public trust Daily Fantasy Sports?

"Within a very short time, it really was very little about Ethan, and much more about the big picture," LSR's Gouker said. "He was just more an allegory. His name got thrown around, but it wasn't him. It was just that people were saying that these sites could be crooked. It very quickly became about oh, Daily Fantasy and evil gambling. It was well beyond just Ethan. I feel bad for the kid. Especially if he didn't cheat. If he did, screw him."

———

The companies did take one smart, badly needed step toward improving their product and reinforcing their legitimacy in those first few days: they banned employee play. At first it was billed as a temporary move, but it stuck. Eccles said that such a move was long overdue—they just didn't realize it until everything hit the fan.

"What we failed to appreciate was that we had tipped over to being a large mainstream brand," Eccles said, stressing that their problems were the result of rapid growth in the industry.

"There was no point where we realized we'd changed," Eccles said. "We're now a big business. It's not this low-level game anymore. It's actually a lot of money going through the system. And it needs to not only be nothing untoward going on, but there has to be all kinds of real controls, and all the appearance that nothing bad can go on. So while I feel confident that nothing bad was going on, we didn't do enough to ensure that nothing could."

The move did little to stem the tide of anger moving against the companies, however—and inside the industry, they were overwhelmed.

Civil and class action lawsuits began trickling in. Eventually the total mounted to more than forty, most claiming some combination of insider trading, illegal gambling, deceptive advertising, and that the bonus system (that galling "we'll match your $200 deposit!" promise) was misleading.

Other states started getting in on the act, as well. Nevada, never likely to be a friend to Daily Fantasy due to its connections to the land-based casino industry, declared DFS to be gambling under its state law on October 15. That required DFS companies to apply for licenses as gambling companies if they wished to continue operating. Knowing that if they did so, it would be tantamount to admitting that they are gambling operations, both DraftKings and FanDuel declined to apply, and pulled out of Nevada soon after.

They soon had more than just lost states and minor lawsuits to worry about, as outside agencies with a bigger reach than New York's Schneiderman took an interest in DFS: federal authorities.

On the night of October 13, I saw a reference on the Twitter timeline of standout DFS pro team Cory Albertson and Ray Coburn, known in the industry as "RayOfHope," to the possibility that the FBI was beginning to question DFS players. I looked into it further, confirming the inquiries, and immediately let my editors at the *Wall Street Journal* know. Our excellent government reporters worked their contacts and we ultimately broke the news the next day that the FBI, working with the Department of Justice, had begun an inquiry into DFS.

Within a few days, that investigation was joined by another out of

New York, led by U.S. Attorney Preet Bharara, the feared prosecutor who had taken down online poker years before.*

It seemed like new problems arose daily. The Fantasy Sports Trade Association tried to respond to each new issue, but they were swamped, unable to effectively play defense with attacks coming from all directions, FSTA chairman Peter Schoenke said.

"The advertising money that those guys spent just created this huge spotlight on the industry," Schoenke said. "So what happened was, anybody who had any issues, tangentially involved with us at all, wanted to jump into that spotlight, and promote their own cause. If it was a casino that wanted to protect their turf, or get more stuff, or a consumer group that wanted to highlight problems—everyone just jumped in front of it, and suddenly we were in everyone's crosshairs. That's just because of how much advertising we had. A lot of that was just misinformed or not about us. But it became this moment that could take down the whole industry."

Inside the companies themselves, they struggled to comprehend the magnitude of what they were suddenly dealing with. In the two weeks since the *Times* story had run, they had gone from dealing with a localized scandal to recognizing that they were in an existential crisis, with government officials scrutinizing them from all angles. It was more than they had ever expected.

Martino, the FanDuel board member and investor, insists that they did expect a legal threat of this sort at some point—had even planned for it. But the ferocity of the campaign against them was more intense than they'd anticipated.

"We always knew that this would happen, but we never thought it would happen the way it did," he said.

At FanDuel, Martino says, they had believed they were protected

---

* ESPN later reported that these weren't the first federal probes into DFS—the first federal inquiry had actually come in the summer of 2015, when the U.S. attorney's office in Tampa, Florida, sent a letter to both companies informing them they were the subjects of a criminal tax probe.

under federal law due to UIGEA. But privately, they always recognized they were on shaky legal ground at the state level. They had expected scrutiny to come, yet figured it would arrive piecemeal, a few states at a time weighing in over a period of several years.

When the Haskell scandal first broke, Martino and Eccles spoke that night, believing this would be the start of those piecemeal efforts against them.

"I remember vividly talking to Nigel that night," Martino said. "Nigel and I had this opinion that, okay, this is going to start getting us some scrutiny. We knew this day would come. This will probably blow over, but let's get ready because the first couple of states are probably going to act."

But they had badly underestimated the level of anger they'd created. And as Martino admitted, it took them too long to realize that they were facing something that was not going to fade away quickly.

"After two or three weeks, we get to the end of October, we're like, oh crap, this is all going to happen at once," Martino said. "We're gearing up, because we're in an existential fight now, not just a slow-rolling state-by-state thing.

"The idea that thirty attorney generals [sic] would act on this in the same ninety-day window was never in anybody's wildest dreams, or nightmares."

As the companies started to grasp the trouble they were in, the involvement of all these government agencies and the near-daily revelations of another probe took the industry to the next level in terms of publicity. Daily Fantasy was suddenly everywhere—even butting into the presidential race. On Wednesday, October 28, the issue came up at that night's Republican presidential primary debate, when CNBC moderators asked former Florida governor Jeb Bush if the DFS industry should be regulated.

New Jersey governor Chris Christie immediately jumped in, cutting off Bush.

"Are we really talking about getting the government involved in fantasy football?" Christie howled. "Wait a second: We have nineteen trillion dollars in debt, we have people out of work, we have ISIS and al-Qaeda attacking us, and we're talking about fantasy football? Can we stop? Enough on fantasy football; let people play. Who cares?"

The outburst earned Christie sustained applause. But the reality is that a lot of people did care, with a tremendous amount of anger directed at the Daily Fantasy world.

Some of it seemed justified. People were mad about the commercials, mad about the unbalanced playing field, mad about the potential for it to be corrupt, whether it actually was or not. But in many cases, the rhetoric and the anger were so overheated that it was hard to take it seriously. One shining example came from Washington State representative Christopher Hurst, as his state—which has laws so stringent that the DFS companies already refused to operate there—considered making its regulations even stricter. Hurst said that Eccles and Robins are "no different than [drug lord] El Chapo in Mexico, advertising heroin or the methamphetamine on our airwaves a thousand times a day to get kids to try it."

That's a bit over-the-top. It's like Christie said, this is fantasy football, not ISIS or al-Qaeda—or El Chapo. But even if Hurst represents an extreme, as time went on and more bad news came out, it became harder and harder for many to feel much sympathy for the companies.

Once Schneiderman's probe got going, it eventually made public all manner of documents and statements that looked really, really damning for the companies. One of the most glaring was the so-called FanDuel memo. It was a 2012 internal document to FanDuel employees who played on other sites, teaching them how to win money without being so successful that they'd anger regular users who might then complain.

"Never account for more than 2% of entries in any tournament of more than 1,000 entries," the memo cautioned. "Never account for more than 5% of entries in any tournament of more than 100 entries. Players who swamp big tournaments with entries frequently become targets of accusations."

There were other suggestions, two of which led to a disturbing conclusion.

"Never use information gained from viewing users' lineups," and "Seek to avoid playing anyone whose lineups you saw for that time period," the memo read.

That essentially confirmed that at least some employees could, in fact, see the lineups of users on FanDuel and then play them on DraftKings or another site shortly thereafter.

Then, a more insidious practice was laid bare, under the "risks" section, listing one of the chief dangers as "Employees targeting weak users as opponents on other sites. This seems to concern users less, but is more of a real threat. In fact, in a sense, it is happening already."

Bingo. This was the real problem with employees playing. It's very different from what Haskell was suspected of—he was accused of knowing player ownership data, which can give an edge, but only a small and situational one. Employees knowing who the true fish are, however? And targeting them? That's a legitimate menace.

As it turns out, it was probably more than just a theoretical danger. This may have really gone on inside the companies, according to the words of a lawyer who represented several DraftKings employees in the government's investigations.

In the spring of 2016, long after the initial Haskell drama died down, attorney Paul Kelly—a former federal prosecutor in the Boston U.S. attorney's office and onetime head of the NHL players union turned white-collar defense lawyer—appeared at a public forum on sports gambling at the University of New Hampshire's school of law. He seemed to think he was just talking to students. But Legal Sports Report managed to get a full transcript of Kelly's remarks, which are astounding.

After saying that "I did want to start by telling you I need to be just a little bit careful here tonight, as I represent certain individuals, managers from DraftKings, in the ongoing investigations," Kelly proceeded to be anything but careful, dropping all manner of fascinating information and conjecture about three ongoing federal investigations into Daily Fantasy Sports.

"We know that three U.S. Attorneys' offices have launched grand jury investigations: Tampa, Florida; Boston, Massachusetts; and the Southern District of New York, which is basically Manhattan," Kelly said. He went on to explain that the feds were looking into two potential violations: the companies themselves violating UIGEA or another federal law, or employees of the companies using inside information to get an edge—so, what Haskell was accused of doing, but probably didn't actually do in the end. But others, Kelly said, certainly had, using company records to seek out the weakest players.

"What the employees were doing is they were taking these spreadsheets and they were then focusing on the losers," Kelly said.

Whoa.

"And what the employees were doing is they were looking at these spreadsheets targeting the losers at the bottom, the people who didn't know what the hell they were doing, right, and then they were challenging these people over email to contests involving specific sporting events, typically baseball games.

"And they were beating these guys regularly because they were so bad at it, the losers, and they knew they were losers, and they were basically putting money in their own pockets. You know, so the DraftKings guys were betting in FanDuel and vice versa."

Forget Haskell, who had repeatedly been cleared of wrongdoing by this point. Kelly, who should know because he's representing several defendants, claimed that employees of the companies were seeking out and actively targeting weak players, a practice called "bumhunting" in both the poker and DFS worlds. He stressed that he didn't believe anything criminal had gone on, or that any charges were warranted—and these practices had certainly stopped regardless when employee play was banned after the Haskell incident. But his words spread quickly anyway, astonishing many.

Kelly walked his comments back the next day, telling Legal Sports

Report that his words were taken out of context (something any readers can easily judge for themselves, since LSR published the entire 3,884-word transcript) and that he was merely "putting hypothetical information out to the audience to stimulate thought and discussion among law students." He also stated, "nothing I said was based on information I have obtained in the course of representing any client."

Kelly wouldn't speak further when contacted, and the DFS companies aggressively disavowed Kelly's words, FanDuel saying he doesn't represent their employees and wouldn't know about their inner workings, and DraftKings saying to LSR, "The comments made by Mr. Kelly about DraftKings and its employees are absolutely false and unfounded."

Except here's the thing: ex–DraftKings employee Mazzone said that those things absolutely went on.

"Let's just say—I wasn't shaking my head at what [Kelly] said, like 'Oh my God, I can't believe this,'" Mazzone said. "I knew these things were happening and were going on. But I was surprised they were made public so fast, by someone representing them."

It was all emblematic of a new and disruptive industry growing at an exponential rate, with no one sure where the line was drawn between right and wrong.

"There was a lot of, not maliciously wrong, illegal stuff, but I'd say a lot of unethical," he added. "And they were unaware of what they were doing sometimes."

Mazzone said that DraftKings grew so fast that it lacked sufficient controls over information. Too many people were able to access lineup data, with very little oversight over what was done with it. He stressed that the company founders probably didn't realize what was happening—but that they hadn't ensured controls were put in place to prevent it, either.*

"What it was back then was that they were such a small company,

---

* Justin Wagner, of the New York State attorney general's office, backs this up. "One of the things that struck our entire team was the lack of compliance culture at these companies. They were among the biggest advertisers on TV, along the lines of Coke and Pepsi, yet if you asked them if they had internal guidelines and policies like a normal company,

that a lot of people had access to a lot of things," he said. "Sometimes they probably didn't need it. Customer service people probably had access to way too much information at the time. It just wasn't a focus for them, because they were all about growth, and they were playing catch-up when they first came into the market."

The easy availability of data at the company made events like the Haskell situation possible, regardless of whether Haskell himself actually used the data for ill.

"The Ethan Haskell situation easily could have been avoided. Even if there wasn't any wrongdoing. And there probably wasn't, truthfully," Mazzone said.

"But there were others who had access to that information, who were using it wrongfully. That information wasn't difficult to get. Ethan Haskell wasn't the only one who had that information. Any number of people could have asked for that and would have been given it. It wasn't hard to get."

When we talked, long after the Haskell scandal, Mazzone said those events made him regard some of his own actions with regret, even though he had no ill intentions at the time, and wasn't actively trying to gain an edge.

"Even myself—looking back now, I realize I was guilty of things, where I shouldn't have done that," he said. "I could look at percentages of players on DraftKings, and then make my team on FanDuel. I wasn't using that data to make my team on FanDuel, but subconsciously, it was still in the back of my head."

Mazzone left DraftKings three months after they bought DraftStreet, in September 2014, to take the vice president of marketing job at the DFS soccer startup Mondogoal,* where he remains today.

---

or what the employee handbook or guidance on things like playing on other sites, or sharing information was, it was vacant, it was nonexistent."

* Mondogoal, as a primarily United Kingdom–facing product, cheerily describes itself as "skill-based gambling."

At the time he left, DraftKings was launching its initial soccer DFS product. Mazzone had been instrumental in designing it.

"The funniest story, and it tied in with all this unethical stuff—the week after I left DraftKings, they launched the soccer product. I was like, oh great—I can play it now—meanwhile I had just built it!" Mazzone said.

"And so I went and played it—and I won the big contest, for ten thousand dollars."

"Oh, shit," I replied, actually breaking out in laughter at the ridiculousness of it. "That's totally shady."

"It really is," Mazzone agreed, also starting to laugh. "I didn't think anything of it at the time . . . but I shouldn't have been allowed to play. Now I'm like, man, this looks really, really bad—I designed the scoring system. When all this other stuff started happening in the industry, I looked back, and I was like, wait, that's totally terrible." *

As October turns to November, enough of these kind of tales leak out, and enough government entities are nosing around, that the public's trust in Daily Fantasy is badly shaken. User numbers start declining, many of those new sign-ups from the ad binge gradually fading away.

It's a fact I can see playing out all around me. After five months of playing—and for me, more than $2,000 in losses—my real-world compatriots fall out of Daily Fantasy one by one. The other reporters who had played through the baseball season with me, guys like Feinsand, quickly lose interest in DFS football once there's any concern that the games

---

* I would have loved to ask DraftKings CEO Jason Robins about, for instance, Mazzone's comments, or for more detail about the Haskell incident, or simply about what he loved about fantasy sports. Or, really, anything at all. I was able to interview the other two cofounders on limited topics, but all legal or Haskell-related questions were referred to Robins, and Robins was never made available, not even after more than a year of good-faith attempts to sit down with him. Eventually, several interviews were scheduled, then canceled by them at the last minute.

might not be fair. Football was already treating us roughly enough, we low-stakes, $50–$100 a week players, and with so much data circulating about how good the sharks are, these guys soon see Daily Fantasy as either too hard, or potentially too sketchy, to keep playing.

Far more damaging is losing John Tomase. He was supposed to be my partner in all this, my link between this unknown world of the gamblers and the familiar safety of journalism. But he's disgusted by the tales of goings-on. The stench of impropriety is all around this, and that's enough for him to want out.

"The shadiness of the entire enterprise has me seriously contemplating just cashing out and calling it a day," he texts me in early November.

I try to protest, but I understand. Not long after, he lets me know he's officially out.

"I'm done with DFS," he writes. "Winning consistently requires time I don't have, and even then the odds are stacked wildly against schmucks like me. Frustrating."

I'm on my own, in enemy territory. Fortunately, I've made one very important ally.

04

As I step off the elevator and head down the hall toward the Ontario apartment of Jay Raynor, better known as "BeepImaJeep," Beep pops out the front door to greet me. My eyes go immediately to his shirt, which bears the gigantic face of a jowly dog. The dog is sporting a ten-gallon sheriff's hat. The shirt says the sheriff dog's name is Hank.

I am, I admit, a little disappointed. I was hoping for a cat.

All the big DFS players have brands. Al_Smizzle wants to be the guru. CSURAM dreams of being the crossover star. DraftCheat is the voice of the independent player.

Beep's brand is cats.

In the world of DFS, there are frat boys in sports jerseys, there are geeks in department store button-downs, and then there is Beep, permanently clothed in cat gear and an off-kilter baseball cap. At the 2014 DraftKings baseball final, where he took home the $350,000 second prize, Jay arrived nonchalantly wearing a T-shirt with a gigantic cat on the front.

"Now I'm kinda pigeonholed as that guy who wears cat shirts," he says, with a smile that doesn't quite go halfway. "It isn't super-optimal."

Others, worried about their man-card status in the testosterone-fueled world of DFS, might have run from this bit of sartorial peculiarity. Instead, Beep went the other way. He embraced it. Soon he boasted a closet full of shirts adorned with animals, mostly cats: big and small, cute and cuddly. Rowdy tomcats. Cats in space. Cats lying on top of pizzas. Fans started making their own versions for him, and he'd wear those, too. Some of the cats resemble Beep's own ten-year-old cat, Sapphire; others are generic. Once, in a fit of inspiration, he ordered a whopping sixty animal shirts at one time, which he now realizes might have been overkill.

"That may have been a miscalculation on my part," Beep admits. "Like, when am I going to wear my forty-second-favorite animal shirt?"

Point made, but I'm still a little sad my arrival didn't merit a feline face on his chest—only a dog named Hank. I'll get over it. Because in addition to being unabashedly, shall we say . . . quirky, Beep is also very, very good at what he does. And for the past four years, that has been to live as a top-tier DFS pro, one of the most inventive and innovative, able to adapt and reinvent as the game has changed and his foes have improved their tactics.

He's been so good that the sites themselves have had to change their rules in response to his strategy exploits. Beep is the creator of the strategy of "stacking," which means dumping nearly all of a single team's players into one lineup. Until Beep arrived, DFSers had done what seemed logical, playing DFS like traditional fantasy sports: they tried to craft lineups featuring the best players from across all teams.

Beep saw it differently. He recognized that if a single team went bonkers on a given night, the rising tide would dramatically lift all boats in that lineup, especially in baseball. In baseball, if an offense knocks out a starting pitcher early and gets into the opponent's weak middle relief, suddenly the cheap sixth, seventh, and eighth hitters can start racking up points as the game veers into double-digit run scoring. Beep began betting on multiple teams to post huge numbers; he would stack nearly their entire lineups in tournaments. When they'd break out, Beep would win big. So big, in fact, that the sites were forced to respond as others began to copy him. In what became known as the "BeepImaJeep rule," players were permitted to stack only a certain number of players from each team, varying by sport, but usually no more than four or five. Beep didn't mind. He moved on to the next innovation.

"I always liked puzzles when I was growing up," he says. "I liked solving things, figuring it out. That's one of the things I love about fantasy sports. There are so many ways to do it."

I first met Beep at the DraftKings NFL kickoff event in Miami, where he was one of the big-name pros flown in via private jet to lend cachet and status to the party. Unlike many of the other pros I met there, however, Beep didn't seem taken in by all the booze and music and bro-citement. This was his umpteenth live event, and he seemed a little bored, really, like he was looking for something new to motivate him.

So when I told him I hoped to shadow him and learn from him, as I tried to live in his strange world, he didn't react as some other pros had, with willing detachment, or wariness.* Instead, he was thrilled. He legitimately couldn't wait to get started as my full time mentor, checking in on my progress as I learned (and mostly failed) at small-stakes baseball and football through the fall.

That's how I found myself in the small city of Kitchener, Ontario, where Beep makes his home. It's November, not long after I covered what would turn out to be my last baseball game as a *Wall Street Journal* reporter. That was game five of the World Series, the extra-inning classic where Kansas City's Eric Hosmer slid home to tie the game in the ninth inning, and the Royals won it—and the World Series with it—in the twelfth. It was a spectacular scene to take in, but even as I walked through the Royals clubhouse, soaked with champagne, interviewing players, watching actor and Royals fan Paul Rudd hold court like he was on the team itself, my mind was elsewhere. I could focus only on unlocking DFS.

Beep and I have already trained in some basic, non-sport-specific pro strategies via Skype, but now I'm here for a full multiday teaching

---

* The connections I'd made at the Boot Camp had proven valuable, but I couldn't transition any of them into full-time mentoring.

session, learning just how it is that Beep has placed in one final after an-other, including winning five seats in the DraftKings baseball final ear-lier this summer. I've picked a good day. Beep is in contention this very night for a semifinal seat to the two-stage DraftKings Fantasy Football World Championship, scheduled for January, with its massive, biggest-in-DFS-history $5 million first prize on the line. Just winning one of the two hundred qualifying seats is worth $80,000, and with only tonight's *Monday Night Football* game left to go—Buffalo Bills versus New En-gland Patriots—Beep sits in a qualifying position. Looking at the stand-ings, however, he doesn't expect to hold on and win the spot, especially with the high-scoring Patriots offense suiting up for many of his com-petitors, and no Patriots on his side. He estimates he has a 5 percent chance of hanging in for the victory.

"I'm going to get bumped," Beep says, looking at the NFL players who might hurt him. "There are five spots—so I have a shot. But I have to fade Gronk, Brady, and Amendola. That's a lot. And Sammy Watkins."

Then he looks at his DFS competitors, just below him in the stand-ings. "FunkiMunki's going to pass me for sure. MrTuttle might pass me, too. Then I'm done by that point. I need no touchdowns—only field goals. We're live, but not really."

Beep makes his home in Kitchener because it's near where he grew up, and where most of his friends still live. Kitchener, and its neigh-boring sister city of Waterloo, have more than 300,000 people between them, and as Beep tells me repeatedly, it's considered Canada's Silicon Valley. But I can only see the kind of gray, drab place that looks like it's very familiar with being cold. Only sixty miles from gleaming, boom-ing Toronto, it lacks any of that city's cosmopolitan vibe, and I was a little surprised when I pulled up to Beep's apartment building. It's nice enough, but remote—just another apartment block next to another sleepy strip mall. Coming and going through the lobby over several days, I never see one person younger than forty-five, save Beep, who is still in his twenties.

We make some small talk as I throw down my computer bag, and it's immediately clear that Beep isn't used to having strangers over to his place—his home, his office, the spot where he spends nearly all of his time. Walking around, I have to admit I'm a little underwhelmed; I thought that one of the best DFS players ever, one of the big-check regulars, would have a nicer place. There's nothing specifically wrong with Beep's apartment—it's just so . . . normal. The spartan one-bedroom apartment opens to a kitchen on the left, where unopened mail waits alongside the protein powders that accompany Beep's workout regimen. The living room is bare, even for a mid-twenties bachelor, and something looks weird about it. It actually takes me a minute to identify what that is: Beep has no couch. Instead, he has installed side-by-side La-Z-Boy recliners, flanked by an end table and a foosball table, all congregated in front of a big-screen TV. This is where Beep does most of his work, building lineups in his recliners, like a nonracist, cat-obsessed Archie Bunker.

"If you're thinking about the money, you won't make the money," he says, explaining why he hasn't upgraded to a penthouse apartment, like MaxDalury did when he claimed Boston Celtics star Rajon Rondo's old pad.

The remainder of the room is filled out by various workout machines, crowded next to one another. There's a rowing machine, and to my great surprise, an inversion table—a medieval-looking device where the user straps himself to a board, fastens collars around the ankles, and then flips upside down to hang by the feet, the head dangling near the ground. It's supposed to improve circulation.

"All the sitting I do making lineups is really bad for you," Beep explains. "So it's really important to take breaks and get the blood flowing around."

He certainly can't take breaks by pondering the artwork; there is virtually nothing on the walls, save a recently acquired autographed picture of famed seventies Notre Dame pipsqueak Daniel "Rudy" Ruettiger, which Beep won via DFS, and a picture of some palm trees. Most people's walls say something about them, both to themselves and to newcomers. Beep's say nothing to him or me, other than suggesting that he might have just recently moved in. (He didn't.)

His floors, however? They're a different animal altogether. The moment I walked in, I noticed that the rugs weren't exactly factory issue. Some have inspirational messages written on them, reminding Beep to work hard every day, to trust himself.

But it's the rug at the edge of the living room that really catches my eye. This colorful piece depicts a scene at an aquarium, where a massive, terrifying, predatory shark lurks in its tank. Families visiting the aquarium line up along the glass to gape at the fearsome killing machine.

Below the picture are two sentences, in bold yellow lettering: "There are lots of fish. But people come to see the sharks."

I point it out to him, raising my eyebrow quizzically as I ask where he'd get something like that.

"I had that custom-made," he says, smiling and showing enough teeth to remind me that even though he's quirky and friendly, I'm now swimming alongside one of the deadliest predators of all.

The tour concludes in his bedroom, outfitted with just the basics: a bed, a dresser—and a keyboard piano. The keys are covered, but a packet of sheet music is up on the stand—open to the theme music to Super Mario Bros. I immediately demand that Beep play it for me. He's quickly plinking away, and despite a few missed notes, manages to bring me back to 1985 and a childhood spent playing Nintendo—before Beep was even born.

"I used to be really good," he says, turning the pages of the sheet music packet and shifting into Pachelbel's Canon for a more serious vibe. "Around the end of high school I could play a lot of the stuff in here."

Beep is a repository of these kinds of odd talents, all self-taught, usually off YouTube videos—the kind of Renaissance Man of the Frivolous that exists only in the Internet age. He can pull off a seemingly impossible foosball shot, the "snake shot," which only professional foosball players have mastered. He is the 2013 Canadian Board Games champion, an honor he achieved after realizing that he should specialize in the forgotten, less popular games in the competition and dominate those. He desperately wants to claim a spot in *Guinness World Records* and has tried to make it in on multiple occasions. He hasn't yet succeeded.

"A lot of times people think breaking a world record is about being the best at one thing, but a lot of it is strategy," Beep says. "I was hoping to break the *Guinness Book of World Records* thing for eating the most Hershey Kisses in a minute. It's only fifteen—but it's surprisingly difficult."

As a partially homeschooled only child, Beep didn't experience much of the childhood socialization that guides us all down a roughly similar path, and it shows. Growing up in the Kitchener area to a family that ran a technical equipment business, Beep was pulled out of school in grade one after, he says, he and his parents felt the other children and his teacher were unduly mean. During that solitary period at home, he dove into math, reading math texts and theory books on his own, while neglecting many other subject areas. He returned to school in fourth grade at a private Christian academy, a budding math prodigy with massive holes in knowledge areas like spelling and grammar.

"I confused things like *witch* and *which* for far too long," he says, still appearing to be embarrassed fifteen years later.

All that alone time, and all that math, brought out other qualities, like entrepreneurship fused with cat obsession. Beep started a business that was more than just the usual lemonade stand: he built catnip bags using his seamstress mother's sewing equipment. He sold them in his father's office to start, but then eventually went door-to-door when the business got bigger.

"I'd fill them with catnip, put a little bow on them, and sell them for three bucks," he says.

By the time he reached college at McMaster University in Hamilton, Ontario, Beep estimates he'd started at least four businesses. He started his fifth partway through McMaster, when he stepped away from school for a year to found a computer repair business called CompuClean—

"Spend your weekend with your friends, not your computer problems," he advertised—which had some success. But the most valuable venture Beep embarked on during that year only tangentially related to computers. It came when his friend Mike McDonald, whom Beep met teaching chess in high school, got him into online poker in a serious way. Mike, known in the poker world as Timex, was a true poker prodigy, one of those fifteen-year-old kids who were the subject of feature stories in the mid-2000s for winning hundreds of thousands in online tournaments. Mike had recently won $350,000 in a massive tourney, and Beep realized he wanted to be part of the exciting life his friend was building.

"I was like, what am I doing with my life, fixing computers? I should be playing poker," Beep says.

The problem was, Beep wasn't very good at poker, and he was diving into something that was already too well established. Even after eight months of shadowing Mike, Beep was still only a middling player at the highest levels, and he didn't have the kind of money needed to keep getting better as he progressed. So he went back to McMaster and eventually finished his degree in business, constantly on the lookout for something that might give him that same opportunity that poker had given his friend Mike.

In 2011, Beep happened upon his first DFS ad.

"I saw this FanDuel ad. 'Football's coming up. Play against your friends for real money.' And I thought, hmm, maybe I can make money doing this," he says.

Yet there was a wrinkle, one that seems like it would have made this venture a nonstarter: Beep knew nothing about sports.

"I didn't really watch any sports growing up," he readily admits, and I can tell you that's an understatement. Even after five years as a professional sports bettor, Beep knows shockingly little about the sports or the players themselves. He mispronounces players' names regularly (Pujols becomes "Pudgles," Altuve morphs into "Al-Toov") and has no idea about pitch counts in baseball, play clocks in basketball, or coverage strategies in football. Even his fellow math-oriented pros laugh at how truly remedial his knowledge level is for someone routinely wagering tens of thousands per day on player performance.

"Underjones told me the other day that cornerbacks don't always cover man-to-man. Sometimes they cover in zones. I had no idea." He shrugs.

At the beginning, however, that turned out to be his greatest advantage. In the early days of DFS, there were no real pros, none of the advanced formulae used today, few advice columns, no basic strategies. People just picked their favorite players, and went on hunches. Beep didn't have any favorite players, and he didn't know enough to have hunches. So he built a system, using commonly available player projections for season-long football, and applied them to the "daily" contests for that NFL season.

"I came up with this system where I'd grab all the projections, and I'd create a weighted average," Beep says.

The model wasn't terribly complex, at least not initially. There were no algorithms, no purpose-built programs, no advanced statistics—just fantasy projections culled from every Internet site he could find, and then dumped en masse into spreadsheets in Microsoft Excel, the bane of interns and office temps everywhere.

"Excel is amazing," Beep says. "That's probably the one thing I took from university, how much you can really do in Excel."

In the infancy of DFS, a little Excel coupled with a little math was enough. He won from the start—small amounts, hundreds of dollars, but it whetted his appetite, and encouraged him to keep improving his spreadsheets and his basic aggregation models. He didn't even think of bothering to try to learn football itself.

"I knew literally nothing. I didn't know what a cornerback was. I was just aggregating the projections and the numbers. I was approaching it from a purely quantitative point of view. I didn't know anything else, so I had to approach it just from the numbers," Beep says.

By October 2011, Beep knew he had a potential career in front of him, even if no one among his family and friends—except for his poker pal, Timex—understood exactly what his new "job" was.

"I knew this was going to be big, and that I was going to make money at it," Beep says. "People were going to pick their favorite players, their favorite teams. Having played poker, I knew that people were going to sign up, play five bucks, and I was going to beat them more than I would lose to them. That was the epiphany I had right away. I wasn't picturing the [massive] growth of fantasy sports, but I was thinking I could make good money at this—maybe fifty thousand dollars a year at the highest point. If I could pay for rent, I'd be happy."

That growth came, of course, and with it, live finals, bigger checks, and more sharp players—many of whom began using methods that far exceeded the rudimentary Excel spreadsheets Beep was employing. He realized he had to raise his game. He studied game theory, linear optimization, and computer modeling. He spent thousands of hours in front of a computer, building and honing models.

As he grew into one of the most feared pros in the business, and that business itself grew more lucrative, he brought on assistants to monitor sports news as he built his lineups. And he hired a computer programmer from Germany to build him models that would allow him to analyze data in ways familiar to any professional sports team's front office staff.

All this kept him ahead of the game. But a few years in, he realized there was one final hurdle left to clear before he could really be great. As much as it pained him, he had to start learning about sports.

"I started out by asking my assistant, who played D-One baseball," Beep says. "I had to learn about platoon splits, and batter handedness. I didn't understand that pitch counts were a thing. I couldn't understand why they'd take a pitcher out while he's doing well. So obviously there were flaws in my models."

With at least most of those leaks plugged (he still had no idea how to pronounce players' names, but didn't care) Beep became perhaps the best DFS baseball player out there, taking the $350,000 second prize in the 2014 DraftKings baseball final, and landing the maximum five seats at the 2015 edition.

That's part of why I've sought him out. If I'm to become a pro, and someday take down the baseball world championship, he's the guy I want on my side. I can see a way through this if he is willing to share his custom-built assessment tools and some of the mountains of data that I'm guessing he has stockpiled.

Yet now that it's time for me to start betting seriously, it's November, and there's obviously no more baseball. Football is winding down. That leaves basketball and hockey. I can't say I know a ton about either of those sports, but at least I played a fair amount of basketball growing up, and covered a few Boston Celtics games early in my sportswriting career. I don't know the players at the end of every team's bench, but I know most of the starting fives, the relevant stats, and the strategies most teams employ. At first glance, that seems like it would be a good winter sport to explore as I make my pro debut.

But the sharpest grinders are wary of basketball. It's the fastest-growing DFS sport, but to the smart money, it's broken. Basketball is too predictable. Figure out points per minute on the court, and account for the impact of last-minute lineup changes, and you're basically done. The regular players have become so good that they've chased out all the fish and are fighting one another for percentage points at the top of the pyramid.

I don't want to swim in that pond, a fresh bit of chum for the sharks, and Beep doesn't want me to, either. Besides, even if we could pull it off, for Beep turning me into a basketball pro would be boring. I can tell that Beep is looking at my training as yet another puzzle to be solved, a way to attack a problem in a different way. What he wants to do is turn me into a hockey pro.

The reason why? I know nothing about hockey. I mean, nothing. My hockey knowledge begins and ends with the 1994 Stanley Cup–winning New York Rangers. The names Mark Messier, Brian Leetch, and Adam

Graves resonate far more with me than those of any current players. Apparently the ageless Jaromir Jagr is still playing, but honestly, I think of him more as a streaking, mulleted sixteen-bit blur in the seminal NHL '94 Sega Genesis game than as an actual hockey-playing human being.

Technically, yes, my wife, Amalie, covers hockey for a living, and one would think that just by osmosis, some of that hockey knowledge would seep into my brain. But to this point, it hasn't. She's been covering it for two years, and I've taken zero interest, picked up nothing. Hockey, to me, just looks like a bunch of dudes skating around chaotically, arbitrarily replaced every few minutes by another group of guys clambering off the bench, in an endless cycle. I can see no rhyme or reason to it.

"I can't be a hockey pro," I explain as we take seats side by side in his two recliners. "I don't know anything about it. I'm just going to be throwing my money away."

Beep is undeterred by my admission. Instead, he's emboldened. Behind Vancouver's Rob Lokken (who goes by "I_slewfoot_U" on DraftKings; I'd met him on the Miami trip), Beep considers himself the second-best DFS hockey tournament player.

"You're going to be fine," he assures me. "You really don't need to know anything about hockey. Knowing all about the sport doesn't really matter."

Before I can protest this seemingly ludicrous statement, Beep stands up from his La-Z-Boy and starts rummaging through a pile across the room. He returns with a second laptop and pops open the screen. He opens up several programs, and I can quickly see that they're custom-made, highly advanced platforms for crunching baseball stats—with hit location patterns, wind direction effects, spray charts, and cluster analyses of pitcher types. It's the kind of stuff I've seen MLB front office staffers use, far ahead of the publicly available tools found across the Internet at sites like FanGraphs or Baseball Prospectus.

Beep is famous for the level of thought and research he has put into DFS. Other players talk in reverential tones about his tactics, strategies, and methods of identifying player performance, and this kind of software is just what I expected to see when I came to visit him. In his quest to crack the puzzle that is DFS, Beep and his German programmer built an entire suite of specialized DFS software programs, Beep drawing on his own experience to craft models that would help him determine exactly what a player is going to do on a given day.

"I spent thousands of hours analyzing data and building software," Beep says. "I can tell, say, how five miles per hour of wind in a given direction and ten degrees of temperature difference will impact Mike Stanton's batted-ball velocity and home run distance in any park in baseball."

I nod, wondering where this is going, and if I should tell Beep that Mike has called himself Giancarlo for three years now. Then he drops the hammer.

"And in the end, it just doesn't matter," he says.

As it turns out, Beep has lost his religion when it comes to DFS. After spending years trying to predict player performance, he tells me he no longer believes that it's truly possible. And he's basically stopped trying.

"I tried to really perfect the process of projecting players," Beep says. "But then I kinda came to the conclusion that, are those few points of difference going to make more of a difference than the strategic factors? The strategic factors ended up mattering more than the projections."

This, to me, seems insane, and I tell him so. The entire point of DFS is that it's possible to predict player performance. The whole industry is set up around that idea—with all the experts promising that knowing, for instance, the blustery conditions in a football game mean that a player should or shouldn't be used.

Beep practically laughs off that notion. To him, that's failing to see the forest for the trees.

"People end up doing that all the time. 'Oh my God, it's going to rain in this football game, don't pick the quarterback!' And sure, that matters, but it doesn't matter nearly as much as making sure your lineup is correlated, for instance," Beep says.

That's why Beep is so certain that I can win. To him, if I build lineups the way that he does—using multi-entry to attack the field with as many combinations as possible, correlating scoring between complementary players, and trying to predict ownership levels and not player performance—I can beat all the people who are trying to win doing what Beep believes is nearly impossible: predicting what individual hockey players will do on a given night.

It's about 3:30 p.m., and with that night's games set to start at 7 p.m., it's time for Beep to begin his day's work. The process is a lot messier than I imagined, and uses only a few simple tools; no customized, proprietary software. First, Beep uses the RotoGrinders mass entry tool to reserve the maximum number of lineups—in many cases two hundred, but generally 10 percent of the field—with a "dummy" lineup, filled with players he has no intention of using, just to hold the spots.

With dummy lineups in place, Beep boots up his beloved Microsoft Excel. He exports the day's player prices off both FanDuel and DraftKings, and then grabs the exportable "daily lineups" document off the fantasy sports website RotoWire. All have Excel versions readily available for easy downloading, and Beep dumps all their data into a hockey template that he's built—an extremely rudimentary one, no bells and whistles here, in his mind.

"It's so messy. It looks like a high schooler made this spreadsheet," Beep says, laughing at his own handiwork. To me, it looks extraordinarily complex. I can hardly keep up with the step-by-step of his process as he pulls data from all corners of the Web. To him, it's child's play, the most basic of systems. It strikes me again how naïve I've been this whole time.

The data flows into a few clear channels, but they aren't terribly complex. The template simply sorts the various lineup possibilities by a player's positional designation. Hockey players appear on the ice in lines—positional groupings where they play together. Each team has a first line, a second line, and so on. In real hockey, lines have a center and two wings. But on DraftKings, sometimes the centers are misidentified as wingers, and vice versa, and sometimes coaches use centers as wingers, further muddling the positional designations. So Beep's primary goal here is to see which teams' lines are listed as having two centers and a wing, two wings and a center, etc. That lets him assign the computer to pair them up into all the available combinations when building rosters.

Everything is about lineup correlation and maximizing point overlap. When a goal is scored, it doesn't particularly matter to Beep which player actually whacks it in. He wants to have the line that scored it—hopefully garnering the goal from one player, and an assist from his two linemates, in some combination. So he stacks three forwards from one team (usually either the center and two wings, or two centers and a wing) with one defenseman from that team, plus the team's goalie. He then supplements that with a three-man line from another team, and then finally adds a defender from a third, random club, the best that the salary allows.

Here's what throws me. He doesn't particularly care which teams these lines come from. Good teams, bad teams, good players, bad players—they're all thrown into the pot as he mass-creates his two hundred lineups. What matters is that the positional groupings match up, and that all two hundred lineups follow his correlated lineup construction formulae. The players, really, don't matter. Only the math does—creating as many highly correlated possibilities as the site will allow him.

"It's nothing magical, nothing crazy. Everyone probably thinks it is, but there's no secret," Beep says.

I'm quiet for a little while as I digest what's happening. Then I venture a question.

"So, is there a name for what's happening here?" I ask.

"I brute-force it. I brute-force all the combinations. And then I Monte Carlo it," Beep says.

"I don't know what any of what you just said means," I reply.

"Brute force means I build every type of combination possible," Beep explains. "You can build a program to do this for you. For baseball, I had a really good program that wasn't messy at all. I'd select the pitchers I wanted, the catchers, the first basemen, create some bundles, and then it would generate a ton of lineups. Then I'd submit the lineups, hundreds. I had settings where I could change the amount of salary I'd have left over."

"Like covering the table in roulette," I say.

"Yes, it's covering the table, though it's eliminating ones that don't fit certain constraints—some positional combos, or if the teams I'm using are playing each other. If they qualify for the things we want, we want every possible permutation," Beep says.

"It's really that simple? You can win this way?" I ask.

You can, in some sports—hockey and baseball, largely, where stacking and correlation matter most, and variance is high. Beep explains that much of the time, most of his lineups are terrible. But some will be combinations that will simply match up—a bad team that no one selects has a player on its second line score a hat trick, for instance, while his linemates notch multiple assists. On those nights, Beep will win the entire tournament, with one great lineup, and 199 forgotten ones. The tournaments are so top-heavy that that one prize—$5,000, $10,000, $15,000—makes it all worth it. The rest of the hockey field is relatively weak, so because he has a bankroll large enough to weather the down periods, a strategy like this will make him profitable over time.

"It's amazing how winning one tournament can make such a difference. Having a nice day can mean a lot. Weather the storm, and wait for the spikes," Beep says.

Beep does do some tweaking after all the lineups are generated—particularly to the most important lineups, those entered into $300 or $1,000 contests. In those he'll use his accumulated knowledge to ensure that his better lineups are used. He focuses on lines that play together more than 20 percent of the game and also align together on the power play, and avoids players who are used on the penalty kill. The spreadsheet has already nixed any instances of two teams facing one another where his scorers' goals mean negative points for his goalies. So it's not fully random, certainly. But it's a lot more so than I expected.

I can't help but notice that Beep is clearly a little embarrassed by what he's shown me. I've pulled back the curtain and found that there isn't a multilayered, impeccably constructed algorithm behind picking the perfect lineups, or a brilliant new tactical approach. Just a well-aimed shotgun blast, firing and expecting to hit a certain percentage of the time. He can read my disappointment, and my would-be wizard asks me if it's all not quite what I was expecting.

"It's actually a little depressing," I admit. "I thought it would be, I don't know, like seeing the Coke formula."

He understands, and I think he actually agrees—he seems disappointed that it's possible to win this way, too. Later on, once I've departed, he fires off a series of text messages explaining just how much work, money, and time he put into learning how simple DFS can be—and saying he almost regretted showing me that the simplest approach can be a winning one.*

"I've invested almost 50k between stats grads, programmers, and helpers, and I'd guess I've dug deeper on stats than 99.9% of people who follow MLB," Beep wrote. "I just hope it didn't appear as 'that was easy' rather than . . . 'Jay is brilliant for simplifying and focusing on the important parts.' I guess I've spent close to 15k hours on DFS by now, and just came to realize numbers matter very little . . . which can only be learned by spending infinite time and money realizing that."

The thing is, I get it. I know Beep wanted it to be the same thing I did—a supremely complicated puzzle that he could solve only after years of study, Rubik's Cube–style. And I guess, in a way, it was? To show him that I'm trying to be sympathetic, I tell him that I think of it a little like the tale of Alexander the Great and the Gordian knot.

In the legend, sometime around 700 B.C., a commoner named Gordius was anointed king of the city of Gordium, in Asia Minor—modern-day Turkey. He and his son tied his oxcart up in the town square

---

* Beep once asked me, "So how much of my strategy will you reveal?" When I told him pretty much all of it, he paused a beat and then said, "Hmm. Well, that's good motivation to develop some new methods."

with a particularly intricate knot and dedicated the cart to Zeus. The knot proved impossible for anyone to unravel, legend grew upon legend, and by the time Alexander arrived in Gordium in 333 B.C., toward the start of his famed campaign into the Middle East, it was foretold that whoever could untie it would someday rule all of Asia.

According to myth, Alexander's counselors told the young conqueror he could not leave Gordium with his standing intact without attempting to untie the knot. Obsessed with position and destiny, Alexander marched up to the oxcart and examined this huge knot.

As the crowd gathered to watch, Alexander pondered the problem, fiddling with the knot unsuccessfully. He stepped back, paused, and pulled out his sword.

"What does it matter how I loose it?" the Macedonian declared, slicing the knot in half—"untying" it in the simplest way possible.

Whether or not Beep follows my metaphoric journey into ancient Greece, he seems to appreciate that I'm trying to understand that something being straightforward doesn't necessarily make it easy. Truth is, I do buy into his system and can see how much work he put in. I don't blame him for seeing how stupidly simple it might be to beat DFS at its core—I blame the companies for letting the system be so easily gamed. They allow far too many lineups to be entered per contest, permitting players like Beep to "brute-force" the win if they have the time, money, and relentlessness to push all those lineup combinations through. The companies need the multi-entry pros submitting all these lineups in order to bring in the cash in their "rake," even if it means the average player with his one, single-bullet lineup is disadvantaged. I can't fault Beep for figuring out the best way to attack a broken system, though it does make him the enemy, sort of. As it turns out, my friendly, quirky pro is just another of those multi-entry demons, covering the board and ending up at the top of leaderboards. I went into this thinking of those guys as evil, as what was wrong with this business. But I like Beep. Heck, it's hard to hate him.

He's seen that internal conflict before. Beep is used to meeting

DFSers who are tired of seeing five of his entries winning big money in contests, using seemingly random, often lousy players whom no sane person would select if they were entering only one lineup. He recognizes that the casual player will, and maybe should, resent him, even if it's hard to do so when they meet the man behind the two hundred entries. I mean, come on, he's wearing a cat shirt!

"People will be like, 'I hated you when I only saw your screen name. But you're not that evil of a person,'" Beep says. "But I would hate me too if I was on the outside."

Now I'm going to replicate what he does, becoming one of those multi-entry evildoers—or, at least, a Mini-Me version. It's time to draft. As I settle into the recliner and open my laptop, Beep ventures into his bedroom, returning moments later having ditched Hank the Dog in favor of a shirt featuring a multicolored cat looming over a jeep. His programmer's wife made it especially for him. A cat shirt at last!

"As much as I like Hank the Dog, this is better," Beep says. "This is actually my favorite shirt of this kind. Now I'm in uniform."

As he hunkers down to build two hundred lineups for the biggest tournaments, I click away at my own rosters. In my first night of hockey playing, I'm going to submit fifteen to twenty lineups into numerous smaller contests, attempting to maximize my options to the greatest extent possible in tournaments where most players submit two to three entries at most.

It is, to be honest, exciting—putting a pro's system into action for my own purposes. It's also terrifying—trusting that his system will work in a sport I know literally nothing about. If he's wrong, or even if it's just a bad night, it's going to cost me money. A lot of it, at least to me. Beep sees me struggling with the possibility that I might soon be lighting a sizable wad of my cash on fire.

"The hardest part for you starting out will be not looking at it as money," he says. "Just look at it as chips. It's how many chips you have on the screen. It's not like you just lost an iPod. Or for me, on a football day, like I just lost a car."

Spoken like a true professional gambler. I am clearly not one of those yet, and it's not just fear, or mentality, it's what the pros call "bankroll." Frankly, I don't have a ton.

Crunching the numbers, it seems that putting a reduced version of Beep's plan into motion for that night's slate is going to require putting in about $750. That's a lot of money. The stress of it is making me nervous, my heart racing fast; I can feel myself start to sweat—and even worse, starting to stink.

Every time Beep leans over to offer advice, it drives home how rank I am. For him, this is a light day. He's betting only $6,500 or so. For me, $750 marks my highest DFS outlay by about $550, and it's got me perspiring badly. I need to take care of this. I excuse myself mid-lineup and head for the bathroom, to perform the venerable shower-in-the-sink tactic: scooping up some soap, adding a little water, and pawing the mixture into each armpit quickly before drying the area with toilet paper. Normally, this desperate measure is something I'd only deployed on long-ago dates, when I feared that a lovely lady might get a whiff of BO and thus send me home early. Now I'm worried that a cat-obsessed Canadian shut-in might think I stink and stop sharing his moneymaking secrets. Strange times.

Beep's bathroom is pretty much what I expected. A plentiful supply of Axe body spray, and attendant Axe bathing products. A John Lennon poster. And the item that really ties the room together: a DraftKings bath towel. I use it to dry my hands as I prepare for the final rush to get the lineups finished before the 7 p.m. start of games.

Frantically combining one hockey line with another, I make a few errors, swapping in the wrong Sedin or Benn or Staal or Hayes before Beep corrects me—why are there so many pairs of brothers playing hockey?—but I eventually get my twenty lineups done, with minutes to spare before lineup lock. My heart pounding, we run through various Internet sites to see if there are any late scratches, and check a list of team beat writer Twitter feeds (my wife's among them, oddly enough) to see if any line combinations have changed in the pregame warmups.

For the night, we've heavily invested in the New York Rangers and the Florida Panthers. We have the Washington Capitals in cash games like 50/50s and double-ups, but not in the big multi-entry tournaments, and we're fading the Edmonton Oilers entirely—meaning we're hoping their players don't score, as we assume they'll be heavily owned. So that's where my rooting interests lie.

With the lineups locked, I suddenly become aware of my surroundings again—and painfully conscious I've spent four hours in exactly the same tensed position in Beep's recliner. To the recliner's credit, it's comfy, but I'd better move around before my butt imprint becomes permanent.

Fortunately, Beep has just the thing for getting the blood flowing—his inversion table. I've always been curious to try one of these devices, and Beep considers it a regular part of his lineup-building regimen, so how can I skip it?

Eyeing it warily, I approach with caution, gingerly strapping each foot into a collar, then leaning against the backboard, preparing to go inverted. Beep, who has been checking over his lineups for errors, suddenly snaps alert, concerned.

"You don't have glaucoma or anything, do you? There's a chance you could bleed from the eyes if you have glaucoma. It's really gross," he says, genuinely convinced this could be a problem.

Just some fairly significant nearsightedness, I assure him. Relieved, he explains how he uses the table.

"You lock in your feet, and want to go parallel to the floor for about thirty seconds to let the blood level out," Beep guides. "And then, you don't have to go all the way inverted, but you can go sixty percent, eighty percent. That'll stretch you out after a long lineup session. I like to swing. Go all the way down, all the way back up. I think that's the best."

When in Kitchener, I suppose.

The blood rushes to my head as I take my first plunge downward, the pressure of it building up in my temples. Maybe it's all that excess blood in my brain, but it strikes me how little in the world of DFS has turned out as I expected it to be, from the ways to win to the lives of the pros.

Am I just naïve? Did I believe in the advertising too readily, or was I not skeptical enough of the companies and the sharks themselves? I started by thinking of them as self-interested to a fault, desperate to keep making more and more money, but not necessarily evil or ill-intentioned. But as I hang upside down, watching Beep check his two hundred brute-forced lineups in a post-Haskell world, I start to wonder whether intention matters. Is that just moral relativism? Isn't it the action itself, not the intent, that is important?

Too much blood to the brain, clearly. I swing down from the board, feeling the pressure in my head abate with a sense of relief, and set to work freeing myself from the collars. Liberated, and with puck drop minutes away, I ask what seems like the logical next question.

"So, where are we going to watch the games?"

Beep looks at me like I'm a third grader, one of those less polished ones who still try to eat their Matchbox cars.

"Oh. I never sweat the games," Beep replies, as if anyone who does is obviously nuts.

From the very start, the most intoxicating part of DFS to me has been watching the games themselves with money on the line. At its most basic, that's exactly what DraftKings and FanDuel are offering— a chance to redefine the sport-watching experience, to make yourself part of it. The heart pounds faster, the adrenaline pumps for a random Chicago-L.A. game like it does when your hometown team is in game seven of the finals. Watching the games seems to be an integral part of the experience—and not just that, but a way to win.

"But don't you pick up things from watching the games?" I protest.

"Not really," Beep says, as nicely as possible. "It means nothing."

More important, as Beep explains, watching the games will make you crazy. DFS is meant to trigger emotional responses. Players living and dying with the swings of each game, thinking about how much money is being won or lost at any given moment, will eventually suffer a breakdown.

"If they're doing it that way, they probably won't survive in the long term," he says quietly, as if mourning long-lost DFS friends.

I admit, inside, I know what he's talking about. Even in such a short time, I've come to crave the highs that DFS offers when watching games, and I feel a little empty if watching a sporting event without a bet on the line. What's the point?

In the DFS world, watching your players try to win your money is known as "sweating" the game—a very different kind of sweating than what my stank self was doing earlier. According to Beep, seeing who sweats games is an easy way to separate the true pros from the amateurs; the pros build their lineups, look at the data, stay active long enough to make late player swaps—and then get the heck away. Amateurs sweat the games and draw improper conclusions from the small-sample, emotionally charged slices of data they see there. At the 2015 baseball final in Las Vegas, as soon as the lineups locked, all the big pros—Beep, MaxDalury, PetrGibbons, CSURAM, and others—left the "sweat room" to the amateurs and went to play blackjack. Even with all that money on the line, they couldn't get away fast enough.

Just this once, however, Beep is willing to make an exception, to satisfy my interest. In sleepy Kitchener, however, there aren't that many hopping places to go on a Monday night. Beep mulls a few options, and eventually we settle on a sports bar called Moxie's, a Canadian chain. We head to the parking lot, and there before me is the blue Jeep Wrangler that gives Beep his DFS username.

As Beep chauffeurs me over to Moxie's, he asks how baseball beat writers eat on the road—whether it's either ballpark hot dogs or lavish five-star dinners. It's a little of both, I explain. When at the ballpark, you're largely at the mercy of the press dining hall, which can vary widely, even year by year. When it opened in 2009, the new Yankee Stadium's press dining was legitimately one of my five favorite restaurants. Skirt steak, tilapia, oodles of dessert options—it was a feast befitting the extravagant image the team was pushing at the new venue. The meals declined in quality each year after that 2009 debut, but Yankee Stadium is still among the best eats in baseball, along with Fenway Park and Atlanta's Turner Field. On the other end of the press dining spectrum? Oakland, Oakland, and Oakland.

When it comes to the food options out in the concourses, however, it's all about the West Coast. San Francisco and San Diego offer great concessions, but in my mind there's no place like Seattle, where I religiously visited a Thai food stand named Intentional Wok and proceeded to crush their Cashew Chicken for at least two out of the three days of a road trip. The third day was reserved for a stop at Ichi-Roll, which, as one would expect, is the gold standard of ballpark sushi. It even kept the name after the famed outfielder was traded to New York.

As we pull up to Moxie's, I explain that on an off night, like day seven of an eleven-day, ten-game road swing, you might go out for a nice dinner in whatever city you find yourself. If everyone's travel schedules line up, that can lead to a group outing among the writers—we never, ever eat with the players; those walls are real and inviolate—but more regularly, it means finding a place to eat alone. I'm very familiar with the solo dinner at the hotel bar, and I've actually come to enjoy the experience. And I've found there's no better place for tracking multiple games at once when you're playing that night's slate.

So as we head in, and Beep looks toward a table in the corner, I veer instead toward the empty center bar and claim two of the seats there, salivating at the wall of television screens arrayed in front of us.

Finally back on Wi-Fi—this is Canada, after all, and I'm not paying for an international data plan—I rush to check the progress of my squads. It's about a half hour into the night's hockey games and I'm thrilled to see that I'm up—almost $500. The way DraftKings does its winnings box is deceptive; it shows what you've wagered as "winnings" as well, so my screen displayed a bogus, yet satisfying, figure of "$1,235" in winnings, which includes my $750 outlay. I'm not in the mood to question it. I flash my phone to Beep, half expecting a pat on the head.

"That's good, for sure," he says, "but it's still really, really early."

To Beep, there's no point in even checking the scores until the night's games are more than two-thirds over. Even then, that's misleading, he says, particularly in hockey. Since most DFS hockey scoring is built around goals and assists, the final minute or two of games, when the losing team often pulls its goalie, can result in massive swings. Empty-net goals are among the cheapest ways to win and cruelest ways to lose in DFS, but they are a nightly reality when playing hockey. So Beep checks in occasionally to get a sense of whether his night is looking positive or negative, but he doesn't pay too much attention until it's all practically over.

There's one game, however, that catches his eye and brings out a little of the dreamer in him. The lone television that isn't showing hockey games is tuned to the NFL—specifically, the Buffalo Bills–New England Patriots Monday night matchup. The one that determines whether Beep will win an $80,000 seat to the DraftKings NFL semifinal in San Diego. It's half over, and we literally haven't even looked at it the entire night— as Beep noted before the game, he expected to be eliminated before the first quarter was over.

As the game comes out of halftime, however, the Patriots have scored a mere ten points, a pittance for their dynamic offense. I think I see a little gambling-related excitement flicker in Beep for the first time all night. Even when you're a pro, an $80,000 win is still enough to light up the right parts of the brain.

"Oh. Wow. We're live," he says. "We might have a sweat tonight after all."

We start breaking down which players need to get the ball, and what outcomes are optimal for his chances, as we wait for our food to arrive. In this we're hardly distinctive. Fantasy is at once nerdy and exclusive, and yet also universal. Everybody of a certain age has a fantasy team, and especially with a game on in the background, "I have so-and-so, too, I need fifteen points to win" is an easy conversation starter when there's nothing else to say.

So it's not a total surprise when the bartender at this sleepy Canadian restaurant ventures into our fantasy football conversation. She's shrink-wrapped into a black leather skirt and diving red top, her gold necklace introducing her as "Claire."

"Do you guys have a lot of players tonight?" she asks.

An attractive bartender wanting to talk fantasy seems like it would be a welcome diversion. The world of DFS is different, however. As soon as she asks about our rooting interests, I feel Beep tense up alongside me— it's clear he doesn't want to talk about what he actually has at stake. At first I think it's superstition, but later he explains that the sheer numbers in play make those conversations uncomfortable. I understand that. Any acknowledgment that he's a DFS pro likely leads to questions about how much he has on the line that day—many thousands, normally—and the assumption that he's a rich big spender. Beep cautions me that he hates discussing money, and gambling in general, with strangers, and especially at places like bars or restaurants; that leads waiters and bartenders to expect a huge tip.

He turns his head away entirely and, sensing his discomfort, I mumble a little about how we don't want the Patriots to do well. With us failing to engage beyond a few minor words, Claire moves off and I take the opportunity to check my own fortunes. They've fallen dramatically, and I'm suddenly down about $100. (Or, in the language of the evil DraftKings app, "winning" $640.)

"What the hell happened?" I wonder out loud.

A lot, it turns out. Goals are being scored across the league, and not enough of my early decisions are paying off. The Rangers game is on right in front of me at the bar, and from their 3–0 lead, I know that at least a few of my lineups are doing well. Yet it's what I can't see that is causing me to fall. The Colorado Avalanche are on their way to a four-goal night, and I have virtually none of their players. They were the "chalk"*—the obvious play—tonight, and Beep's whole philosophy is to play contrarian and bet against the chalk. Tonight the chalk is winning.

---

* Most DFS terms are adopted from poker—but Beep says *chalk* is a DFS original, one of Al_Smizzle's many contributions to DFS culture.

"This is how it goes," Beep notes. He's about even—one of his many, many lineups is sitting near the top of a big tournament for $5,000, which should keep him relatively steady on the day no matter what else happens.

His $5,000 doesn't make me any less pouty. I had dreams of a big score tonight, benefiting from my access to such a renowned pro. But I don't have the number of lineups or the bankroll he had invested; my bastardization of his shotgun system is a poor peashooter approximation, and it relies far more on luck—one of twenty lineup combinations striking gold—than the real thing, where so many more permutations are covered.

My fate begins to feel a bit less important the longer this Bills-Patriots game wears on, though. As we eat, the Patriots score again and are leading, but none of the players Beep fears—Tom Brady, Danny Amendola, Rob Gronkowski—are contributing much. At the beginning of the night, Beep put his chances of claiming a seat at 5 percent. Now, with the fourth quarter under way and me egging him on to feel a little excitement, he gives himself a little over 50 percent odds to claim the $80,000 seat, plus its promised 1-in-200 shot of winning $5 million at the January final itself. I think I'm more excited than he is—after all, if he lands a spot, I bet I could tag along, at least to the next stage in San Diego in December, the semifinal. Everybody wins!

Nothing's really tying us to Moxie's any longer. I long ago finished a surprisingly good lobster pasta (what, ordering a fresh fish dish at a landlocked Canadian sports bar is a bad idea?) and Beep tore through a wings special, so we can head out whenever. Beep wants to sweat the rest of the game with his gambling mentor, Mike McDonald, aka the famous poker pro Timex.

As Beep had explained earlier, Timex was the embodiment of the teenage poker pro raking in cash from his bedroom—the difference was, he turned that into a career playing live poker. At eighteen, in 2008, Timex became the youngest player ever to win a European Poker Tour event when he cashed in for $1.37 million at the German Open in Dort-

mund, according to his Wikipedia page. He followed that up with a se-
ries of six-figure wins, made the final table at the famed World Series of
Poker, and has been ranked as high as number five on the Global Poker
Index. His winnings totaled more than $12 million at the end of 2015.

"He was always supersmart, but with poker, he keeps figuring out
how to improve his game, and adapt. That's what the best do," Beep says
of his friend.

Now twenty-six and no longer poker's young ingénue, Timex has
transitioned into adulthood and maturity with an ease and wisdom uncommon to many of his wealthy gambling brethren. Case in point? His
choice of autos.

"He has a Lamborghini—but it's used," Beep says.

Timex now presides over a swanky multi-bedroom apartment full of
smart twentysomethings, all hell-bent on outdoing one another. Over
the years, a revolving door of high-achiever types—including Beep—
has come in and out of the pad as roommates, making it the Kitchener equivalent of a Silicon Valley incubator. In addition to Timex and
Beep, two of the roommates went on to found start-ups valued in the
tens of millions. Another member of the posse, Jake Meyer, known as
DJ Vekked, is one of Canada's top DJs and won the 2015 DMC World DJ
Championship. Timex is the one who ties them all together, this odd
Canadian power group where call signs like Timex, Vekked, and Beep
replace real names.

Now Timex is texting, imploring us to get to his pad so we can all
sweat the final minutes of the game together. We jump into the Wrangler, racing through Kitchener's empty streets.

Timex greets us at the door, and with only a few minutes to go in the
game, shepherds us inside quickly. Timex is thin and fit, with a Celtic
baby face that jibes perfectly with his real name. His incubator/salon
is set in a modern apartment building, boasting granite countertops,
stainless steel accents, and blond wood trim. Honestly, it's more what I
expected Beep's apartment to look like. Spacious, classy, more obviously
smelling of money. Timex catches us up on the standings—FunkiMunki,

who it turns out is a real-life poker pal of McDonald's, has passed Beep as expected and is going to take first place in the qualifier, but Beep is just barely hanging on to the fifth and final $80,000 spot. The Patriots are winning, 20–13, so they're unlikely to throw the ball, meaning that Brady, Amendola, and Gronkowski are no longer significant threats. As Beep and Timex pore over the standings, they realize the real danger is Bills receiver Sammy Watkins. When the Bills get the ball back, a Watkins touchdown, or even just a series of receptions, will vault several players ahead of Beep.

So that's our enemy: Watkins. As soon as Buffalo gets the ball back with 1:39 remaining, we lock in on the dreadlocked Bills receiver and point out exactly where he is at all times.

"Lined up on the top!" I shout out before one play.

"He's going across the middle," Timex chimes in soon after.

Bills quarterback Tyrod Taylor misses Watkins on a deep ball and we let out a mass sigh of relief. But two plays later, Taylor hits Watkins for eight yards on a pass that looks to be incomplete. It's within the final minutes of the game, however, and everything is under review. We sit silently, each of us dissecting the replays, trying to reason out our own take on whether it was a catch, biased as all hell. The NFL officials, who are presumably more impartial? They rule it a catch, for eight yards. Two or three more of those and Beep is done for.

A few failed plays later, the Bills are down to seven seconds left, time enough for one more shot. Beep stands right next to the television, jumping up and down as Taylor hikes the ball.

Taylor looks to Watkins—of course!—and fires the ball to the second-year receiver. It's caught—it looks like fifteen, sixteen yards. Watkins manages to crawl out of bounds untouched, which should stop the clock and give the Bills a chance to throw again.

Timex rushes over to the computer, reporting that Beep is still just barely ahead—with it all coming down to the next play. But then, the cat-gods smile on Beep; the referee calls the game over. He didn't see that Watkins snuck out of bounds, and so the ref didn't stop the clock.

The Bills are protesting like mad, but it makes no difference. The Patriots are all over the field, the coaches are going for the traditional handshake, the game is final.

"Wait, it's over?" Beep asks all of us and the television at once.

"I think it's over," I respond without any real insight beyond what we all see on TV.

"It's over!" Timex declares with authority, prompting us to leap out of our chairs with guttural, manly shouts, meeting in the middle for high fives and fist bumps aplenty.

"I really didn't think it was going to happen," Beep says, giddy from the win. He's now tens of thousands richer and heading to San Diego in mid-December to be one of the two hundred semifinalists vying for a seat in January's ten-man final. I'm psyched, too, because it means I might just be able to tag along as Beep's guest. Timex whips out a high-end blender to make margaritas and Beep says it's time to "celly"—to celebrate.

Hey, wait a minute, I've got my own money in play! The last time I checked, I was down $150, and it's terrifying to look at my phone—what if it's far, far worse? What if it's zero?

I peek at the screen.

"Hey, I'm up seventy dollars!" I say, realizing how ridiculous that sounds in a room where we just celebrated a win of nearly six figures. They're all nice enough to humor me with talk that "any win is a good one," and the like. And Beep seems genuinely relieved that I didn't lose all $750 I put in today, probably thinking I'd blame him if I did.

We sit around sipping our margaritas (plus a second round) as we rehash the win. It's 2 a.m. when we finally call it a night and I head for the austere comfort of the local Holiday Inn. We have another training session scheduled for the next day, and I need my rest. With $70 in my digital pocket, and Beep's $80,000 irrationally bolstering my own confidence, I feel like with a few more cracks at this, I might do okay after all.

But as a New Yorker, I may not get the chance to try.

05

The disembodied head of New York attorney general Eric Schneiderman bobs up and down above a sea of protesters, veering to and fro in a chaotic dance that must make even this placard version nauseous. Leering down at me with dead eyes, the oversize cardboard head is draped in a neon-green T-shirt courtesy of the staff of FanDuel; on the front, the shirt reads "#Fantasyforall." On the back, "Protect your right to play."

The attorney general has looked better.

In my years as a news reporter, I covered a lot of protests. They are all a bit contrived; the best ones have some element of theater to them, and that's okay. Protests are a media show, intended to draw eyeballs and attention to the problem at hand, usually some bit of human suffering that could benefit from some whipped-up press.

Of course, some shows are better than others. Sometimes the human drama is absent and it's clear that what's unfolding is actually far closer to a comedy. On those rare, cherished moments, it's best to just sit back and soak it in.

On the brisk, sunny morning of November 13, 2015, it's apparent pretty quickly that I'm lucky enough to witness drama and comedy rolled into one. FanDuel and DraftKings have hurriedly organized a protest outside the lower Manhattan office of Attorney General Schneiderman, managing to get more than two hundred people onto the sidewalk at 8 a.m. to push back against Schneiderman's all-out legal assault on Daily Fantasy Sports. Two hundred people that early in the morning is a pretty strong turnout for any protest, especially one defending something as esoteric as fantasy sports. The attendees came armed with all the tools of the protest trade—signs, the neon-green shirts, even the aforementioned Schneiderman heads floating up and down across the picket line. All the right pieces are in place for an effective, meaningful protest, one the organizers hope will focus anger against Schneiderman and what they see as his headline-grabbing crusade to create a nanny state.

But then . . . then they start chanting.

"Game of skill! Game of skill!" come the cries from the crowd. Followed by "Schneiderman! Drop that bill! DFS is a game of skill!" and then repeated refrains of "Let us play! Let us play!"

I'm trying not to laugh. I've got to keep up that reporter's detachment. But I can't. It's just too delicious.

The signs are equally cringe-worthy: "Schneiderman should focus on real problems," "Let's get real, it's just fantasy," and the coup de grâce, "Get your laws off my lineup." (Though I have to give credit to whoever came up with the excellent "If only politics were a game of skill.")

Then there's the question of who exactly these two-hundred-some-odd people are. I rode the subway down to the protest from Times Square with about thirty protesters, mostly attendees from a conference organized by the DFS website RotoGrinders, an event billed as the first-ever "DFS Players Conference." That group are legitimate DFS players, without question. But the masses filling out this protest are . . . different. Most of them I don't recognize, and there are far, far too many women for this to be a staunch group of committed DFS grinders. As I ask around and try to talk to them, few will give their last names, which is weird—I've found DFS players to be a relatively open bunch one-on-one, MaxDalury-name-masking issues aside. I put this question to one of the players I'd ridden down with, a Nashville-based software engineer named Jason Green, who goes by the DFS name IHaveAReputation.

"I think they're mostly FanDuel employees," he says. "The office is right nearby."

Looking around, that makes more and more sense. This is FanDuel's event—not just created and organized, but actually populated by employees of Nigel Eccles's company and its affiliates. Wandering the perimeter, I find a pair of cardboard boxes, which turn out to be the origin point for all those neon-green shirts making the rounds. The boxes are earmarked for distribution by "FanDuel Emily"—FanDuel PR assistant Emily Bass. Poking around a little further, it seems like more than half the attendees are employees of either FanDuel or another DFS company, like numberFire or Scout.com.

Sidling up to one of the plainclothes cops "protecting" the attorney general's office at 120 Broadway from this group of riffraff, I bring my old Rhode Island accent out of storage—cops always love that one, it's very salt-of-the-earth—and ask the officer if he's ever seen anything like this.

"I've been here for some funny events, but this is better than all of them," he says, smirking as more chants of "Game of skill!" serenade us in the background.

We're not the only ones to see the humor. *The Daily Show*, the satirical news program made famous by Jon Stewart and now hosted by Trevor Noah, sent a correspondent to the event, and he's now mingling among the protesters, waving a sign that reads "Bro lives matter" and chanting "Bro! Bro! Bro!" He's cracking me up. The protest organizers aren't quite so amused.

Silly and contrived as it is, it's not like I blame FanDuel for putting this together. Schneiderman came at them hard, and they need to both parry his attack and strike back themselves. In the month since the Haskell scandal broke, numerous threats to Daily Fantasy's viability have emerged, from the revelations of FBI and Justice Department investigations to class action lawsuits naming both the companies and prominent players like MaxDalury and Drew Dinkmeyer as defendants. But none of those had quite risen to the level of clear and present danger until Schneiderman dropped his legal bomb earlier this week.

The first connections between Schneiderman and DFS came in the days immediately after the Haskell scandal broke, in early October, when his office began its probe into the Haskell insider trading situation. But by the beginning of November, it appeared the storm had broken. Everything went quiet for a time. It even seemed like the world of Daily Fantasy might be settling into a new normal—weakened, certainly, but not irreparably harmed. There was talk of legislators writing up bills to take to state legislatures, and early forms of soft regulation. People within the industry were beginning to speak with cautious optimism about the road ahead.

That mood was shattered on the evening of November 10. FanDuel and DraftKings received calls from members of the media earlier that day, asking them for comment on something big coming out of the New York attorney general's office. It was bigger even than they'd initially feared. That Tuesday, Schneiderman issued cease-and-desist letters to both companies, labeling them illegal gambling operations and ordering them to stop serving customers in New York State. This was no shot across the bow, no mere PR move. This was an all-out assault from the top legal officer of one of the most important states in the nation—and the second-biggest Daily Fantasy market—and he wasn't exactly mincing words.

"Daily Fantasy Sports companies are engaged in illegal gambling under New York law," Schneiderman said in a press release. The sites are causing "the same kinds of social and economic harms as other forms of illegal gambling, and misleading New York consumers."

Schneiderman made it clear that he wasn't looking for some sort of settlement. He wanted the companies out, and for people to know them as villains. And lest anyone somehow miss the point, he shifted into full man-of-the-people mode.

"DraftKings and FanDuel are the leaders of a massive, multibillion-dollar scheme intended to evade the law and fleece sports fans across the country. Today we have sent a clear message: not in New York, and not on my watch."

As over-the-top as that statement might be, there's no mistaking its intent. Schneiderman has chosen this hill to die on, and he is going to employ the full resources of the New York attorney general's office to bring the companies to heel. The previous two attorneys general, Eliot Spitzer and Andrew Cuomo, used the attorney general's office as a direct springboard to the governor's mansion. Schneiderman, despite his five years in office, didn't have a signature issue yet, one that might give him the kind of name recognition necessary to make that leap. DFS was going to be his crusade.

The companies were blindsided, Eccles says, and alarmed. They couldn't afford to lose New York. New York represented 10 percent of FanDuel's customer base and 7 percent of DraftKings'.

"It was a big surprise," the FanDuel founder says. "There was an investigation. That investigation was into the claim of insider trading. There was no indication that that investigation had changed to the legal ity route as well."

If the online poker bogeyman was Preet Bharara,* then Daily Fantasy's chief nemesis is now one Eric T. Schneiderman. Born on New Year's Eve, 1954, Schneiderman was raised on Manhattan's tony Upper West Side before heading to Massachusetts for college at Amherst. Harvard Law School came next, followed by a prestigious clerkship at the U.S. District Court for the Southern District of New York, leading to fifteen years of private practice at the firm of Kirkpatrick & Lockhart.

Schneiderman made his first forays into public office in 1998, running as a Democrat for the state senate seat representing his Upper West Side home. The local boy made good spent twelve years in the state senate, helping to reform the state's drug laws and clamping down on tax cheats. Along the way, Schneiderman became something of a man about town. He runs in rarified circles, claiming fund manager David Einhorn, rap mogul Russell Simmons, and actor Alec Baldwin among his friends.

Now he's dreaming of bigger things, and Schneiderman couldn't

---

* Bharara presided over the famed "Black Friday," which shuttered online poker in 2011.

have picked a better time to drop his bomb on the DFS companies. The RotoGrinders Players Conference, the first of its kind, brought 150 serious DFS players to New York this weekend for seminars, a trade show, a movie screening, panels, and more. Once Schneiderman made his move against the companies public, the conference became the focal point of resistance. Suddenly the conference attendees became foot soldiers for FanDuel's protest, and both FanDuel founder Eccles and DraftKings founder Jason Robins agreed to do Q&As at the conference to speak out against Schneiderman's action as soon as the protest was over.

All this turned the conference into a ready-made media event for any outlet that wanted to send a reporter or two (or in the case of Reuters, eight) out to the scene to get some easy color, even if they'd missed the protest. Suddenly, and quite unexpectedly, the RotoGrinders team—Cal Spears, Riley Bryant, and Cameron MacMillan—have a major media circus on their hands.

"We're literally the biggest event in New York this weekend," says a stunned Spears. "I guess that's a good thing?"

The RotoGrinders conference is a three-day event, headquartered at the Marriott Marquis in Times Square. The evolution of Times Square—from the seedy, nasty peep show hell of my youth, to the glitzy symbol of New York's rebirth, and then finally into this twisted Disneyfied version full of freaks in cartoon character costumes demanding tips—probably says something about the human race. I'll leave that to the sociologists, however. All I care about on my way back from the protest is getting off the A train and through this glut of tourists in time to get to the RotoGrinders event before Eccles starts to speak.

RotoGrinders* occupies a vitally important place in the world of Daily Fantasy. It's at once the entry point for most players and their first

---

* An amalgam of *rotisserie*—a word that harks back to the very origins of fantasy—and *grinder,* a term for a serious, everyday DFS player.

teacher; the primary source of DFS-related advice and content; the arbiter of who is the best of the best, via player rankings; and the community's town square, through its widely used forums. It is truly the one-stop shop for all things DFS and has a unique role and sway in the community.

For many curious potential players who see a DFS commercial and wonder about signing up, RotoGrinders serves as a kind of digital Ellis Island: processing them, helping them choose a new name, and giving them the basic tools to be on their way inside DFS. It's how I entered—if you sign up for one of the major sites through RotoGrinders' links, you get oodles of free content, from how-to guides to daily advice columns to specific programs that help players, like lineup entry tools and bankroll management add-ons. Entering DFS is intimidating. RotoGrinders promises to make it slightly less so.

The RotoGrinders founders came from the poker world, where this group of Vanderbilt University grads became well known for building a poker website called Pocket Fives. What set Pocket Fives apart was its rankings system, which used an admittedly subjective rating to determine who the best online poker players were—and encouraged debate over those ever-shifting rankings. The site thrived but was still a niche player in the vast poker world. When the Unlawful Internet Gambling Enforcement Act of 2006 (UIGEA) tore apart the poker industry, they sold the site and began casting about for something new. A few years later, they stumbled upon Daily Fantasy, and when the community had grown to the point where they felt they could replicate their poker formula—rankings, content, forums—in DFS, they launched RotoGrinders in the summer of 2010.

"Daily Fantasy is a puzzle—and every day is a new puzzle," Spears says. "The poker puzzle is always the same puzzle—it evolves slowly over time as people get more aggressive, but Daily Fantasy is always a new puzzle. That's part of the fun of it. Putting together that new puzzle every day."

Because of this approach, (almost) everybody likes RotoGrinders.

The site offers players a forum for airing grievances, real help, smart advice—and the founders and creators are at once good guys and serious DFSers, so they are relatable to the common player. The Nashville-based company's role in offering small-time players a voice when the sites can appear hell-bent on catering only to the big spenders and high-volume pros is invaluable.

Yet while it functions as quasi-industry media, RotoGrinders has long had a deep and direct financial interest in the success of the two major companies. Because users sign up for FanDuel and DraftKings via RotoGrinders' links, the sites pay RotoGrinders a fee, indefinitely, every time one of their referred users plays DFS. So when a MaxDalury bets $150,000 in a given day, a huge percentage of his post-expenses rake goes directly to RotoGrinders.

"Cal Spears is frankly making more than anyone in the industry, because he's taking forty percent of so many players' commission, or rake, from all the referrals," MaxDalury tells me. "What RotoGrinders primarily does is refer people to DraftKings or FanDuel, and they're getting that forty percent for that. That's a huge business. They're the ones who are really winning."

Industry insiders say it's more like 25–35 percent, and the arrangements are sometimes onetime up-front payments instead of the perpetual deals. Regardless, that cash is why they can afford events like this money-losing "Players Conference." RotoGrinders is in the business of growing, promoting, and now protecting DFS. If nothing else, their conference serves as a place for the bewildered professional players to congregate and try to figure out what the hell has happened to their industry in the last five weeks.

Throughout the first phase of the DFS scandal, it seemed to me like the companies had their heads in the sand—like they didn't realize just how much hatred they had stirred up, and how deeply much of the American public wanted to see them fall. They publicly hemmed and hawed on the idea of regulation; they said their internal investigations found no wrongdoing; they continued to stress not blaming Haskell. Their public statements rang with a combination of hubris and denial. They simply didn't seem to recognize the danger they were in, and the level of schadenfreude that existed as a result of all those commercials.

Sometime around the filing of the Schneiderman lawsuit, something changed. It may have been the lawsuit itself; or that very smart people are now guiding the companies (DraftKings, for instance, hired legendary lawyer David Boies for its legal defense and contracted with, among others, the crisis PR firm of FTI Consulting to help with their public image); whatever it was, the companies appear to finally recognize that a new tack is needed.

Eccles's post-protest Q&A at the Marriott Marquis, with the well-spoken Dan Back, RotoGrinders' media director, marks a turning point on multiple levels. From the moment Eccles sits down at the front of the hotel's conference room and begins answering Back's questions, it's clear that his company, at least, is now taking a reasoned public response to these crises. Fresh off the bombastic, comical protest, Eccles gives intelligent answers that exhibit a real understanding of the mess his industry is in. When Back asks Eccles, for instance, about his feelings on regulation, Eccles doesn't say that he'd grudgingly accept it, as industry voices have often done; instead, he embraces it.

"Appropriate regulation of the industry is not something we should fear," Eccles says. "It gives us the certainty that someone isn't going to wake up one morning and say 'You know what? I think this is a game of chance, and I'm going to shut it down.' Self-regulation can't do that. State-by-state regulation can do that."

Maybe these guys are going to survive after all.

From there, Eccles lays out a new path for his company, officially bringing the "commercials" era to a close and acknowledging that the time of growth is over, in favor of retrenchment and survival.

"There's definitely been a shift in the market, and a shift for us as well," Eccles says. "We've definitely been mega-growth for several years, which is exhilarating, but exhausting. But what we're seeing now is a shift—our priority over the next twelve months, candidly, is about regulation."

Eccles also explains that while FanDuel isn't making money now, it could instantly do so just by slashing its massive, bloated advertising budget—"If we wanted to, we could be profitable tomorrow," he says.

I find myself nodding along as he speaks, finally hearing some measured comments coming out of a top DFS official. Yet the most important thing to happen during Eccles's session isn't anything he says. It's something his company does, signaling a new era in the fight over DFS.

FanDuel and DraftKings are going on the offensive.

As Eccles speaks, the reporters around me start reaching into their pockets to check their phones, en masse. This is a dead giveaway that some sort of news alert has dropped, that editors are calling, texting, and emailing to discuss coverage plans.

Dragging my iPhone 6s out of my front pocket, it doesn't take me long to see what the other reporters are looking at on Twitter: FanDuel and DraftKings are filing separate lawsuits against the state of New York, attempting to stop Schneiderman's efforts before they're fully under way. It's a bold, aggressive move and, if true, represents a massive escalation. There'll be no going back now, no middle-ground, negotiated solution.

I sidle over to FanDuel's director of communications, Justine Sacco, in the back of the room.

"Is this real?" I ask.

She nods, promising more details once Eccles is off the dais.

Thanks to the wonders of the Internet, I can pull up the lawsuits almost immediately and look through them. The lawsuits are emergency measures, asking the courts to issue injunctions preventing Schneiderman's cease-and-desist orders from taking effect. FanDuel's contains measured, conservative language arguing why the company should remain open for business in New York, reasoning that an immediate shutdown is an overly drastic move. DraftKings' suit makes the same point, with more electric verbiage—accusing Schneiderman of trying to "bully" the companies.

These suits, and their hope for immediate judicial relief, mean that a court hearing is coming in the very near future, probably a week's time. The first DFS legal showdown looms, the first chance for all the arguments made in the press—game of skill versus illegal gambling, criminal scheme versus legal new-economy tech enterprise—to be tested. But in the interim, Eccles and his company are playing it safe. While attacking via the courts, FanDuel is pulling out of New York for the time being, declining to take paid entries from New York players. DraftKings, true to form, is going to stay active in New York as long as possible.

Finishing his Q&A to applause from the friendly audience, Eccles comes off the stage nonchalantly, not exactly swaggering like I might be if I had just sued the state of New York and gone to war with the attorney general. After a few questions about the lawsuit from the assembled reporters, Eccles heads off to his next stop and the crowd in the conference room thins out. Robins will do his own Q&A later that afternoon, but for now the legal show is over—and there are actual DFS-related strategy sessions for the paying customers who had shelled out $600 to attend this conference.

Pulling out the schedule, I see there's one that might be interesting to attend later—MLB tournament strategy with Dave "CheeseIsGood" Potts sounds worthwhile—and am about to head off in search of lunch when I'm stopped by a man in his mid-twenties who sticks out his hand and introduces himself as Mike Zheng. Mike explains that he's a pro who plays under the names MBomb44 on FanDuel and Underjones on DraftKings, and that he's friends with Beep—he's heard how Beep is training me, and he wants to say hello.

Underjones, it turns out, lives in New York City, and though he wasn't at the protest earlier in the morning, he probably should have been. As a full-time, high-volume DFS player for the past few years, his world has been turned upside down in the last four days. Mike realizes that he's going to have to leave New York as a result of Schneiderman's campaign—otherwise, with FanDuel already pulling out and DraftKings likely to follow at some point, staying in New York means he'll effectively lose his job. Not that anyone is going to be particularly sympathetic, but there really are people impacted by the potential end of DFS in New York.

Underjones is weighing a few options. He'll either move to New Jersey or perhaps get an office there. If he goes the office route, he'll commute out to Jersey every day, set his lineups, and then head back to the city.

"It'll be like having a regular job, going to work every day," he muses.

Some of these DFS pros aren't that lucky, in that they don't have a "friendly" state within commuting distance. Later that afternoon, I meet a DFS pro named Brit Devine, an ex–poker coach with spiky blond hair who says he wears RotoGrinders shirts to the gym in the hopes of starting up DFS-related conversations. He used to work in customer service at the now-defunct DFS site FanThrowdown. Beep had already mentioned him to me. He had gotten to know him well, dealing with him frequently when the site would have technical issues. Beep would need Brit to make changes to his lineup before it locked, letting Brit see exactly which players Beep was going to use on FanThrowdown that night. Then Beep would find himself playing Brit in head-to-head matches that same night on FanDuel. Man, DFS.

Now Brit is just another pro who might soon be out of a job, and a funny one at that. At a reception shortly after, he perches himself by a display of Dove ice cream bars and pretends to hawk them to passersby to make extra cash.

"The attorney general took my job away. I'm charging ten dollars for an ice cream—I need the money," he wheedles.

Brit lives near Syracuse, deep in the heart of New York State, not exactly a quick jaunt to the DFS-friendly areas of Pennsylvania to the south or New England to the east. His girlfriend just bought a house in the area and has a stable job, and so he can't move. He's resigned to the idea that he will soon be unemployed, though he isn't crying poverty.

"I have enough stored away that I can hang back for a while and wait to see how it plays out," he says.

Not everyone is handling this with Brit's equanimity. Some of the pros and regs are furious at Schneiderman for what they see as overaggressive and unfair politicking; if DFS is illegal gambling, they insist, then this or that legal pursuit must be, too. I can't count how many times I hear one DFS shark or another compare Daily Fantasy to real estate speculation. One genial newcomer to DFS, a tall black man named Roman, engages me in a long and rambling conversation where he tries to argue that Daily Fantasy is just like the stock market, which is probably the most common comparison made by DFS players and supporters.

"They're exactly the same," Roman argues, stridently. "Tell me how they're different."

These arguments always ring so terribly hollow to me. Okay, sure, DFS is like the stock market in that there's money put forward toward uncertain outcomes, and that you're trying to find undervalued assets. But the stock market is also highly, highly regulated, overseen by government agencies that monitor it for fraud, excess, or everybody's favorite, insider trading.

Look, the stock market probably *is* gambling—but that's why the regulation around it exists in the first place, I tell Roman. Also, the stock market serves a purpose in the economy: to capitalize the companies selling pieces of themselves as stock. What purpose does owning a player in DFS serve, really, other than one's own hopes of making money by betting against other people?

This does not seem to sway new friend Roman. We agree to disagree for the moment.

There's one person at the conference who is more practiced, and more invested, in playing the "DFS is like . . ." game than any other, and that man is the reason I'm still hanging around the conference through the late afternoon: DraftKings CEO Robins.

It will be my first chance to meet the DraftKings boss, who is the unquestioned head of the company's three founders, the face of the business while Matt Kalish and Paul Liberman stay in the background.

In the month since his employee, Haskell, screwed up and committed the data leak that would change the DFS industry forever, Robins has been all over television, print, and radio, defending his company and his industry. At times he's done that by invoking the stock market analogy, or by comparing his game to chess.

He also, likely to his later regret, has described the industry in poker terms, something Schneiderman's lawsuit seeks to use against him. In a 2012 Q&A on the website Reddit, not long after DraftKings was founded, Robins explained DFS and DraftKings using gambling language.

"The concept is different from traditional fantasy leagues," Robins wrote. "Our concept is a mashup between poker and fantasy sports. Basically, you pick a team, deposit your wager, and if your team wins, you get the pot. Fantasy sports has a carve out from the 2006 gambling regulation because its [sic] considered a game of skill. This concept where you can basically 'bet' your team will win is new and different from traditional leagues that last an entire season."

Even more thrilling to the attorney general, he also wrote, "The concept is almost identical to a casino.. [sic] specifically Poker. We make money when people win pots."

I mean, he's right—that's exactly how I'd describe it. And I'm sure he could never have predicted that those casually typed words would ever be used against him by the state of New York.

But little about Robins's life in the last four years has been predictable.

Growing up in Kendall, Florida, a southwestern suburb of Miami, Robins was a typical geek, one after my own heart. He loved sports but stunk at them, flailing about in his soccer, baseball, and tennis efforts in local leagues and at the JCC. But more than the players or the strategies, it was the numbers of sports that consumed him, and he quickly realized that he was better at memorizing great statistics than at producing them.

Sports were one of the twin passions of the Robins household. The other was technology. His father, an economics professor at the University of Miami, was always up on the latest tech, and his son learned at his knee, working at home on the family's PC and beginning to train in basic programming at age thirteen, according to a profile in the *Miami Herald*. When he stumbled upon online fantasy sports, everything came together.

Fantasy sports had been around, and growing, through his entire childhood, but it was when it made the leap to the Internet that people like Robins and myself ate it up. I first played an online league during the 2000 baseball season, riding Todd Helton and his .372 average to a third-place finish. Robins started even earlier, then took his passion for fantasy with him to Duke University, graduating with a double major in economics and computer science, and set out into the world with hopes of becoming a tech entrepreneur.

He took a job in business analytics at Capital One, where he met Kalish, the second of the three eventual DraftKings founders. After five years the pair moved to business card and marketing company Vistaprint, in Boston, where they met Liberman, and the triumvirate that would start DraftKings was whole.

From there Robins and his cofounders began an ascent that would eventually bring them to the top of the fantasy world and land Robins on the cover of the October issue of *Fortune* magazine. Scoring a magazine cover at age thirty-four is quite an accomplishment, especially for someone who isn't exactly oozing with charisma. Robins is pleasant and genial, but there's an awkwardness there that's hard to describe— though that shouldn't be confused with a lack of confidence. The *Boston Globe*'s Neil Swidey, who gave my journalism career its true start when he helped me get an internship at the *Globe*'s statehouse bureau in 2000, described him beautifully in a December 2015 profile.

"Robins is slender, has deep-set eyes, and is generally serious but occasionally flashes a wide, crooked grin. His voice is monotone, and he never seems to raise it, though he sometimes tosses off mattress-size paragraphs that can leave his interlocutors unsure about where they might jump in," Swidey wrote.

But none should think he's some wallflower. As Swidey continued, "Though neither a backslapper nor a particularly charismatic speaker, Robins is an extrovert, comfortable introducing himself to people and confident before a crowd."

That confidence is what has made him such an effective fund-raiser; if there's one thing that DraftKings did better than every other DFS site ever, it's raise money, and that's a direct tribute to Robins, as Kalish noted.

"We probably met five hundred different people, investors, partners, in that first year, and he's just tireless—he never gets tired of that," Kalish says. "He loves meeting people, talking about the idea, putting things together. He was very clearly the leader of the group from early on."

I'd add that his quiet demeanor camouflages a hard-charging ferociousness, the kind that people call bold when it works and reckless when it doesn't. With Robins at the fore, DraftKings has consistently pushed the boundaries in its rise to the top. It offers sports that FanDuel won't touch (MMA, NASCAR, golf) for fear that doing so might not be legal under UIGEA. It spent more than four times what FanDuel did during the infamous advertising blitz. It chose to stay operational in New York when FanDuel and most every other DFS operator pulled out. Its public statements on every legal development in the DFS world often ring with the hot fury of an angry child stamping its feet when it knows it's about to be sent to its room.

As the DraftKings CEO enters the room to start his Q&A, I'm struck by the contrast between this rumpled yet relatable everyman and the more polished head of FanDuel. Eccles—shiny and smooth in his loafers, his fitted sport coats, his Britishness—seems stoic and upbeat through all the DFS turmoil. Robins is clad in a green sweater and slacks and he looks impossibly tired, worn down to the nub. That morning, Eccles had exuded positivity, a sense of marching forward despite the numerous setbacks. As he sits for his own Q&A with RotoGrinders' Dan Back, Robins sounds a tone somewhere between frustration and depression, the quiet sadness of a man who has been beaten down.

He sounds human.

As the room sits and watches at the end of a bizarre day full of protests and lawsuits, Dan Back probes what it's been like for Robins to go from darling of the business world to national target.

"No one enjoys dealing with accusations that hurt, that make you feel lousy. No one likes dealing with pressures, and stresses," Robins says, slowly and quietly, making me actually feel a little sorry for him.

But he can also be prickly, as when he delved into perceived media bias and the "Is it gambling?" question that he constantly faces.

"Here's what I'm sick and tired of—is when people ask a commentator, or someone in the news media, 'Is this gambling?' The answer they're giving is their own answer based on a subjective view of what constitutes gambling in their mind. There are people that say that playing a game of chess, if you challenge your friend for ten bucks, is gambling. There are others who will say that something like online poker absolutely is not gambling."

I think we know my feelings on that by now, but I'll let Robins keep the floor for the moment.

"What I will say is that's not the right question," Robins continues. "The right question is, is it legal or not under the laws of the state in which you operate? That's something that I think is the more relevant question."

If I were his PR person—and thank God I'm not—I'd probably tell him to be a little less candid, at the risk of sounding disconnected and tone-deaf. But more than that, I'd tell him, simply, to be more positive. Robins is one of the two faces of this industry, and so his hangdog routine has repercussions; his words carry weight, especially those that hint at defeatism—like when he closes the Q&A by acknowledging the possibility that all this turmoil might mean the death of DFS.

"This is sometimes the price of success," Robins says. "Unfortunately, it's happened in a way that I didn't anticipate and I'm not enjoying. But we'll deal with it, and make sure we get on the right side of it, and if we don't? We die trying."

When Robins comes off the stage, I wait for him to finish chatting with a few industry types. Looking to introduce myself, I corral him on his way out, we shake hands, and in a few minutes of chitchat, I explain to him who I am and what I'm doing—living in his world, playing on his site, trying to tell the story of what I generously call "the rise of DFS."

No fool, Robins quickly picks up on what was left unspoken.

"Maybe the rise and fall," he says, flashing that wide, crooked grin.

"Sports?" the bailiff shouts, prompting most of the people crammed near me in the courthouse hallway to raise their hands. They are, almost uniformly, a well-coiffed bunch, spiffy in jackets and ties and skirts and pantsuits.

"Flu?" she yells next, and an entirely different population—favoring sweatpants—raises theirs, as the bailiff tries to find a way to organize everyone into two distinct groups.

It's the day before Thanksgiving, nearly two weeks after the sidewalk protest and the RotoGrinders conference, and the first DFS legal showdown has arrived. The state Supreme Court* is set to hold a hearing on Attorney General Schneiderman's request for an injunction to stop FanDuel and DraftKings from doing business in New York while both sides wait for a full trial to play out. DraftKings and FanDuel have teams

---

* The name is a little deceptive; in New York, Supreme Courts aren't the court of last resort, like the federal Supreme Court. Instead, it's just the highest level of trial court, akin to a superior court in most other states.

of lawyers filing briefs in their defense, and it will all be decided in the drab, low-ceilinged Manhattan courtroom of New York State Supreme Court justice Manuel J. Mendez. Mendez plans to hear arguments from both sides and then probably render a decision within a few weeks— with the potential to level a death blow to the industry, one that could trigger a domino effect of state after state following New York's lead and barring DFS.

But first Mendez has to deal with another case: a challenge from the anti-vaccination set, fighting New York City's requirement that pre-K children be inoculated in order to attend school. The flu crew and the DFS crowd jam the hallway outside the courtroom in one big mass, media and lawyers with their briefcases and laptops, and anti-flu-shot advocates with their "No shot!" stickers and signs, all jumbled up together. Trapped in such close quarters with the anti-vax crowd? I'm totally going to get sick.

I spot Robins off to the side, sitting with one of his lawyers. We exchange pleasantries, and I tell the DraftKings CEO how I had recently visited with BeepImaJeep and learned how he builds lineups. Robins and Beep know each other well enough and spent a day on a fishing boat together at a previous DraftKings event. Robins lights up when he hears where I've been.

"Then you saw firsthand what a game of skill this is," he says immediately.

There it is again—"game of skill." The companies take cover behind that term like it's their all-purpose shield, one that will make them impervious to all threats and legal actions. But what does it mean? And why does it matter?

To anyone not employed by a DFS site, Daily Fantasy Sports is gambling, certainly in the casual sense of the word. Players risk real money on an uncertain outcome, against other players doing the same, in a contest where they lack total control. Just like in poker, anything can happen in the short term, but in the long run, better players win and poor players lose their money. Regardless, the house—in this case, DraftKings and

FanDuel—takes a cut and disburses the cash to the person with the best outcome at the end of the contest. It's a familiar scenario to anyone who's ever set foot in a sports book.

Legally speaking, however, it's not quite so cut-and-dried.

"The issue here is not whether this is gambling in some kind of colloquial sense," DraftKings' lawyer, Boies, explained in a conference call I sat in on days before the Supreme Court hearing. "The question is whether this is unlawful gambling under New York law."

The answer to that question leads us down a road where we're suddenly parsing what the definition of "is" is, Bill Clinton–style. At the federal level, UIGEA protects fantasy sports well enough. Yet gambling law has mostly been left up to the states, and trying to navigate those brings us into a thicket of archaic and varied state laws across the country.

At its most basic, if a contest is classified as a game of skill where skill is the primary determinant of the outcome, it is usually not considered illegal gambling and can operate without restriction in most states. But if it is considered a game of chance, where luck is the main factor in the outcome, then it's probably going to be considered gambling in the legal sense. Yet nearly all games have some elements of both chance and skill—if they didn't, the outcomes would be either totally random, like the lottery, or fully predetermined, like pro wrestling. It's a spectrum, and for most games the line between chance and skill is drawn somewhere in the vast middle. But where, exactly? That's where it gets complicated, and much of it depends on which state we're talking about.

There are a handful of states where even a minute element of chance makes a game gambling, and not coincidentally, most DFS companies refused to operate in these even before the Haskell scandal. On the other end of the spectrum, there are about twenty-five states that say luck or chance must predominate in order for a game to be considered gambling. For the time being, DFS is mostly safe in those states.

But in the rest, things start to get murky. In about a dozen states, including New York, games must pass what is called a "material element" test. In New York, this means that a game is gambling if "the outcome depends in a material degree upon an element of chance."

So what exactly is a material degree of the element of chance? How much is that? That's at the heart of all this. No one on either side disputes that there is skill involved in Daily Fantasy. No one really disputes that there is chance involved, either. But where that line falls, Boies argues, is the arbiter of legality. The Daily Fantasy companies have sought to make the entire court battle about that question.

"In every game of skill, there is some chance, even in chess," Boies said. "Even with games that are predominantly of chance, there can be some skill involved. So the question is a practical one: does skill predominate, or does chance predominate?"

Somewhat ironically, one of DFS's problems helps solve another. The fact that a few sharks can consistently dominate helps support the idea that it is a game of skill, and both companies have submitted affidavits and studies citing this.

Schneiderman, for his part, seems to be seeking traction in other areas. In comments leading up to the hearing, he sought to largely sideline the "game of skill" debate.

"Games of chance often involve some amount of skill; this does not make them legal. Good poker players often beat novices. But poker is still gambling, and running a poker room—or online casino—is illegal in New York," he wrote in an op-ed in the New York *Daily News* days before the hearing.

These statements preview the arguments that the two sides plan to make in court: for the companies, that the skill element makes it legal, and for the state, that it doesn't really matter if there's some skill involved: the basic tenets of DFS are similar to other types of illegal or otherwise regulated gambling.

Hanging outside the courtroom with former *Sports Illustrated* reporter Joe Lemire, who is there to cover the hearing for *USA Today*, we hear the angry moms of the anti-vax posse railing against the dangers of vaccination. One testifies that she is "anti-poison." I resist the urge to yell out that I am "anti–contagious epidemics."

As morning turns into afternoon, Mendez finishes with their case and the bailiff calls "Sports" again, triggering a stampede of journalists and lawyers pushing to the front, trying to shove their way into the sixty-five-seat courtroom before the final few seats are gone. Elbows and press passes fly left and right as we jockey for position at the all-important doorway. I get there in good position to make the final push, but once at the gateway, it tightens up; the throng squeezes me like a python crushing a mouse and I go low to escape. Sliding sideways and down through the pack, I pop out into fresh air and the relative calm of the courtroom itself, straightening my blazer and coolly claiming the last seat in the left side of the gallery. A full fifteen people still stand crammed in the doorway, blocked by the all-business bailiff, who expertly holds the crowd at bay. Behind the unfortunate group in the doorway are dozens and dozens more, those unwashed masses who either weren't positioned for—or weren't game for—that brief rugby scrum I managed to win. Lemire, sadly, is left far behind, but I promise to send him my notes from inside.

Robins and his cadre of lawyers take seats right in front of me, with quite the star-studded group present. Alongside Boies is former New York City deputy mayor Randy Mastro, and for FanDuel, respected litigator John Kiernan, the current president of the New York City Bar Association. If I was building a DFS lawyer squad, these guys would all be high-salary, cap-busting picks.

I'd have to compensate by matching them with the midlevel salaries of the attorney general's team, led by the chief of Schneiderman's Internet Bureau, Kathleen McGee. A graduate of Boston University School of Law, McGee worked in the Bronx district attorney's office prosecuting sex crimes and domestic violence cases before running a unit tasked with handling quality-of-life issues, like illegal hotels and counterfeit trademark activity. A strong resume, but not quite the star power of the DFS legal team.

Presiding over it all is Mendez, a Dominican-born Fordham Law grad and veteran of the New York court system, who rose from criminal defense and personal injury work to the legal bench. He gestures to prosecutor McGee that it is, at last, time to begin. She stands a few feet from Robins and his team of legal hotshots and reads from an expansive opening statement, one that pulls no punches as it seeks to explain why Daily Fantasy Sports is simply gambling by another name. Sure, she says, playing DFS requires skill—skill at gambling.

"What DraftKings and FanDuel really offer is a way to bet on sports," McGee says succinctly.

In many ways, McGee argues, Daily Fantasy resembles prop betting, where gamblers wager on the outcome of specific events within a game. They are still staking something of value over an uncertain result separate and apart from the outcome of a game over which they lack control.

"Whether you call it an entry fee or a stake, it's something of value," McGee says. "I place my bet. I pick my team and then I watch TV. The rest is up to the athletes."

Chance is everywhere, she says, and DFS players don't have the kind of control they may think they do.

"The defendants' contests are not a bunch of clicks of the mouse or taps of an iPhone—it's what's happening beyond the computer screen. Chance pervades Daily Fantasy Sports—an athlete injury, a slump, a lucky shot, a streak, dropped pass, even the weather on any given day, especially if the game is rained out," she says.

Importantly, McGee stresses that the attorney general's office has no issue with season-long fantasy leagues. They're not a focus here.

As she sits, it's now on Kiernan, FanDuel's lawyer, to rebut her claims. He ventures this way and that, defining DFS games as "true contests" like fishing competitions or even spelling bees, those where contestants pay entry fees with the hope of winning a prize. Those contests also feature unexpected events—a change in the weather, or encountering a word that a spelling bee participant didn't study. That doesn't mean they aren't games of skill, Kiernan said.

Those comparisons ring hollow to me, and seemingly to much of the audience. Attendees shuffle quietly in their seats and chuckle to one another at the spelling bee reference.

But Kiernan does make an interesting point—that the focus has been on the wrong contest. The contest that is at play here is not the game on the field, Kiernan argues. The contest is entirely one of roster construction among fantasy participants, those who are creating lineups and pitting them against one another; defining it like this, in theory, would allow them to skirt New York State law that defines gambling as a "contest of chance" or a "future contingent event not under [the participant's] control or influence."

"What Fantasy Sports contestants believe is that they're developing skill at the game that they're playing, which is selection of a roster of players that they believe will outperform another set of rosters of players selected by other people," Kiernan says.

That makes some sense, though it would seem there are levels to that contest, and that the fantasy contest can't exist without the real-life sporting event to determine the winner. Just as I'm pondering that, Mendez interjects with his first question of the day, asking how such a contest would work without the games actually being played.

There may be skill in the roster construction, Mendez says, but "now you're relying on someone else's skill to play the game."

It signals that he ain't buying FanDuel's argument, at least not entirely. Kiernan stammers through a recovery, but I can sense the mood in the courtroom shifting. People are bored, or at least not energized by the DFS companies' arguments, as we break for lunch.

During the lunch break, I run into a few fellow reporters from the *Wall Street Journal* and hear about more bad news for the reeling Daily Fantasy industry. My colleagues have learned that Major League Baseball—the most important of all DFS partners—sent a letter to DraftKings informing them that it was considering severing their business relationship. It appears that the letter was a procedural step, not a final decision, and with MLB being uncooperative and DraftKings actively trying to kill the story, we couldn't get enough on it to bring it to print on that November afternoon. But it exists, and represents another potential blow for companies already on the ropes.

When we reenter the room after the lunch break—I slip in a bit more easily this time—there's a real buzz in the air. With the break over, David Boies is slated to give his arguments, and in a crowd of journalists and lawyers, this amounts to a celebrity guest appearance.

In the world of big-name attorneys, Boies is perhaps the biggest. The seventy-four-year-old delights in the most prominent and interesting of cases, and wins them more often than not. Once a fixture at the peerless firm of Cravath, Swaine & Moore, Boies left and started his own practice in 1997 because Cravath refused to let him represent Yankees owner George Steinbrenner, who was suing Major League Baseball and, by extension, one of Cravath's other clients, Atlanta Braves owner Time Warner Inc.

Leaving Cravath did Boies no harm; a legal generalist now free to amble to whatever court he pleased, he took on a slew of famous cases and clients. He eviscerated Bill Gates at the front of the government's legal team in its 1998 antitrust case against Microsoft, and later won a record $4 billion settlement for American Express in its own antitrust case in 2008. But it's hard to top his most famous case: representing Vice President Al Gore when the 2000 presidential election was fought in the courts over a few hanging chads on Florida ballots. Boies, and Gore, lost that case before the U.S. Supreme Court, but he would never lose the luster that comes from litigating with nothing less than the presidency at stake.

When Kiernan spoke, the momentum seemed to favor the attorney general's side, and it appeared the DFS companies were headed for a loss. But as Boies stands to take his turn, it's like all that built-up malaise is swept away in one motion. He instantly sets to work hammering the attorney general's argument, first restating and expanding on Kiernan's contention that the contest in question is the fantasy game, not the real-world sporting event.

"The New York attorney general wants it said that the contest is those real-world games," Boies begins. "The problem is that isn't the contest for which the player has paid an entry fee. And that's not the contest for which the prize is awarded. When you're betting on sports, you're getting a prize for what happens in that real-world sports contest. When you're playing fantasy sports, you're getting a prize for what happens in your fantasy contest, and that's a contest where the player controls the result."

Next, Boies lays into the premise that season-long and daily fantasy sports can be treated differently from a legal standpoint. As there are many paid season-long leagues where a prize is distributed at the end, Schneiderman can't go after one while happily accepting the other, Boies argues.

"The fact that they concede seasonal fantasy sports are lawful and not gambling is fatal to their claim here," Boies says. "They cannot have it both ways."

At that, the pair of suits seated next to me, who are clearly on the attorney general's side, grimace. "He might have traction on that one," one says. I swear I saw Mendez nodding along slightly as Boies spoke.

Then Boies attacks the premise that a temporary injunction is warranted—that there's sufficient immediate public harm here to essentially torpedo the Daily Fantasy industry without benefit of a trial.

"The issue here is that you had a long-standing status quo, that they're trying to upend with a preliminary injunction," Boies says. "It's not an appropriate situation to shut down a company that's been operating lawfully for four years without a trial."

Impressive. One of the attorney general–connected people next to me murmurs that Boies was "strong on the preliminary injunction front."

Mendez seems to pick up on one part of Boies's argument above the others, because when McGee gives her rebuttal, Mendez lobs his second question of the day at her.

"Why is it that traditional fantasy sports would be allowed, whereas daily fantasy sports wouldn't?" Mendez asks. "What's the core difference?"

McGee stumbles at that, first saying that season-long contests don't offer prizes—which many do—before offering that some season-long contests might also be illegal if they took entry fees and offered prizes in a similar fashion to Daily Fantasy games. A solid recovery, but the DFS legal team seems to lean back in smug satisfaction after the exchange.

With the arguments winding down and time growing short, Mendez brings things to a conclusion, promising a decision "very soon," which apparently in legal terms generally means anything from three days to three weeks. After it's over, Boies and Kiernan hold court on the sidewalk outside the courthouse for a good fifteen minutes. They're in good spirits. They feel they've taken the attorney general's best shot and perhaps turned the tables.

On the subway uptown with me is the ubiquitous Florida lawyer Daniel Wallach, who says he thinks the DFS lawyers might have done enough to prevail, even though he doesn't believe the law is really on their side.

"They may have been able to buy a victory, just on the strength of their legal team," he says "I'm not exactly sure that's how it's supposed to work, but it may have been enough here."

That's what I thought, too. I'd put the odds of FanDuel and DraftKings winning—winning meaning holding off a shutdown until a full trial—at 60–40. Sixty percent isn't bad. In DFS, you'd take those odds in a head-to-head matchup any day.

06

It's a sunny, breezy day along the San Diego shoreline, and footballs whiz by my head as I crane my neck around, searching for my mentor, Beep.

I finally spot him, finding him hunched over on a park bench, his face inches from his phone, eyes intently studying its screen. I peer down over his shoulder at what he's reading. It's a WikiHow entry titled "How to Kick a Field Goal in 12 Steps."

"This doesn't seem too bad," says Beep, ever the self-made expert. "All I have to do is remember the proper sequence of steps in the moment, and it should be fine."

"It's not actually that easy," I warn, imagining him flipping over as he tries to kick the ball, à la Charlie Brown.

Beep smiles and pretends not to hear me as he scampers off to join the other DFS players tossing, catching, and kicking footballs all around us, as they warm up to take a run at conquering the FanDuel Football Combine.

At Embarcadero Marina Park South, looking out on Coronado Island, FanDuel has built a course that's a cross between a McDonald's playground and an American Gladiators arena—with a little bit of football field thrown in for good measure. There's a foam rubber pit for making leaping catches, a drill where players hop through tires while dodging sandbags, a set of six trash cans arrayed as a giant beer pong formation, and a football goalpost, for kicking field goals. Oh, and two Hall of Fame quarterbacks: Joe Montana, stationed at the beginning of the course, and Dan Marino at the end, gamely lobbing passes to star-struck DFS players.

The football combine is the centerpiece event of FanDuel's NFL final weekend in San Diego and the unofficial start of what many in the DFS world call "finals week." Ever since football season began, both major sites have loudly trumpeted their NFL finals as the culmination of their football offerings; each one boasts the biggest prizes either site has ever handed out. FanDuel is awarding $3 million for first place, and DraftKings, ever bigger, is giving $5 million to its winner. Between them, the two finals offer a stunning $27 million in prizes, after the sites combined to dole out $17 million the year before.

Both finals were originally scheduled to take place in Las Vegas. But after Nevada required DFS companies to apply for licenses and register as gambling operations in October, both DFS giants pulled out of the state. They subsequently moved their signature events to San Diego, scheduling them for consecutive mid-December weekends.

For the big-time pros, that's remarkably convenient. Most of the top players managed to qualify for both finals, so they've grouped up and rented beach houses to serve as home bases over the entire finals period. MaxDalury told me he's spending seventeen straight days in San Diego, at a house in La Jolla that he's sharing with CSURAM. Beep didn't qualify for the FanDuel final, only for DraftKings, thanks to our Bills-Patriots sweat—but he's here for the duration anyway, as the guest of Underjones, the New York pro who is working on finding a DFS office in New Jersey in the post-Schneiderman era. Underjones has a whopping five seats at the FanDuel event, plus three for DraftKings. Beep and Underjones, close friends in the DFS world, are staying at a house out on Mission Beach, along with RotoGrinders founder Cal Spears and a Los Angeles–based pro named Jeff Collins, who goes by the username

JeffElJefe. I've convinced them to let me spend the week with them on the beach, tagging along as the fifth roommate and trying to soak up what DFS knowledge I can.

Most players arrived in San Diego on Friday, December 13, and were greeted by a package that included a black and gold FanDuel football jersey with their last name across the back. With the final and its $3 million top prize on the line on Sunday, the top players will be staying home on Saturday night, fine-tuning lineups before the main event. But Saturday afternoon, FanDuel has drawn more than one hundred of them out to a spit of land off the city's waterfront for the chance to put on that jersey and, at least momentarily, feel like actual football players, not just football gamblers.

The football combine is the brainchild of FanDuel founder Nigel Eccles. I spot the wiry, energetic Irishman wandering the event grounds and head over to say hello. Eccles is wearing his own FanDuel football jersey, similar to those he's had made for every participant. The company founder reports that he's run the course himself already. I start to wonder how I'd do—the egotist in me thinking that this doesn't look that hard, and that I can surely beat most of these slightly overweight DFS basement dwellers (excepting the occasional superjacked one, of course). Eccles, in his early forties but in the same kind of lean shape that I am, relates that it was tougher than expected—especially the field goal part. I'll get used to hearing that over the course of the day.

"Is this supposed to make them feel like they're the athlete, like they're in the game itself?" I ask.

"Yes, exactly!" Eccles says, his eyes lighting up. "We want to give them that experience, that feeling. That's what DFS is all about, really."

Right. It's male wish fulfillment. It's gaining a role in—a feeling of control over—the sporting events on television every night, however illusory that involvement really is. I remember a conversation I had with Draftcheat a month earlier about how he'd love to be working in the Minnesota Twins front office, or as a scout, but that isn't happening. So

DFS offers him the next-best thing, a way for him to feel involved in the sports he loves.

Draftcheat, by the way, is warming up nearby, bragging to the other pros that he's a former high school kicker. I figure he's got a pretty strong shot to win it all. I'm sure somewhere around here someone is taking bets on this.

Eccles marvels at how many reporters are here to cover his final. In the world of DFS, it's become impossible to even admit that I'm a reporter without players or execs noting how much they've come to distrust or dislike mainstream DFS coverage, and there's a lot of mainstream media here. There's a *60 Minutes* crew headed by Armen Keteyian, there's a *Sports Illustrated* reporter, and there's a former Grantland editor and now freelance writer for the *New York Times,* Jay Caspian Kang, whom I'd met at the Schneiderman protest a month earlier.

The players distrust the *Times* most of all. The paper, to them, has become synonymous with the unfair media—the nameless, faceless people who are out to get all DFS players and companies. With Eccles, despite his sophistication, it's no different, and he immediately launches into a story about how comically biased he considers the paper's coverage to be. He's particularly energized about a column that ran recently, by William C. Rhoden, about how fantasy sports dehumanize athletes. That, to him, was the tipping point that proved the *Times* was out to get DFS, one way or another.

"That's when I just had to laugh," Eccles says. "I was like, what are they doing?"

What has really angered him, and many others in DFS, is that the *Times* is trying to conflate DFS operators and offshore sports books, melding them together as part of a yearlong investigation into online gambling. He predicts that at some point, the *Times* will have to change its tune on DFS, as newspapers in his native Britain have to sometimes do when they start taking heat because their coverage of an issue is clearly too slanted.

"Have you ever heard of the 'reverse ferret'?" Eccles asks.

When I plead ignorance, he explains that the term is a reference to the tenure of editor Kelvin MacKenzie at the *Sun,* one of London's top tabloid newspapers. MacKenzie liked his reporters to go out and stir things up by, metaphorically, sticking a ferret into the trousers of their subjects and seeing what happened. If it tore things up and resulted in a big story, then mission accomplished. Yet there were times when, despite the *Sun's,* well, ferreting, the story or the subject wasn't quite what they thought it was. It might turn out that, editorially, they found themselves on the wrong side. At those times, MacKenzie would come sprinting out of his office and into the newsroom, shouting, "Reverse ferret! Reverse ferret!"

"That's what I think the *Times* is going to have to do at some point— a reverse ferret," Eccles says, laughing. Ferrets! Those zany Brits.

The funny thing is, I'm not media anymore, or at least not in the same way. A week before, I'd given my notice that I was quitting the *Wall Street Journal.* I'd told my bosses my plan to live in and document the world of DFS full-time, and they understandably said I couldn't be both a heavy gambler and also an active sportswriter, and denied my request for a book leave. I had no problem with that. It made sense. So after fifteen years in print journalism, that was that. As part of this change, I'd be moving to Boston—partly because New York was a banned state for DFS, but mostly because my wife lived in Boston and our jobs had kept us apart for a few years now, with me covering the Yankees, her covering the Bruins. My last official day is a few weeks off. So starting the new year, I'll be a full-time DFS player. And so far, a really, really lousy one. I tell Eccles my plan, and he beams at it, apparently not as concerned as my mother is that I'm making a completely crazy decision. Maybe he hasn't seen that study that only 1 percent of players really win?

This weekend should be Eccles's finest hour, the culmination of a football season that saw significant growth for his company. Instead, conversations about the latest legal actions, the state of the industry, or the perceived media bias loom over everything. When I'd arrived at the

DraftKings Miami kickoff event in September, it was a different world. If there was talk of the larger industry outside that room, it was focused on how much bigger DFS was going to get—how it was going to grow, grow, grow, from the prize pools to the user numbers, until it had completely changed the way we watch and consume sports. Everyone there believed that blindly, and to say otherwise in that company earned you blank stares. Forget drinking the Kool-Aid— that was a room full of Kool-Aid producers, sellers, and marketers, and at the time it was hard to argue with them. They had ample reason to feel the way they did.

A mere three months later, all has changed, and paranoia is the order of the day. Instead of talking about how much money they're going to win, players discuss the most recent anti-DFS articles, calling them "hit pieces," and the latest legislative and regulatory efforts. It's been a big week for DraftKings and FanDuel, legally. Friday, just as contestants were boarding their planes for the final, Judge Mendez issued his ruling, granting Attorney General Schneiderman's request for a preliminary injunction against DraftKings and FanDuel, halting them from operating in New York State. Mendez sided entirely with the attorney general, ignoring the skill-versus-chance debate completely, declaring the companies harmful to the public good and ordering them to cease operations in New York immediately. For a few hours, DFS was dead in New York. But later that afternoon, just as I was boarding my own flight for San Diego, appeals court justice Paul G. Feinman granted a stay of that injunction, putting the matter on hold until a larger panel of the appeals court could address the issue in January. That amounted to a big win for DraftKings and FanDuel, and both companies took an immediate victory lap—FanDuel even deciding to resume operations in New York after three weeks of barring New York players from its site.

With this all in the air, Schneiderman's name comes up frequently, usually preceded by some variation of "fuck." There are other regulatory efforts under way—in Massachusetts, Attorney General Maura Healey is drafting regulations that would apply multi-entry caps and introduce other consumer protections, and the companies are largely on board.

Here on the West Coast, the California legislature is holding a hearing on DFS later in the week, and the California-based players are trying to find out what it means: Is it just informational? Will they try to pass something? Is it the precursor to more legal actions? What's the attorney general doing? What's the state's legal standard for games of chance—is it a "material element" of skill, or any element of skill? A group of lay-abouts who make their money on sports knowledge and computer skills are suddenly experts in the most arcane of legal distinctions.

I plan to ask Eccles why exactly he felt the New York decision—which is basically just a delay, not an overturning of Mendez's ruling—was reason enough for his company to jump back into business in the state, but he is tapped on the shoulder and yanked away to do an interview with the *60 Minutes* crew, so we agree to talk more later.

I wander off in search of fish tacos and happen upon Jay Caspian Kang, there shadowing a few players of his own for his *Times* magazine piece. Like me, Kang recognizes the allure of the game, that it really is a lot of fun. We both have a little bit of degenerate gambler in us, and we're of the same mind that much of the coverage of DFS is hysterical, Chicken Little–type stuff about rigged contests and insider trading. Perhaps more important, we also agree that DFS's real problem actually lies more with the people all around us—and how the companies long allowed these top sharks to run roughshod over the casual player, letting them dominate in a way that is probably bad for the industry as a whole, and certainly ruinous for poorly bankrolled, mid-stakes players like Kang and me.*

---

* Some of those thoughts would eventually manifest themselves as pieces of Kang's article, which would come out in early January and introduce much of the non-DFS world to concepts like bumhunting, computer script exploitation, and the companies' willingness to alter rules to accommodate the top pros. Bumhunting—the practice by pros of targeting weak, casual players in head-to-head matchups—got most of the attention, but to me the biggest takeaway was the admission by the sites themselves of the degree they catered to high-volume players. Unfortunately, it was slapped with a nasty, over-the-top headline, and the DFS world felt Kang got a few things wrong—conflating bumhunting with being auto-matched by the site when lineups lock, for instance—allowing those who most needed to heed his message to dismiss his article as just another misinformed

As the contestants run through the course all around us, Kang and I are concerned with a much more pressing issue: what are Marino and Montana getting paid to be here, smiling through gritted teeth in the name of an appearance fee? Being the good DFS-related media that we are, we decide to put a wager on it: $10. I pick $60,000 and instantly regret it, realizing it's far too low. Kang goes with $150,000, and a third reporter jumps in with an even higher bid. Sleuthing it out, we learn that it's over $100,000, and Kang, closest to the pin, takes my money. At least giving him my cash doesn't grate as much as when MaxDalury takes it.

I see faces and names I recognize running through the course, including my diminutive Canadian pal Slewfoot, who can't seem to avoid the sandbags on the tire drill; Cal Spears, who bites it hard on the ramp; and finally Draftcheat, who, despite his braggadocio, shanks the field goal badly low and left. Glad I didn't bet on him.

At last, we see Beep line up for his chance to run the course. Despite having touched a football only a few times in his life, he is bubbling with confidence thanks to his Internet crash course in gridiron basics—that, and the new sneakers he bought this morning for the occasion. He takes his place at the starting line and gives us a thumbs-up, as Slewfoot, his wife, Sheana, and his friend/personal assistant Garrett and I all roll our eyes, certain we're about to witness a colossal and impressive failure.

Instead Beep wows us all with an unexpected display of just-good-enough athleticism, catching passes, hopping through tires, running up ramps, and firing footballs into trash cans with surprising ease. The final challenge is the field goal. Beep sets himself up, clearly running through the proper sequence in his head, before (Step 5) "taking his approach steps," (Step 6) "positioning the plant foot so that it points at the target," and (Step 9) "following the kick through to the target." The ball flies forward, just clearing the uprights, and Beep improvises his own Step 13: "Celly!"

---

hit piece. And it wasn't that. People who don't want to hear bad news will find a way not to.

His score puts him in a tie for first with another player, and a playoff is announced. But as Beep stands at the podium, awaiting his rival, we learn that the other contestant has already left, perhaps not realizing how well he'd actually done. Conferring over the next step, the FanDuel organizers decide they'll give Beep the win if he can just catch one more pass from Dan Marino.

But this isn't going to be just any pass, as we could tell from Marino's mischievous grin.

That's because Beep and Marino have a history.

A few minutes earlier, kind, charming, innocent Beep had managed to piss off the impeccably tanned, perfectly coifed, enviably fit fifty-four-year-old Marino. As Beep finished his run through the course, he had been catching passes from the Hall of Fame quarterback—gentle, soft throws—and the career Miami Dolphin took it easy on the obvious novice. Beep, genial sports know-nothing that he is, walked over afterward to thank Marino for throwing to him.

"Thanks a lot, Joe," Beep said to one of the most famous NFL quarterbacks ever to play. Unfortunately for Beep, this was not Joe Montana, who was also nearby, throwing passes to other FanDuel DFS finalists. This was Dan Marino, and Marino didn't like being mistaken for his fellow Hall of Famer—especially a guy who actually won all the Super Bowls that Marino missed out on.

So when Beep found himself in the surprise one-catch-wins-all tie-breaker, Marino was overheard telling Montana that this guy didn't even know which of them was which—and that he was going to give him a heckuva ball to catch.

Now Marino, a football in his massive right hand, points to the spot where he wants Beep to jump. It's square in the middle of a pit of foam rubber blocks meant to cushion his fall, allowing Beep to try for the leaping, diving catch.

Beep nods nervously, takes his running start, and stretches out over the pit, snagging Marino's pass just as he falls into the foam's cushioning embrace. Really, though, it's not fair to say he snagged it. It's more like he absorbed it. Marino rocketed the ball into Beep's chest, hard enough to leave the area bruised and sensitive days later.

The catch seals him as the surprise champion of the football combine, winning him an impressively sizable trophy and a $1,000 FanDuel contest ticket. It is not lost on my Canadian mentor how unlikely it is that he caught that ball at all, much less that he won the entire competition from a field of more than one hundred contestants.

"I'd say I have about a twenty percent chance to catch that ball, normally," he says, before adjusting for the "Dan Marino hates me" factor. "Under the circumstances, it may have been as low as eight percent."

The best part? Beep didn't even know which Joe he was mistaking Marino for. Forget Joe Montana—he believed it was another famous, retired quarterback.

"So that's not Joe Nay-moth?" Beep asks innocently, his trophy in hand. "Oh. My bad."

With the sun setting, we head back to the Grand Hyatt San Diego to show Underjones the loot and rib him for missing out on all the fun. Between the FanDuel football jersey on his back and the trophy in his hand, Beep gets a lot of looks as we stroll through the lobby and board the elevators. As we ride up, a couple in their forties takes an interest in Beep, and the husband asks if Beep actually won FanDuel's $3 million first prize, the one that's the subject of those signs all over the hotel.

"No, no," he explains. "This is just for the football combine—it's just a little thing, we were basically just throwing footballs around. I didn't win the grand prize."

"Oh, okay," the man says, seemingly satisfied, as we reach his floor. "FanDuel—that stuff's all rigged anyway."

Saturday night, the pros are hunkered down preparing lineups for the final the following morning, but this is San Diego! Perhaps my favorite town, it's a perfectly casual mix of California weather, food, and culture, without the L.A. traffic and excess. It would be criminal to sit in my hotel room on a Saturday night. So I throw on a light jacket and venture out into San Diego's lively Gaslamp Quarter to meet up with Eccles and the FanDuel staff, who have gathered to watch a UFC fight. Side-stepping eager panhandlers, veering bike cabs, and oblivious twenty-three-year-olds in tube tops, I arrive at Bub's, a sports bar in the shadow of the Padres' Petco Park, and spot Eccles almost immediately, even among the crush of Saturday night partiers. He waves and I venture over.

It's no exaggeration to say that Eccles is the most important person in the history of DFS. He wasn't one of its original founders, like Kevin Bonnet of Fantasy Sports Live or Chris Fargis of Instant Fantasy Sports, but without his innovations and drive, the industry would never have skyrocketed into what it is today. I think of him more like the Henry Ford of DFS—he took an existing product and made it accessible to the masses. FanDuel was the first major DFS operator to break through the start-up phase and become a viable, established company, and it quickly became the industry standard, the company everyone else was chasing. Much of that is due to Eccles himself, as unlikely a DFS star as you will find.

Raised on a dairy farm in Northern Ireland, Eccles had a background in the English betting industry, and at the consulting firm McKinsey, when in 2007 he and several associates founded HubDub, a Web-based platform for predicting future events, mostly in politics. HubDub wasn't a bad idea, but it was clear fairly quickly that it wasn't going anywhere. The market just wasn't there. As 2009 dawned, they were all aware of the feeling of stagnation.

"We had a few unpleasant board meetings," Eccles says.

While casting about for something new, Eccles took a ten-hour flight from London to Austin, Texas, for the South by Southwest festival's tech carnival. As a Brit, he knew little about the American sports scene. But he knew math, and he thought he knew money, and he believed that there wasn't enough money being made off American sports. On that fateful flight, Eccles read through the 2006 law banning online poker,

UIGEA, examined the exception for fantasy sports, and was struck by what would literally become a billion-dollar idea. There was already a nascent industry here, but the companies either were flawed or had little backing. If he could move his company into the DFS space and stay within the parameters of that carve-out—the contests must cover more than one game, prize amounts must be set before the games begin, point spreads and game scores can't factor in—he could build a juggernaut. He and his team met at South by Southwest and solidified the idea.

Thus in the summer of 2009, FanDuel debuted, and Daily Fantasy Sports entered its modern era.

Eccles and I shake hands as all around us, the bar simmers along with the early rounds of this UFC fight night. This is no ordinary UFC bout—this is the international coming-out party for Conor McGregor, the cheeky Irish featherweight who has taken the fighting world by storm with his power and his charisma. As a Northern Irishman, Eccles, who otherwise doesn't follow UFC, is paying attention.

That's a rarity for him. Like so many others I've met in DFS, Eccles didn't come to it as a rabid sports fan. He's slender, prim, fond of elegant sweaters and skinny jeans. He's certainly no jock or bro. His family—he has three children, and his wife, Lesley, is one of his cofounders—splits its time between Edinburgh and Brooklyn, and while he used to follow English soccer, American sports always eluded him.

"I had only ever watched maybe two football games in my life" before starting FanDuel, Eccles says. "I'd watched one baseball game, and I don't think I'd ever watched a basketball game. I had never played fantasy sports."

While sports are now his life, starting FanDuel hasn't made him a bigger sports fan—on the contrary, looking under the hood of sports, and founding a company that has made it ever more about individual performances, has made him even more detached from the process of following teams. He has a hard time grasping, or even relating to, traditional sports affiliation.

"You start to realize that it doesn't really matter that much. Which is kinda sad, but it's like, 'Oh, woo, my team's won. Whatever,'" Eccles says, his accent making everything he says sound weighty, even the "woo."

After so many years of watching baseball, I can empathize.

"You're rooting for laundry," I say, trying to show my understanding. In covering baseball, I came to root for the players whom I liked as people, and rooted against those I disliked covering. The team's success or failure really didn't matter, even though no fans ever believed me when I explained that. Fantasy sports are a mass-market manifestation of that idea, exalting the individual and not the team, and Daily Fantasy magnifies it further. Eccles and I arrived at the same destination from vastly different avenues.

Tonight's sport is particularly alien. I don't watch UFC, and Eccles doesn't, either. As I sip a Red Trolley Ale, and Eccles a Diet Coke, we're both surprised at how brutal it can be. In one of the early bouts, one fighter pins another to the ground and pounds away with elbows as blood spatters the octagon. A couple nearby stand up and leave, disgusted.

"Won't they stop this at some point?" I wonder aloud.

"I think maybe when he drops his hands," Eccles says. "So, John McCain is a big opponent of MMA, and I often wondered, did they ever think, let's get him alone and try to convince him, it's not as bad as he thinks?"

He nods up at the carnage on the screen. "And then you look at that."

What really has him surprised, however, as we watch the early bouts, are the constant reminders of DraftKings' partnership with UFC, plastered all over the fighting octagon. FanDuel doesn't have a deal with UFC, although Eccles says they were approached about one and quickly declined. The reasoning is twofold. The first is that minor sports like UFC don't bring in much revenue—though according to multiple sources, DraftKings threw money at them anyway. That stuns Eccles, who says those ads can't be worth it.

"The deals don't make any sense," Eccles says. "Like this one, for the signage, they're definitely paying a couple of million. But they'll make hardly anything from this thing. If they make over a million a year from UFC, I'll be amazed. It's mind-blowing."

There was a far more important reason for FanDuel to stay away from UFC, however. UFC—like golf, and like NASCAR—is a legal gray area as far as DFS is concerned. Those sports exist primarily as one-off, self-contained events—a monthly night of fights, a golf tournament, a single race—not multiple games on a daily slate, as in the four major American team sports or in English soccer. At first glance, that makes single-event sports like UFC or NASCAR appear to violate the UIGEA carve-out that allows DFS to exist in the first place, which requires that prizes are awarded based on *"accumulated statistical results of the performance of individuals (athletes in the case of sports events) in multiple real-world sporting or other events."*

For this reason, Eccles said his board and legal team argued they were risky endeavors, and FanDuel stayed away. When DraftKings did its deal with NASCAR, their lawyers apparently felt it was less of a risk. What was perhaps more surprising was that NASCAR's lawyers seemingly agreed. Which is something that NBC wondered about, too, after the NASCAR and DraftKings deals were consummated. A person with knowledge of the negotiations told me that when NASCAR signed off on the deal, they were asked by NBC where they got their legal advice.

"Oh, we used DraftKings' lawyer," was the NASCAR rep's response, the person said.

While Eccles and I chat, the FanDuel crew is happily drinking nearby, unconcerned with such matters of business. These finals seem to be a working vacation for the companies' staffers, almost like attending a convention. It's probably a welcome respite from the drama in the industry. Eccles is used to being the target of animus by now, and he mostly shrugs it off. But there are a few digs and jabs that hit a little too close to home. I bring up, perhaps unnecessarily, the brilliant twenty-minute-long John Oliver skit on Oliver's HBO show, *Last Week Tonight*, that brought in celebs like Seth Rogen to skewer the world of Daily Fantasy. Oliver & Co. gleefully mocked the companies' claims that DFS isn't gambling and perfectly captured all of DFS's tropes, from the overeducated pro winning with algorithms to the poor sap who is convinced he's about to hit it big when he's just had to sell the TV to make rent. I see Eccles cringe when I remind him of it, and almost feel bad.

"That was really funny—it was too good," he admits. "I was hiding behind the sofa during that one."

The undercard fights are wrapping up at last, and the main event is close to getting under way, McGregor against Brazilian José Aldo, who hasn't lost in ten years.

Eccles and I turn our attention to the television. We look up just in time to see the bell ring, and it's a good thing. The two start trading kicks and punches, and I pull out my phone to check the time. As I look down, the room erupts. Thirteen seconds into the fight, Aldo is on the ground, unconscious. McGregor is standing over him, having leveled the Brazilian with one punch. The fight is over. I missed it. What a schmuck.

Eccles is dumbfounded, and bemused.

"What the hell?" he says. "I waited all night for that?"

I shake my head as they show replays of the punch that last longer than the fight itself.

"That is simultaneously the best and worst thing I've ever seen," I say.

"That was pretty exciting, I guess. It was cool," Eccles says, pondering it for a minute. "Though if I had paid and waited that whole night and then watched this, I'd be disappointed."

We realize that this early ending is probably a good thing—with football starting at 10 a.m. on the West Coast, we both have to be up early and into the watch room to chart the action. So a thirteen-second UFC fight between two people I'd never heard of before this week isn't such a bad result. We shake hands and get ready to head out—but Eccles, cracking a smile, has one question first.

"So what do you think, should we offer this on FanDuel?"

We laugh.

The pros are all hanging out in the back. They are having a bad day.

In the front of the cavernous ballroom at San Diego's Manchester Grand Hyatt, amateurs hoot and holler as their players rack up points. One particularly well-tanned trio in jerseys and zip-up hoodies are screaming at the quiet groups around them, taunting their foes as their entry continues to climb in the ranks.

"Lay off the steroids, boys," comes a crack from one of the pros around me.

The most aggressive bro in that group starts leaping around and bashing into his friends like he's in a mosh pit, spilling beer everywhere. Garrett, my Canadian pal Slewfoot's assistant/manservant/researcher/lackey, makes an astute observation.

"That guy is why people hate Americans," he says. I can't exactly disagree.

A few hours into the FanDuel $12 million final, everything is going wrong for the pros and regs. They crafted precise, intelligent lineups featuring unique, contrarian picks, and they're watching these darling lineups go down in flames. The chalk picks are winning the day, and for the most part, only the random amateurs with single seats picked those players. Underjones? Five entries, all of them losers. Cal Spears? Second to last, out of 120. Assani? Flirting with irrelevance. MaxDalury? Literally in last place.

In their stead are a group of overjoyed single-entrants, the kind of people for whom the tenth-place prize of $150,000 is life-changing money, to say nothing of the $1 million third prize, the $1.5 million second prize, and the $3 million first-place check. The leaderboard is full of names unfamiliar to the pros—"RickyWaller1982," "Longbottoms," "Light125Steve," and more. Three of the top-ten contenders are women, one in her fifties.

Those happy few stay up by the front, near one of the eight massive wall screens, or by the circular center bar, manned by a half-dozen busy barkeeps. The pros have retreated to a set of high-top tables in the back of the room, near the snack spread with its Hershey bars and cakes and bags of chips. Comfort food, I suppose. They sip their Bud Lights in silence, watching others live in their world for the briefest—yet most important—of moments.

The mood in the back isn't somber solely because of the scores, however. This is the first big live event I've attended since the football kick-off party in Miami, and there's no doubt that the atmosphere here is muted for other reasons. Despite all the money in play, the most ever for FanDuel, the event is uneven, a pall hanging over it. There's so much talk of the industry, and the future of it. Where once there were dreams of frenzied growth, there's now only a hope of holding on to what they have, and maybe not even that. A $3 million prize to first place? No one thinks there will be one of those next year, if there is a next year.

Still, those one-off amateur entrants provide enough energy to carry the day—they're happy to be here, and excited to meet the people they consider Daily Fantasy celebrities. CSURAM, who is here as a guest of MaxDalury, joins me as we leave the high-top tables and their pervading darkness to go take a walk in the San Diego sun, but we can't get five feet without one fan after another coming over to shake his hand and grab a little face time. His success in the industry, and his role making DFS picks on ESPN, give him a stature with this group that few, if any, can match. I've been around famous athletes who don't have as hard a time traversing a room.

"I played you in a head-to-head last month—you crushed me," one man in a plaid button-down comes up to report.

"Dude, you are so money on ESPN, I watch your college picks every week," another tells him, touching off a brief discussion about CSURAM's role at the cable TV monolith.

CSURAM turns to me apologetically—we're going at a foot-a-minute pace.

"It isn't usually like this," he says. RotoGrinders needs to create another of its silly titles: "President of DFS." This guy would win.

He isn't just glad-handing and kissing bro babies, however. He actually offers up advice and commentary. One well-wisher asks him how he's doing in NBA DFS this year. CSURAM gives him the same speech that Beep gave me, that the NBA is a broken ecosystem—the pros have gotten so good that most of the little fish are gone.

"It's just pros butting heads against other pros," he tells the other man.

When he runs into another shark, CSURAM actually apologizes. With so many demands on his time, he's recently committed a minor faux pas in the pro community: he hasn't been withdrawing his untaken high-stakes head-to-head games before lineups lock. The top pros all post $5,000 or $10,000 head-to-head games, hoping a wealthy fish who doesn't realize how strong they are will come along and try to play. (A professional NASCAR driver who shall remain nameless was actually considered one of the juiciest of these.) The pros try not to pick up each other's games, of course, both because they don't want to simply pass money around the pro community and because that competition is too stiff. But if the games remain available when lineups lock, the system will auto-match the remaining unmatched players—so any pros with games still hanging out there will be forced to play one another. The custom, then, is to unreg: to withdraw the contests in the minutes before lineups lock if they remain unfilled. CSURAM has apparently failed to do that a few too many times of late, and he apologizes to the other pro for being so careless, saying he didn't want to end up playing against him.

"It's my fault, too," the other pro says, and the moment is past, forgotten.

We finally clear the crowd and make it out of the room, talking about the state of the industry. CSURAM is afraid, more so than most people I've talked to. He thinks those in Daily Fantasy are so focused on the headline grabbers like Schneiderman that they're perhaps missing that there might be an even bigger gun being aimed at them—something federal, I'm left to assume, or the class action lawsuits that directly name CSURAM's friends and associates, like Drew Dinkmeyer and MaxDalury.

"To be totally honest, I'm really concerned about that," he says. "There's some interesting stuff going on. I'm worried. The whole time I was. This is my livelihood. I got to ESPN, I established my career. I worked really hard. I worked ninety hours a week for years and years. To have the industry crumble underneath me would be devastating."

Yet he knows there's nothing he can do to stop it, if it's coming. So after years of single-minded focus on trying to be the king of this industry, now CSURAM is trying to enjoy this crazy ride he's on, in case it all comes to an end soon.

We wander back into the watch room, where blaring television broadcasts overlap one another and pockets of cheers rise from one corner or the next. The games are winding down, and it's clear that the winners will come from that corps of first-timers. The pros are pouty, acting like they suffered bad beats in poker, but I'm actually encouraged. This is how it's supposed to go—the little guy can win the big prize. According to the board, "Longbottoms" is likely to hang on to his lead, and cameras are already starting to zero in on him.

I follow their focus toward a tall black man in his forties, distinctive in a long, flowing shirt in autumn colors, speckled with what look like dandelions on fire. The mob is starting to crowd him, people slapping him on the back, holding up their cell phones to take pictures, *60 Minutes*' Armen Keteyian angling in for an interview. When I get a closer look, I recognize him—I realize it's that guy Roman Edmond, whom I'd met at the RotoGrinders conference in November. We'd discussed whether DFS was like the stock market. Ha! I guess he really paid attention in those tutoring sessions. Even though there's still five minutes left, and a pick-six by the Denver Broncos defense could easily knock him out of first place, Roman is acting like the win's in the bag, which the pros around me think is crazy—they've seen how many times a late shift has undone big money. But Roman is undeterred. He's on the phone now, presumably with someone close to him.

"Our lives are about to change," he tells the person on the end of the line.

There are more cheers—Roman looks up and sees his player, Eddie Lacy, cross the goal line, giving him a touchdown that should truly lock up the win. Now it's fair to celebrate, and the party begins. Amid all the backslapping I wander in and nod at Roman, who looks at me and then beams with recognition, extending his hand.

"Congratulations, Roman," I say as I shake his outstretched hand.

"Thank you, brother," he responds with the contented smile of a millionaire three times over.

Soon Roman is up onstage, posing with the famous Big Check and delivering a well-manicured speech about how he plans to be an ambassador for the industry. That trio of jersey-clad morons who spent the whole day screaming manage to finish in the top three as well, and they take advantage of their time with the microphone to yell at Joe Montana about how they can't believe they're standing so close to him. But not everyone is boorish. My favorite winner is the ninth-place finisher, Tamika Bearden, a bubbly thirty-five-year-old woman from Houston who won her seat on a $2 bet and didn't even realize what a "live final" was until FanDuel emailed her the day after she'd won. Did she use advanced analytics to draft her team? Nah. Rumor had it she picked her team based on who she thought were the best-looking players, which she happily confirms.

"That's absolutely true," Bearden tells me. "Cam Newton was my quarterback, [Danny] Amendola, [Thomas] Rawls from Seattle, very good-looking. Jimmy Graham, very good-looking."

Now she's reveling in this life-changing money.

"From two dollars to a hundred and fifty thousand." She shakes her head. "I just got engaged in September. We can now plan the wedding; we can buy a house. I'm so thankful."

As the beaten pros take in this scene, I'm reminded of baseball players leaning morosely against the dugout rail after a playoff loss, watching the other team celebrating on their home field. They trickle out in groups or one by one, off to lick their wounds at dinner or drinks in the Gaslamp Quarter. The FanDuel final is over. But the reality is, for nearly all of them, Finals Week is just beginning. There's more work to be done.

———

Like a dad picking up the kids from soccer practice, I roll up to the Hyatt the next day in my giant white Dodge SUV, rented from my pals at National Car Rental by the airport (best car selection in the business!). Three big-time DFSers—Beep, Underjones, and Cal Spears—throw their bags into the back, toting a surprisingly large amount of luggage for such a small group. The fourth, Jeff Collins (JeffElJefe), will meet us at our destination.

With the FanDuel final complete, we're off to Mission Beach, northwest of downtown San Diego, to start the next phase of Finals Week: preparing for the DraftKings NFL semifinal this coming Sunday. This crew has rented a beach house, where they'll spend the week researching and planning their lineups for the semifinal and perhaps even getting some much-needed sun. As big as the FanDuel final was, with its $3 million top prize, the DraftKings final is even bigger, in keeping with the company's desire to one-up FanDuel at every turn.

DraftKings took a new approach in creating the industry's first-ever two-part final. These two hundred semifinalists will vie for ten spots in a really-final-final, to be held in January in Los Angeles. That contest boasts a $5 million first prize, $2 million second prize, and $1 million third prize, the biggest pot in Daily Fantasy's brief history. Back when everyone in Daily Fantasy saw only dollar signs, those enormous prizes figured to be marketing gold for the DFS industry. Now it just seems like more evidence of excess.

Yet somebody's got to win all that cash, and the people in my backseat would be thrilled to be Example 1A of industry hubris. Right now, they're still smarting from their losses this weekend. They all did badly, even beyond just missing out on the prizes in the FanDuel final; their other lineups all tanked as well. Underjones estimates he probably lost $350,000 over the weekend, but to his credit—I think?—it doesn't seem to faze him. He says the ups and downs of Daily Fantasy—down $400,000 here, up half a million there—don't register much after five years of living through them.

"You get desensitized," he says. "I don't even feel it much anymore."

Underjones is an interesting guy. In some ways, he's exactly what outsiders assume all DFS pros are—a late-twenties Asian male with a degree from Penn and a background in investment banking at Citibank, who builds Excel spreadsheets to dominate the competition. He dislikes the spotlight—he created his DFS usernames on Internet random-name generators to ensure greater anonymity—and can be awkward in social situations, saying that they tire him out. But there's more there. He's unafraid of taking risks, is whip-smart, and is aggressive when he needs to be. He is no pushover, and he's talented—Beep believes him to be the best DFS player active today, and that his desire for a low profile is what keeps others from realizing that he's up there with Condia and MaxDalury. More than that, I've found him to be caring, friendly, and loyal once he lets his guard down.

An alumnus of Hunter College High School and a true New York City kid, he was forced out of Manhattan when Schneiderman began his Daily Fantasy purge, and he retreated to New Jersey. He rented an office in Hoboken, New Jersey, and is miserable commuting there every day. He's desperate for the courts to declare DFS a little safer so he can return to New York City.

For the week, at least, he doesn't have to worry about it, as we leave downtown San Diego and cruise toward sunny Mission Beach. Cal Spears, doing the navigating in his gravelly voice, directs me to get on the 5, toward SeaWorld, promising that Mission Beach will come up soon after. One of my favorite things about California is how you can't say the name of an interstate without adding the prefix "the" in front of it. It's a really distinctive convention. Of course, if someone back east told me they were heading from Boston to New York on the 95, I'd slap them.

Mission Beach is an old summer community dating to the 1920s and 1930s that eventually became a year-round destination. It takes us about ten minutes, plus a few more for a wrong turn (I blame the navigator) to make it out there, as we cross a causeway and come up on the beach itself. As we approach the water, we're greeted by a white, wood-frame roller coaster and a sign proclaiming that we've discovered historic Belmont Park. Belmont Park was built in 1925 by the area's original developer to lure tourists and would-be future buyers to the slow-developing area. The Giant Dipper roller coaster is still standing, and operating, though it fell on dark times and was closed from 1975 through 1990, according to a handy-dandy history posting I find outside a local restaurant. From what I can tell, Mission Beach is sleepier and less upscale than its cousins up the coast, like Redondo Beach or Manhattan Beach in Los Angeles, but not nearly as seedy as East Coast beach towns on the painful Jersey Shore. It appears to be a pleasant middle ground, I think, as we wind down the tight, narrow streets toward our new beachfront home. Perched on the end of Mission Beach at the entrance to Mission Bay, our two-story house overlooks a set of volleyball courts on the broad, flat, yellow-sand beach, and people are out playing at almost every one. We gaze out at the beach, noting that the house is situated perfectly to let sunlight cascade into the living room from seemingly every angle.

Among this crew, however, it quickly becomes clear that all that natural light isn't exactly a selling point. The sunlight creates glare for all the computer screens that need to be set up. The blinds are quickly closed, not to be opened again. Computer screens matter. Vitamin D, less so.

And there are a lot of computer screens. I finally realize why all the pros travel with so much luggage—they bring full computer setups with them wherever they go. Underjones opens up a suitcase and pulls out a full-size monitor, I'm guessing twenty-plus inches' worth of screen. Then out comes a keyboard, a large power strip, a mouse. Soon that setup is joined by four high-powered laptops, a variety of headphones, and wires and cords running everywhere. Beach party USA!

All that processing power is needed, because computers are at the heart of what makes this group great at DFS. Once Underjones is set up, he opens his Excel spreadsheets, which are the core of his analysis system. He, like Beep, has custom-built programs that will help him make his daily picks, and they're as good as they come. Scarily so.

When outsiders rail against the pros with algorithms who make DFS such an uneven playing field, this is exactly what they're talking about. Underjones has built a system that takes into account numerous variables—advanced stats, weather, salary info, matchups, Vegas odds, and much, much more, weighted to reflect how important he thinks each variable is—and spits out projections for each player, ranking them in terms of who the best options are today.*

Most high-level players do this in Microsoft Excel—"If you're good at DFS, you're probably pretty good at Excel," Beep says—but there are some, like MaxDalury, who have taken it a step further. Max came from a coding background, and so he built his own prediction programs using Python, a high-level programming language. In the end, it's all variations on the same theme: programs built to automate the selection process and do it better, or faster, than a human could.

Some players then have programs that will auto-build various lineup combinations using these predictions, and the completed lineups are then dumped en masse into DraftKings or FanDuel, hundreds of diverse, uniformly dangerous lineup combinations suddenly appearing at the click of a mouse.

Most top players say they make some tweaks after seeing the predictions and lineups the computer offers, but in the end, at a certain level it really can be one player's algorithm against another's. There are ex-

---

* Most of these stats are publicly available, but some, like MaxDalury, buy proprietary stats at great expense from the same companies that provide data to professional sports teams.

ceptions to this, to be sure—many top players eschew algorithms—but most of the biggest names have built their own models and employ them daily.

Professor Kurt Eggert of Chapman University has studied the growth of algorithms in DFS and predicts that they will only get better and more adaptive in time, particularly in terms of information gathering.

"Once the AI-driven algorithm teaches itself how to acquire information and experiments regarding what information is most useful to acquire, the spoon-feeding of data to the algorithm might be much less necessary," Eggert said in testimony submitted to Congress. "Players who do not use algorithms might find themselves competing against computer programs that are not only better able to manage and create portfolios of lineups from data, but may also be much better at acquiring the data itself."

I'm not as concerned as he is that sentient robot overlords are about to conquer DFS, but there's no question that algorithms and custom-built programs are integral to the success of most of the top players, certainly the volume players. I wonder if this is in my future, if I am ever to get any good at this. I hope not.

As we tour our house, it's clear it's not as ritzy as the one MaxDalury and CSURAM are renting up in La Jolla, but hey, those guys are multi-millionaires. I think my posse top out at just, uh, millionaires, though I haven't quite confirmed. Cal, clearly comfortable leading the group, starts to divvy up the rooms. The house is split into nearly identical upstairs and downstairs apartments, with a large master bedroom and a smaller guest bedroom in each. For whatever reason, while the downstairs guest bedroom is normal, the upstairs one is dark and creepy, with odd knickknacks everywhere and stained glass windows giving it a weirdly religious feel. I keep expecting a pair of twin girls to pop up and write "Redrum" on the mirror.

"Obviously nobody wants the scary room," Cal says. "Should we set up a private contest on tonight's NBA slate, winner gets first room pick, and so on?"

While that might be perfectly appropriate for a bunch of DFS pros, the NBA slate will be over too late for unpacking to begin, so it's determined that a game of DFS's elder cousin, poker, will be used to determine room precedence. But JeffElJefe isn't here yet, so for the time being, people simply squat in the better rooms, leaving the murder room for him.

Unpacking is put on hold for the moment anyway, because there's work to be done—for all of us. The DraftKings semifinal is a mere week away, but not every one of the two hundred finalist seats has been claimed. There's one more qualifier tonight, with the $80,000 seat up for grabs. Underjones already has three entries in the semifinal, and Beep has the one we won that night in Kitchener, but Cal needs to get in on the action, and he's gunning hard. He and Underjones quickly set up at their workstations and start crunching stats for tonight's Giants-Dolphins *Monday Night Football* game, which will determine who gets the seat.

I'm trying to finish my drafting for the day, too. With access to pro tactics and advice, I've got to use this time to make strides in my own game, betting both hockey and basketball while I'm here this week.

I'm up to betting about $300 a day in hockey, though I'm still doing poorly. I've spent the last month intensively studying hockey statistics, players, and concepts, trying desperately to get my knowledge of the game itself up to speed. I've got the basics down by now, and I'm starting to become more proficient in judging publicly available inputs. For instance, I start my DFS day by assessing the Vegas lines projecting the scores of each game, and then delve further by going through the individual player projections produced by fantasy sites like RotoWire and numberFire. I'm adeptly employing Beep's correlation strategies without having to prod him for reminders every afternoon, but I still make dumb mistakes. For instance, there are days I pick the exact right lines but neglect to check every team for updates in the half hour before games begin, and so fail to see that the backup goalie is actually playing instead of the regular starter. Lineup fail. So I've started following all the hockey beat writers on Twitter so that I can account for late scratches and line changes in the crucial minutes before the games start.

It's a process, a difficult one, and the results still aren't there. I can't flood the field with entries like Beep had without spending tons—new entry limit restrictions are making strategies like that far less effective anyway—and my hockey knowledge just isn't to the point where I can build a few great lineups successfully. All those tactics I just mentioned? For a good hockey DFSer, those are rudimentary, obvious things to do. So, every once in a while I have a good day, and I feel like I'm getting there, but it's rough going. Despite Beep's good advice, I'm slowly pissing away money. My records show I'm down more than $1,000 on hockey since November, which puts me at close to $5,000 down on DFS overall since this adventure began. Shortcut to riches my ass.

Cal is taking his time tweaking his lineups, but Underjones, Beep, and I soon finish for the day, so the three of us walk along the beach toward the amusement park in search of a place to both watch *Monday Night Football* and eat some dinner. It's windy and chilly, and I immediately regret not packing more warm clothing. Still, there are a few surfer-girl types in wetsuits nearby, and the conversation turns to the success that Slewfoot's butler/man-at-arms/indentured servant/pal Garrett is having on Tinder, the mobile dating app, while in San Diego. The entire weekend, women have been sending him naked pictures, videos, you name it—he hardly has to try and he's raking them in. It's stunning. I was clearly born in the wrong era. Don't tell my wife I said that.

Being in their late twenties, these guys are of a perfect age to take advantage of the Tinder phenomenon, but it's been more than a year since either of them has had a real girlfriend.

"I couldn't even imagine having a girlfriend and doing this job," Beep says.

Beep, who my wife says isn't a bad-looking guy, made a few random forays onto Tinder, but it's his Canadian ex-roommates who really use it to clean up. One, a strapping, country music–loving firefighter, succeeds for obvious reasons. But Mike McDonald, the poker pro Timex, has thrived in a more interesting fashion. As this crew tends to do, he approached Tinder as a systemic problem to be solved, where women aren't individuals but rational actors who follow set patterns of inputs and outcomes. Reading online guides, he learned to open with only a smiley-face icon, to be mysterious yet put the ball in the woman's court. Then, based on her response, he follows a branching decision tree that lays out his next statements exactly, leading to high success rates of dates. I guess I shouldn't be surprised by now that this group has broken down modern romance into a series of moves and countermoves—it's just another version of "how to kick a field goal in twelve steps."

Shivering our way down the beach, we pass the amusement park and spot a sign for a gastropub called Draft on the other side, good enough for food and football.

We slide into a table near two massive wall screens. Cal and Jeff won't be along for a while, so we've got time to get comfortable, and Underjones and I order wings and beers. The waitress then turns to Beep to get his choice.

"Do you have milk?" Beep says, earnestly He's decided to quit drinking because . . . just because. The waitress looks at him for a moment, the two of them locked in a game of chicken to see who will break into laughs first. But Beep doesn't blink, or smile, and she eventually realizes he's serious.

"Umm . . . let me check," she says, turning and heading to the back.

The sun is setting, which on the West Coast means *Monday Night Football* is about to start. Underjones is happy with his lineup for their qualifier contest but Cal is still tinkering with his. Underjones reports, in fact, that Cal has sent him a text saying that he's going with the quarterback–wide receiver combo of Odell Beckham Jr. and Eli Manning, instead of Ryan Tannehill and Jarvis Landry.

"You know that's illegal, right?" Beep asks. "You can't share information like that. Knowing his lineup could make you change yours."

Underjones clearly hasn't thought of that, though Beep is of course right, even if *illegal* is the wrong word and it's not exactly clear that exchange even violates the murky site rules. But it's definitely something that should be avoided. Theoretically, two players could gain a significant edge by sharing information and working together—picking opposing lineups and sharing the profits when one hits, or simply knowing a little bit more about ownership percentages in a small contest with big rewards. In a $3 contest with thousands playing, who cares? But in a small, expensive qualifier with $80,000 at stake, where only a few teams are in striking distance of the top prize, this stuff matters.

"Well," Underjones stammers, "my lineup is already set, and he knows I'm not changing it. He was just telling me who he's going with."

He's obviously telling the truth, and after an uncomfortable silence, we move on. The waitress returns with a tall, cold glass of milk—skim, whole, or low-fat is not specified—and Beep thanks her profusely. Partway through the first quarter, Cal and Jeff show up, and it's already clear that Cal's lineup is doing well, well enough to actually win. Cal vows that if he lands the seat, he'll take a midnight dive in the frigid ocean, and we all support this plan. Before long it's apparent that we're going to have another sweat under way, and Beep starts calling me a good-luck charm—every time I'm around, someone has a real shot to qualify for this semifinal. I start to wonder if I should have thrown in a lineup, before remembering that the entry fees were four figures. Um, no thanks.

Cal is leading, but the sweat turns tense as Miami's Jarvis Landry keeps catching balls, threatening to ruin Cal's chances. As the anxiety builds in the final minutes, Cal knocks over his beer.

"Dude, have you ever had a sweat before?" JeffElJefe ribs him.

It comes down to the very last minute, but thanks to the efforts of Beckham and Giants tight end Will Tye, Cal hangs on to win the seat. As the final whistle sounds, we go bonkers, leaping around the bar area as the few other unlucky patrons look at us like we're crazy. No one here cares. "We're going swimming!" Cal proclaims as the Giants ice the victory.

Cal, $80,000 richer, orders us up a round of celebratory shots, some good tequila. Even Beep assents—his temperance movement clearly isn't that strong after all. Though after we've raised our glasses and downed the shot, he looks like he wishes he'd remained a teetotaler.

"Do you know if tequila and milk aren't supposed to mix well? I don't feel very good," he asks before heading off to the restroom.

The rest of us hardly notice; we're on a high from winning, even if only one of us really won. I suppose we all did, in a way, since Cal picks up the tab for dinner, which easily stretched into the hundreds. He doesn't seem to care. He's thrilled at the seat, and at the fun he had winning it.

"This is what it's supposed to be like," he says as we head toward the door, pushing out into the December chill. It is cold. Legitimately, nipple-hardeningly cold. I had been weighing joining Cal on his polar bear plunge, but as my testicles pull up into my stomach I start to reconsider. I'm lucky that I can do that. Cal has no such out, knowing that we'd never let him live it down. When we get back to the beach house, he gamely pulls on his bathing suit, grabs a bottle of celebratory champagne (the cheap stuff), and heads out to the water. We stand in a circle as Cal makes a toast, and then—how did I not see this coming?—pops the cork on the champagne bottle and douses us all with it. Satisfied he's soaked us all well, Cal turns, splashes his way into the water, and then dives all the way in.

"It's not even that bad," he calls, obviously suffering the effects of hypothermia already. "It's warmer in here than outside."

Maybe if I'd won $80,000, I'd agree with him. As it is, I'm just cold and reek of champagne, the good-luck charm who can't seem to make any luck of his own.

The next few days fly by in a flurry of lineup building, trivia quizzes, video games, and poker, as well as the worst game of beach football ever to sully the sands of Mission Beach. Trying to maximize the presence of the pros, I play some DFS basketball (largely just asking JeffElJefe for smart plays) and actually win $350 on it, while taking home another $400 on a two-game hockey slate the same night—my biggest one-night win to date. Beep has been training me in game selection tactics—why, in cash games, it's better to play head-to-head contests than 50/50s or double-ups, for instance.* I don't know if it's a tangible advantage or mere luck, but I certainly feel smarter and better at this when I'm drafting around these guys. Bouncing ideas around the room, talking about which players might be good values, which lineup concepts are winners—it all helps, there's no question. Maybe if I could live with them full-time, I'd someday be back to even.

But there are other ways, I soon learn, to make money at DFS even if you're not very good yourself.

One afternoon, as we're drafting hockey lineups and half listening to a California legislature hearing on DFS regulation, Beep offers me a proposition. He's willing to sell me a piece of his action for the DraftKings semifinal.

For those who didn't grow up with a deck of playing cards in their hands, selling action is a big part of the poker world, and one that exists deep inside DFS but is rarely talked about. The surprising reality is, those people holding up the big checks at live finals are hardly ever actually winning that much. Usually they are winning a small share—and paying the rest back to their investors.

The entry fees for the qualifier tournaments are so prohibitively high—sometimes as high as $5,000 a shot—that players can burn through their whole bankroll and never win a seat. Or if they do, they

---

* If you have one standard cash lineup you deploy among all your cash games, as most players do, playing in head-to-heads over 50/50s can help you mitigate losses when you have a really bad night. For instance, if you have a bottom 40 percent cash lineup on a given day, that lineup will lose every single 50/50 or double-up it's in. But that same lineup should lose only around 40 percent of its head-to-heads, allowing you to recoup some of those losses.

could easily spend $100,000 "successfully" winning the $80,000 seat, making the whole thing a net loss.

"Nobody is bankrolled for these qualifiers. Maybe three people in the whole industry are—MaxDalury, RayOfHope, and CSURAM," Beep says. So top players sell pieces of themselves in exchange for funding to compete in these qualifiers. Investors will buy a percentage of each player, usually at a minor markup—Beep usually sells at 1.03 percent— and that gives the player the funding he needs to fire numerous entries at the qualifiers. Of course, if he wins, he has to pay back the investors out of his winnings.

At the 2014 DraftKings baseball final, Beep and CSURAM were on-stage, holding up their giant checks for first and second place, $1 million to CSURAM, $350,000 to Beep. CSURAM leaned over and cracked to Beep, "I swapped so much action that I think you probably won more than I did." As it turned out, though, Beep had sold enough—he owned only 30 percent of himself—that he barely cleared six figures off his win. His investors—primarily Timex, his poker pro friend—were the ones making hundreds of thousands off his win. That was painful, but he believed it was the right move. It also helped explain why, after all his big wins, Beep wasn't actually rich, at least not in the way I'd assumed he was.

"It's not about profit maximization. It's about loss minimization," he says, adding later that "anyone who wins the whole big check probably isn't a very good player."

Now Beep is offering me the opportunity to be one of those investors, buying into his and Underjones's seats for the DraftKings semifinal. He knows I'm not exactly well-off, so he suggests a 1 percent buy-in— which sounds ludicrously small, but might offer a big payoff. I ask him how the math works—do I just get 1 percent of whatever they win? Like, 1 percent of $5 million is $50,000. That sounds good to me. He explains, however, that that's not quite how it works, and gives me a crash course on finals economics. I quickly learn that the numbers on these seats aren't exactly what they seem, thanks to what they call "variable equity," which basically represents future potential winnings.

"You'd buy the variable equity," Beep says. "That's where the skill is. That's everything above min payout. The variable equity is $55K on this tournament. The seat's worth $75K, the variable equity is $55K, because of the $20K min payout [and the $5K trip value]."

What that means, I soon realize, is that when Cal "won" $80,000 the other night, he didn't really. He won $20,000 guaranteed, and DraftKings was counting the chance of his winning more, that "variable equity," as part of that win. Of course, if he finishes in last place in the upcoming tournament, that variable equity is zero, and he wins nothing more than the $20,000 minimum payout. It seems a little ridiculous to me, but it's an ingrained and accepted part of this world.

In this case, I'd still have a shot at a big win if I buy 1 percent of Beep for $565 ($550 plus his usual 1.03 percent markup), but he thinks it would actually be a better idea to spread my action around. As I learn, Beep isn't just rooting for himself in Sunday's semifinal, he's cheering on Underjones, too, because he's bought 7 percent of Underjones's total action. And he's willing to sell me some of what he's bought.

"What I think would be smart would be to take a tiny piece of myself and Underjones's three seats," Beep explains. "I could sell you a piece of his. That way, rather than putting $550 on one bullet, you have your $550 spread between four bullets. So you have .25 percent of four lineups. Which sounds like just a little bit, but if someone wins $5 million, that's still 12,500 bucks if one of us wins. That's much better bankroll management."

Even with all of Beep's hedging, chances are I'll still lose money. If one of those four seats doesn't land in the top ten I'm probably out most of my investment.

"You might cash a bit of seventieth, you might cash a bit of fiftieth, and those add up," Beep says, before admitting, "But yeah, the expected outcome of this is that you probably lose three hundred dollars."

I don't care. The chance of having a piece of a $5 million win is too much for me to pass up. It's exciting—I feel like I suddenly have something real at stake this coming Sunday. Not just a few lineups that might make a few hundred bucks, but something really big. I tell Beep I'm in, and we shake hands as we become business partners.

And that, to my surprise, is pretty much it. There's no contract, no signed, written agreement, despite the massive amounts usually at stake in these sales. For that reason it's crucial to sell only to people who are completely reliable.

"I only do it with people I trust. That's the biggest thing," he says. Though that's not the only factor that determines who he sells to. Selling to someone who's too close a friend can be just as bad, he's found—especially when it comes time to tell them you've just lost their money.

"I used to sell to my parents and friends, but it's so much work and emotion when working with people who aren't used to gambling. It just sucks losing people who aren't used to gambling's money," Beep says.

When the winning happens, however, there are a few legal boxes to check. I'm actually surprised, because so much of DFS seems to take place on a handshake basis, but this buying and selling is big enough that it can't escape the notice of the federal government. Eventually, come tax time, all of this goes on the record, as Beep explains when he describes how Underjones will pay him if he wins.

"He'd declare it on his taxes. I'd file with the IRS to collect that money. For him, it'd be an expense. Because it's an investment. He files that when he files his taxes. I won this much, and one of my expenses was 'Jay.' They withhold the money for me," Beep says.

There are fantasy-focused accountants who specialize in these kinds of transactions, though half the time, as Underjones tells me later, they're making it up as they go, and most regular accountants, no matter how expert, are flummoxed at dealing with the kind of issues professional DFS players introduce.

"There's no precedent for any of this, so they're guessing. I have to bring up new things to them all the time, and they're like, 'Oh, I hadn't thought about that,'" Underjones recounts.

For the moment, none of that is my concern, as I'm dreaming of what owning a piece of these two pros might mean come Sunday. Beep thinks I've made the right move.

"You're not betting on some crappy horse," he offers as we pack up our stuff to get ready for dinner. We've got plans with MaxDalury up near his place in La Jolla, and one doesn't keep the biggest horse in all of DFS waiting.

When MaxDalury speaks, everyone else at our table immediately goes silent.

At a dinner full of some of the industry's top players and voices, it's incredible to watch this otherwise superconfident and accomplished group—Cal, Beep, Underjones, JeffElJefe—all defer to Max. Whenever he speaks, laconic and measured, the rest hang on his every word. MaxDalury grandly issues a statement or two and then goes back to presiding over the action. He's like a Godfather figure—his prowess and power so respected that even this group is cowed by him. And he's clearly gotten used to it.

When Max and I had first talked, in June, the pro was in the crosshairs of the DFS world, representing the evils of mass multi-entry and scripting to many. He was just taking over the top ranking as the best DFS player from the even more feared and resented Condia, the original great DFS pro, and we had that strange moment where I realized he'd taken his name from the real Max Dalury, the Tufts guy. Honestly, when talking to him then he seemed nervous, skittish, uneasy.

But now that all feels like long, long ago.

Meeting up with Max and his girlfriend, Cynthia, at the posh La Jolla eatery Whisknladle here in December, the Amherst grad is well established alongside CSURAM as one of the biggest brands in Daily Fantasy, and is known to all as the most dominant player. He shed his anonymity in the fall, admitting that he was actually Saahil Sud, and is now beginning the process of making SaahilSud his username and getting past the whole MaxDalury mess. Along the way, *Saahil* won more than $3 million in 2015 and is starting his own subscription-based analysis and DFS tools site, RotoQL, to parlay his name value into even greater riches and exposure.

In a Bloomberg News article in September, the one where he first revealed his identity, this mild-mannered computer whiz was slapped with a new label: he was described as an "apex predator" in the world of DFS. It seemed that, somewhere on the path to winning multimillions, he's embraced his role atop the food chain, confident and secure in his power.

The funny thing is, smart DFS people like Saahil. Saahil became the undisputed best through a month of high-stakes head-to-head play where he beat Condia so badly it prompted Condia to take the next few months off DFS. Condia had been so merciless in trying to quash all competition that Saahil as the new king is somehow a kinder, gentler regime. Now the undisputed top dog, Saahil is still in every $20 three-man, all over every big tournament, but he doesn't scoop head-to-head games at low levels in the way Condia had. He wants to win, but seems to understand that he can't be the only winner. Meet the new boss, same as the old boss—except a little less apex-predatory.*

Right now our new fantasy overlord is using his bully pulpit to make proclamations about the truly precarious state of the industry. He's been getting into soccer DFS, for instance, because he sees the two major companies establishing themselves in Europe, and even if DFS dies in the United States—what he calls "the seventy-fifth percentile outcome"—then it will still likely survive abroad, providing him an avenue to use his skills and win money.

"Everything could be totally different in a year." He shrugs.

Trying to keep the mood light, with the Old Fashioneds flowing,

---

* Sharks such as Beep don't even consider extreme-volume players like Saahil and Condia to be of the same species—they call them "whales" instead, because they cruise around, their maw open, gobbling up all possible action like baleen. Sharks, fish, whales—I wonder if there's a DFS analog for jumbo shrimp.

Cal needles Saahil about never coming to visit the RotoGrinders offices down in Nashville. Saahil won't take the bait, however.

"I'll come visit when DFS is dead," Saahil says with a slight smile.

Saahil's gloomy predictions take the other pros by surprise.

"You're a lot more down on DFS than I thought you'd be," Underjones says.

Saahil looks at him like he hasn't been paying attention.

For an industry holding two finals totaling over $25 million in prizes this very week, it's a little surreal to hear them lapse into talk of the "good old days," but that's exactly where they drive this conversation. The chatter turns to finals past, only a year or two before, which really seem to have been the Wild Wild West days of DFS. All the events were in Vegas, or at the Playboy Mansion; there were no girlfriends or wives around like there are now; and the site staffers would join the pros on trips to the strip clubs. No expense was too ridiculous, no extravagance too grandiose. On a week where two men dressed as Secret Service agents will carry a glass box full of money into the DraftKings semifinal for maximum effect, these pros bemoan how the glorious times of DraftKings and FanDuel throwing money around indiscriminately are actually over, despite what the boxes of money might suggest.

"The days of that kind of discretionary spending are done," Saahil intones.

The dinner winds on, crossing the three-hour mark as the waitstaff cleans up the restaurant. Every time I think we're done, and the conversation is dying, Saahil chimes in with something else—most of it smart and incisive, by the way, but it's still late. Finally, the waitress arrives with the check, signaling that they've gotten tired of either waiting for us to leave or for Saahil to buy the restaurant.

The many excellent dishes—plus all those Old Fashioneds—add up, and the bill tops $600. I start to pull out my credit card to pay for my share, when Saahil suggests we do a little gambling for the bill: a game of credit card roulette. For those unfamiliar, the waitress will pick one of our credit cards out of the billfold, and the "lucky" card owner foots the entire bill. As Saahil reminds us, we have a 5-in-6 chance of getting a free dinner.

I blanch at the idea of what happens if that one-sixth whacks you, however, and start to stammer something about preferring to do it another way. Fortunately, JeffElJefe joins my protest, and it appears that's enough dissent to ruin the fun.

Saahil sighs and collects the credit cards, handing them all to the waitress at once so we can split the bill evenly.

"Sorry for making this unnecessarily complicated," he says, looking at me pointedly. "But some of us aren't gamblers."

Sadly, I wouldn't be around to see how the gamblers did on my behalf. On Thursday we packed up the beach house and I drove the crew over to the Hard Rock Hotel, where Cal, Underjones, and Beep would spend the weekend as official contestants. I, however, had a red-eye to catch back to the East Coast for a wedding on Saturday. Bryan Hoch, one of the Yankee beat guys, was getting married out in Bethlehem, Pennsylvania, at a *Back to the Future*–themed wedding (yes, really, complete with a DeLorean and Marty McFly and Doc Brown impersonators), so I couldn't miss that, no matter how much money I potentially had on the line.

And I was missing the beat writing crew already. When you spend years flying around the country with a group of guys following a baseball team, you come up with your own language, a million inside jokes, an entire culture shared among ten sports-mad travelers. Leaving those guys was one of the hardest parts of deciding to quit my job. I'm finding a cut-rate version of that camaraderie in the world of DFS, but I still feel like an outsider there, even if Beep had made me a slight part of things.

Back on the East Coast, though, I'm surprised to feel a little bit of loss at missing out on the Sunday sweat that I had watched the DFSers train and prepare for. Driving back from Pennsylvania to New York on Sunday, after the wedding, I force Amalie to give me updates on how our guys are doing, by following along on the standings chart. Yet as we drive home, every check of the standings brings a certain amount of embarrassment, that maybe my guys weren't the sure bets I thought they were. From the start, all four of our lineups—three by Underjones, one by Beep—are far, far down in the standings. And they keep falling. Toward the end of the 1 p.m. games, three of the four lineups are below 180th place, and the one "contender" is piddling about in roughly 50th, with most of its player minutes used.

I feel like a failure in so many ways. Even my chosen pros seem to stink. All I do in DFS is lose, even if it isn't directly me doing the losing this time. Another $565 down the drain.

Then something odd happens. My wife checks the standings again when we're almost home, and she virtually yelps with surprise. Something had happened. Or, a lot of things had happened. Our guys were rocketing up the standings chart with remarkable speed—so much so that Beep is now seventeenth, and Underjones has two lineups in the top thirty. Cal Spears is even in the top ten! Maybe I am a good-luck charm after all.

We rush home, turning on the television to watch Underjones's lineup make a late push, giving him eighth place, with its $100,000 minimum payout and chance at the $5 million top prize next month. The famed and despised Condia had come out of nowhere as well to take first by a commanding margin. But I didn't particularly care, or notice. All I know is that I've got a lineup in the top ten, a shot at taking home as much as $12,000, and as a financial backer, I'm going to be heading to San Diego for the final itself, as part of Team Underjones.

Looks like I picked the right horse after all.

07

Former U.S. representative James Leach is a teacher now, holding an endowed chair at the University of Iowa's law school. His students generally know the basics of his background—that the Iowa Republican spent thirty years in Congress, and that he left office after he lost to a Democratic foe in 2006. There's another piece, though, that he doesn't usually publicize: that his efforts, unwittingly and accidentally, led directly to the creation of Daily Fantasy Sports.

Leach doesn't want that to be his legacy.

It's one of the great unintended-consequences moments of the Internet era: that a sincere attempt to rein in most types of gambling online would lead directly to a niche type of Internet gambling flourishing in a massive and unprecedented way.

"A decade ago no one envisioned the manner [in which] fantasy sports would morph into today's cauldron of daily betting," Leach says.

That unlikely metamorphosis would have been even more astounding to the men who first imagined fantasy sports when they created it as a hobby more than fifty years ago.

While there have long been simulation games like Strat-o-matic, along with a few efforts in the 1950s to track golfer stats in a manner that resembles today's fantasy sports, organized fantasy leagues first appeared in the early 1960s. The original fantasy football league was founded in 1962 by Oakland Raiders part owner Bill Winkenbach, a millionaire businessman. Winkenbach was bored, stuck on the East Coast on a long Raiders road trip playing the New York–area teams. In a hotel room one night, a group that included Winkenbach, the Raiders' PR director, and the *Oakland Tribune*'s beat writer—a trio that would never hang out these days—hashed out the concept for a league using real players' stats to generate points, and they soon invited their friends to join up. Their mouthful of a league, the "Greater Oakland Professional Pigskin Prognosticators League," featured the same basic tenets as fantasy leagues today, though it was much simpler—touchdowns and field goals were the main instruments of measure. There was a trophy for winning, and a dunce cap for finishing last. Fantasy football had arrived.

On the opposite side of the country, a few other smart people were coming around to the same idea. At Harvard University in 1960, baseball-obsessed sociologist William Gamson laid out the framework for the first fantasy baseball league, using wins, ERA, batting average, and RBI. It was called the Baseball Seminar, a name so intentionally dry and technical that they figured no one would mistake their enterprise for gambling, or confuse the participants with bookies or gamblers as they tried to track down all the relevant stats. His colleagues joined in, and Gamson took the game with him when he moved on in 1962 to teach at the University of Michigan. Among the new players was a history professor, and later noted film scholar, named Bob Sklar.

But neither Winkenbach's nor Gamson's leagues ever really captured the popular imagination, or boomed into anything bigger—they were hyperniche movements known about by a few hundred people, really just games among networks of friends.

That all changed when Dan Okrent entered the picture.

Okrent had been a student of Sklar's at Michigan, and the two became friends. Years after Okrent graduated, Sklar laid out the basic concepts of the Baseball Seminar to his onetime mentee at a get-together in New York. It took hold. By the late 1970s Okrent was a well-respected and well-established writer, a sometime member of the New York media scene—and a baseball nut. He desperately wanted to get even closer to his passion. In 1979 he started to draw up plans to do just that.

Working from the old model for the Baseball Seminar, Okrent expanded the categories to include home runs, stolen bases, saves, and a stat of his own invention: WHIP, walks + hits/innings pitched. He then took the concept to a group of fellow baseball obsessives and New York media members at a regular gathering held at an unimpressive local bistro with a name that has since gone down in history.

My old boss at the *Wall Street Journal,* Sam Walker, recounted those early meetings in his 2006 book, *FantasyLand:* "Their regular venue was a Midtown restaurant called La Rotisserie Francaise, which, if not for this particular party of regulars, would have vanished forever into the mists of culinary mediocrity. (About four years later, to the surprise of no one, the Rotisserie would serve its last croque monsieur.)"

Okrent recruited other baseball-mad luminaries of the New York literary scene into their aptly named "rotisserie league," and soon they were under way—with a $250 buy-in, lest anyone think money and fantasy haven't been linked from the start.

They drafted, they followed, they became obsessed. But these "roto" fanatics weren't professors, or even football executives—they were media members. And their friends were media members. As soon as a few other reporters heard about this crazy pastime that their pals had developed, they wanted to tell the story. The *New York Times* ran a piece, as did the *CBS Morning News.* The secret was out. At the end of the first season, Random House editor Peter Gethers and Glen Waggoner, later founding editor of *ESPN The Magazine,* were crowned champions. As Walker wrote:

> At the awards banquet, Gethers and Waggoner arrived in rented tuxedos accompanied by their girlfriends, who wore cheerleader costumes. In real clubhouse celebrations, Champagne is the preferred bath of champions. But in this case, the winners were marched into

Cork Smith's bathroom and told to lean over the tub, where they were drenched in something more in keeping with the spirit of the league: chocolate Yoo-hoo. As the cold, syrupy goo slipped under his collar and trickled down the length of his back to puddle at his belt, Waggoner stared off into the distance, his face aglow. "I've never had more fun in my life," he says.

Others wanted to have that kind of fun, too. So when a follow-up piece on the league by Okrent in *Inside Sports* listed the full rules to the game, a new crop dove in. From there, Rotisserie baseball took off—except it did so under another name. The original founders had trademarked the name Rotisserie and protected it zealously. So anyone who wanted to write a guide or start a league without paying them their share had to find another term. Before long, they had happened upon the phrase *fantasy baseball*—which seemed to do the job, and soon became the popular way to refer to the booming pastime.*

Over the next decade, fantasy sports exploded, aided dramatically by the rise of personal computers and the Internet. By the late 1990s, fantasy had become so commonplace that the sports leagues themselves even started to come around; before that time, they had stayed away, viewing it as a bastion for nerds at best, and a gambling enterprise at worst.

"Back then the concerns were way less legal concerns, and more so the fact that the leagues didn't like us. Back then the leagues themselves viewed us as gambling," said Peter Schoenke, chairman of the FSTA and founder of powerful fantasy news and information site RotoWire. "It took years before the leagues were okay with us—not just liked us, but were even neutral to us. And the media companies, like ESPN, wouldn't touch us; it was just total geekdom to them."

---

* Okrent, by the way, has distanced himself from the rise of DFS, telling the *Boston Globe*'s Dan Shaughnessy that he's "bemused" by the way his creation has mutated. "I feel like J. Robert Oppenheimer, having invented the atomic bomb. . . . I meant it for peaceful purposes."

Fantasy sports wasn't the only industry aided by the Internet boom, of course. One of the many other beneficiaries was its distant relation, online gambling. Internet gambling was in its infancy in 1997, just starting down the path that would lead to the online poker boom a few years later.

Enter Arizona senator John Kyl. The Republican had won election to the upper chamber in 1995, the start of what would be an eighteen-year career in the Senate. The conservative Kyl quickly set his sights on the budding scourge of online gambling, though few knew it even existed at the time. Kyl wanted online gambling barred before millions were seduced into throwing away money online. His movement's pithy slogan? "Click your mouse and lose your house."

His antigambling bill was extremely aggressive and broad in scope, whacking pretty much any online venture that offered cash rewards for any sort of contests. Whether Kyl meant it to or not, that included fantasy sports. And fantasy operators noticed, realizing that there was a danger there. They'd expected something like this for a while.

"We kinda knew," Schoenke said. "We knew that there was kinda a gray area, and if some aggressive prosecutor, or legislator, or attorney general, wanted to make a case out of it, even though we think we're legal as a game of skill, we knew there would always be some uncertainty."

They called a meeting in St. Louis to organize their opposition, a kind of G-8 summit for the fantasy world. CDM Fantasy Sports brought together other industry leaders, including SportsLine, Prime Sports Interactive, Sports Buff Fantasy Sports, and the *Sporting News*. They realized they needed to work together to oppose threats like Kyl's legislation, and in 1998 they created the Fantasy Sports Trade Association. The group played a minor role in successfully fighting off Kyl's efforts, and his bill failed. During congressional hearings on the bill, fantasy operations were discussed in the halls of Congress for the first time as lawmakers debated whether to exempt fantasy from the proposed online gambling regulations.

Florida State University associate professor Ryan Rodenberg has extensively studied the congressional efforts that culminated with the passage of UIGEA. He traces the first carve-out for fantasy sports to July 1998, introduced into Kyl's antigambling bill of that year by Democratic senator Richard Bryan of Nevada. The 1998 discussions on fantasy were surprisingly extensive, considering that fantasy had yet to truly boom. There was testimony from both sides of the issue: a representative of the Major League Baseball Players Association testified that it should be exempted; the Department of Justice weighed in that it should not—that when it is played for money, fantasy is effectively gambling by another name.

"[W]e do urge Congress to carefully [craft] legislation to ensure that gambling on fantasy sports leagues and contests is not legalized on the Internet, when all other gambling is banned," the Justice Department wrote in a memo.

Kyl's bill didn't pass that year, but the fantasy exemption was included, over the DOJ's objections. And once it was in that 1998 bill, it would eventually find its way into the final version of every subsequent bill introduced to fight Internet gambling.

"The very first example of the fantasy carve-out is remarkably similar to what eventually got passed into law; there are some tweaks, but it's very, very close," Rodenberg said. "It's a historical anchor. It was in there as early as '98, and it just kept getting recycled into every one of these bills."

That was true all the way through the introduction of the bill that would effectively end online gambling and pave the way for Daily Fantasy Sports, the Unlawful Internet Gambling Enforcement Act of 2006. In the late summer and early fall of 2006, after years of failed efforts, the campaign to pass an anti-Internet-gambling bill was finally gaining traction; as online poker had grown in popularity, so too had the outcry against it. Now antigambling lawmakers in Congress were getting close, with the bill now known as UIGEA. UIGEA didn't actually ban poker or online gambling per se; it instead placed restrictions on payment processors and U.S.-based credit card companies, regulating how they could process gambling-related transactions. That would effectively choke off the Internet gambling industry. The bill had the support of key legislators in both houses, and the online poker industry was running scared. The sports leagues were pushing hard in favor of UIGEA, lobbying for the bill both openly and privately, because they believed banning Internet gambling was vital to preserving the integrity of their games.

The professional leagues went so far as to send multiple letters in support of UIGEA, every communication slapped with the official logos of all four major pro leagues plus the NCAA—a level of unity rarely seen, Rodenberg said.

Still, UIGEA was not a slam dunk, and similar bills had died before. As the bill moved forward, its supporters, conscious of previous failures, wanted to make sure that no thorny side issues derailed their legislation.

Chief among these was Leach, the current Iowa professor and former legislator who was the bill's sponsor in the house. Partway through the legislative process, Leach began hearing concerns from legislators that fantasy sports might be impacted by UIGEA. It's not clear who raised these concerns, and Leach himself says he doesn't know where the issue originated. Several sources have said that congressional staffers who played fantasy suggested to their bosses that fantasy needed to be protected, pointing out that it was in previous versions of the bill and hence shouldn't be an issue. Regardless of where it came from, when Leach began hearing the slightest concerns about fantasy, his response was to simply put the fantasy exemption into UIGEA—to him, fantasy wasn't a big enough issue to warrant any additional controversy on an already difficult bill.

"My principal memory relates to the sense of frustration and exasperation that I felt when informed that concern had begun to be registered on the Hill about fantasy sports," Leach told me. "Given the lack of enthusiasm leadership had for the bill and the problems that could quickly emerge and be magnified in the Rules Committee and the House floor, let alone in the Senate, the consensus seemed to be to let it go and limit on a timely basis as much controversy as possible."

The push to add the 2006 exemption certainly didn't come from the fantasy industry itself. Schoenke says that his group, the FSTA, hardly knew that fantasy was at issue, let alone that they needed to lobby for it.

So, relatively early in the process, the fantasy carve-out was included, recycling the language used in earlier anti-online-gambling bills.

"There's this narrative that the fantasy carve-out was thrown in at the last second. There's not anything in the congressional record that backs that up," Rodenberg said.

What was unquestionably last-minute was the passage of UIGEA itself. In order to get it passed, congressional leadership tacked UIGEA onto a port security bill, ostensibly as a means of fighting terrorism by protecting against the movement of funds by offshore terrorist groups—a bit of politics that irritated many UIGEA opponents who felt like supporters had snuck the measure in. The port security bill passed in the final hours of the session, and President George W. Bush soon signed it into law, dragging UIGEA with it.

It's clear that the sports leagues' support of UIGEA was helpful in getting the bill passed, and that thus they indirectly helped to lay the foundation for DFS. But Rodenberg said that a narrative has developed after the fact—when online poker and other interests were fighting back against UIGEA, and trying to amend or repeal it—that preserving fantasy was a bigger part of the leagues' priorities than it probably was. The *New York Post* first makes the connection in an article from October 2006 about the NFL's using well-known and well-connected lobbyist Marty Gold to push UIGEA through; the article highlights the fantasy connection as a major reason why the leagues wanted UIGEA passed.

Since then, the leagues have hotly contested that connection. Even before fantasy was controversial, or Daily Fantasy existed, they have consistently stated that they pushed for UIGEA to go through because of their larger worries about Internet gambling, not because of fantasy, which at the time was a far, far smaller business than it is today. Current

MLB commissioner Rob Manfred has repeatedly insisted on the record in the past year that the leagues weren't pushing fantasy, and people I've talked to privately in the league office are adamant that this is actually the case.

Rodenberg's analysis backs that up. The last on-record mention of fantasy in relation to UIGEA or online gambling is the 1998 testimony by the MLBPA, and he has found no other evidence that the leagues were hot on the fantasy issue, beyond the *Post* article.

"To their credit, there's nothing that I've found where they were specifically pushing this," Rodenberg said.

That said, it's probably a little naïve to think that no backroom dealings went on. Some certainly might have, as Rodenberg acknowledges.

"Of course something could have happened behind the scenes, [then–NFL commissioner Paul] Tagliabue taking John Kyl out to lunch, you get Marty Gold in there, he sends some curt email. That's certainly possible. But with all the emails and letters sent [on UIGEA], you'd think they would have put something in there on the record [on fantasy] if that were the case."

Regardless, UIGEA was now reality, and Internet gambling in America would never be the same.

RotoGrinders founder Cal Spears was running the popular poker website Pocket Fives at the time. He and his coworkers happened to be away at an event in Aruba, monitoring the progress of UIGEA from afar. They thought it was headed for failure, so much so that with the session almost over and with no immediate news of its passage, they started celebrating.

"We flew back home, and it had passed when we were on the flight. I land in Miami and my phone is blowing up. Uh-oh. The publicly traded companies, like Party Poker, pulled out the next day. It was very clear to me this was an industry you didn't want to be in anymore," Spears said.

Much of the U.S.-based online poker industry closed up shop immediately, but others held out, continuing to operate in defiance of the law. That eventually led to the 2011 "Black Friday," where the few remaining operational poker sites and several payment processors were indicted and the funds of online poker players were frozen.

But in the wreckage, some saw opportunity. UIGEA was wide-ranging. But it had also carved out a few exceptions: horse racing, for instance. And fantasy sports.

Not long after UIGEA passed, young entrepreneurs, many from the poker world, began to look over the fantasy exemption, and realized that if they were to adhere to the letter of the law, they could craft short-duration fantasy sports contests for cash prizes. It would be, effectively, fantasy sports wagering, done over the Internet.

One of the first of these was a University of Nevada, Las Vegas graduate and part-time poker blogger named Kevin Bonnet. Saddened by the death of online poker, Bonnet combed over UIGEA hoping to find a loophole that would allow online poker to be brought back in some form. He didn't find one. What struck him instead were the possibilities that the fantasy sports carve-out might create. Bonnet figured out quickly that a whole new world was possible if he applied the rules of UIGEA to fantasy sports. The guidelines were simple, just as UIGEA laid them out: all prizes and contest sizes must be decided beforehand; all outcomes must reflect the knowledge and skill of the multiple participants in multiple real-world sporting events; game scores and point spreads may not be a factor in the winning outcomes.

"It hit me that the multiple players and multiple-game requirements could be met with as little as two games held on the same day," Bonnet wrote in his DFS how-to book, *Essential Strategies for Winning at Daily Fantasy Sports.*

"Congress was thinking that this requirement would require a full season of traditional fantasy sports to be met. I was realizing that it actually allowed for a new type of legal sports betting based on fantasy sports," Bonnet wrote.

A few tiny sites had offered some version of a Daily Fantasy game before, but none that were crafted in response to UIGEA, and none that

offered the kind of fully legal cash prizes and sports betting Bonnet envisioned. Borrowing concepts from online poker sites, Bonnet managed
to get a little start-up funding and prepared to launch his new site, Fantasy Sports Live. In a 2007 blog post announcing the dawn of DFS, Bonnet explained how wagering cash on short-term fantasy contests was
possible on Fantasy Sports Live.

"We realized," Bonnet wrote, "that we could offer contests that lasted
as little as three hours, just the length of a single game or event, as long
as other games started and finished in the same time frame. We could
take the early football games on Sunday for example and create fantasy
teams using just the players from those games. We could form contests
up in real time, like a sit and go, collect entry fees, and pay cash prizes
however we like as long as we guarantee the prizes before taking the
entries."

On June 22, 2007, Bonnet's site went live, and DFS was here to stay.

Bonnet wasn't the only one realizing UIGEA's potential. A few months
after the birth of Fantasy Sports Live, the first true competitor popped
up, in Chris Fargis's Instant Fantasy Sports. He was another high-level
poker player trying to find a way to live in the post-poker world.

"It wasn't something I came up with on my own," said Fargis, who is
now DraftKings' director of product. "A lot of us were talking about it at
the time. It was, hey, there's this fantasy sports carve-out, what can we do
to make this into a business?"

Fargis's site emerged as a true competitor to Bonnet's, but both remained minuscule. Bigger money, however, was noticing the potential
in DFS.

Over at NBC, a young executive named Rick Cordella looked at this
burgeoning space and realized that a company with resources like his
could grow one of these start-ups into a giant. NBC was rebounding
after years of trailing its rivals in sports programming and had dipped
its toe into fantasy with its purchase of content provider Rotoworld.com
in 2006. But it was far, far behind Yahoo!, the undisputed leader in fan-

tasy content and eyeballs. NBC needed to latch onto the next big thing if it was going to surpass Yahoo! and the growing fantasy presence of ESPN. They wanted in.

Fargis had no idea how to make his niche company into a big business, so he was willing to sell.

"I knew it was a really good idea. I knew if you could package it and market it, it could really work. I don't know if I imagined a five million, three-dollar buy-in tournament," Fargis said.

In the summer of 2008, NBC bought Fargis's Instant Fantasy Sports and soon rebranded it as SnapDraft, adding resources and positioning it to challenge Fantasy Sports Live as the leader in this tiny but growing market. The arrival of NBC was transformative in the growth of DFS, legitimizing the space and encouraging others to jump in.

"I think everyone always knew that this was on the edge—is it legal? Is it not legal?" Schoenke said. "Everyone looked at the game play and said, is this really fantasy? But to me, the big thing was when they took it to the NBC lawyers. I thought, they're never going to approve this. Not because it's illegal, but because they're risk averse, it's a big company. And then they came back and said, 'Yeah, no problem.' After that happened, then everybody else said, 'Okay, we're good here.'"

With Fantasy Sports Live and SnapDraft now well established, it appeared that one of these two small companies might be the one to make the breakthrough, hitting the mainstream.

Instead, the crossover success story would be Nigel Eccles's FanDuel, as the Scottish company jettisoned its failing election-predictions model, HubDub, established itself in America, and entered the Daily Fantasy space in 2009.

"In 2009," Eccles says, "we liked the sector. With SnapDraft, it was like, NBC and GE own this. That gave us the comfort that major corporations with expensive lawyers were comfortable with it."

Eccles may not have known much about sports, but he knew how to showcase his vision. He convinced British companies Pentech Ventures and Scottish Enterprise to take the lead on a $1.4 million Series A funding round in 2009, allowing FanDuel to get off the ground. It started slowly but took off once the 2009 football season hit, quickly surpassing SnapDraft and Fantasy Sports Live to become the market leader, partly because it showcased salary cap format games over a draft format, and partly because it simply explained the product in a way that neither of the two existing leaders had. Daily Fantasy didn't make sense right away to the majority of players. Most would go through a process that went something like this: It's fantasy, but it lasts a single day? Why bother? Oh, wait, I can bet money on it? Oh. Huh. Okay.*

The existing sites made a user figure that process out on his own. FanDuel was very hands-on and explanatory, and when users would make suggestions, FanDuel implemented them almost immediately. The company wasn't reinventing the wheel; it was just making it user-friendly.

"I think what separated us was that we were a start-up with engineers as cofounders," Eccles says. "We had very, very fast cycle time, and very, very fast development time. Whereas a company like SnapDraft was owned by NBC, and just couldn't update quickly enough. We could just keep iterating, and keep making the product experience better."

FanDuel's success led to new competitors, including Brian Schwartz's DraftStreet in 2010 and Jeremy Levine's StarStreet in 2011. But FanDuel was breaking out, introducing new features that were both building the DFS marketplace and solidifying the company's grip on the top spot. In 2010 they added tournaments and introduced the first live final in Las Vegas.

In 2011 they faced perhaps their darkest time, when player lockouts in the NFL and NBA and increasing competition threatened their very

---

* I actually realized deep into this process that I had encountered Daily Fantasy once before, when I didn't understand what it was. During spring training 2014, a DraftStreet employee reached out to ask me if they could pay me to promote their site, describing it only as "one-day fantasy sports." I didn't comprehend their business, and couldn't understand why anyone would want to build a fantasy team for one day, and quickly passed. Wish he'd told me back then that it was basically legalized sports betting!

existence. They had trouble raising money, with U.S. investors spooked by the obvious gambling parallels and unsure if UIGEA really protected them.

Paul Martino of Bullpen Capital, who was among the first U.S. investors, was interested in the site's potential, even though others were passing.

"At that point, I'm like, okay dude, how come no U.S. investors are in this company?" Martino asked. "And Nigel said to me, somewhat perplexed, everyone's afraid of this category.

"I called up a venture buddy of mine, and said, 'What am I missing?' I'm the only guy saying yes. Nigel told me he's gotten seventy-seven nos. I'm the one yes out of seventy-eight tries—I was honestly sweating a little at night, saying, 'What am I missing?'"

FanDuel's numbers, however, were simply too good to pass up.

"My investment memo is almost comical," Martino said. "This guy is making a million dollars off twenty thousand users. There are forty million fantasy players in the United States. I had the luxury of investing when the thing already worked at small scale and is in a massive market with nothing but acquisition in front of it. I may never see one as easy as this again."

FanDuel stayed afloat with a $4 million Series B funding round led by Pentech in the fall of 2011, and continued growing with an $11 million Series C round just over a year later. FanDuel was now the undisputed king of this growing industry, having gone from $1.15 million in revenue and 17,000 active users in 2011 to $10 million in revenue and 70,000 actives by 2012. DraftStreet was the clear number two, followed by StarStreet and others.

In a spare bedroom of a Watertown, Massachusetts, condo, however, a challenger was taking shape.

Jason Robins, Matt Kalish, and Paul Liberman were employees at the Lexington, Massachusetts, office of online printing company Vistaprint—not close friends, at all, but coworkers with a few things in common: a love of entrepreneurship, of solving puzzles, and of sports, particularly fantasy sports.

Kalish, the true fantasy nut of the bunch, knew nothing about FanDuel or the early DFS industry. But he believed season-long fantasy sports could be improved by shortening the duration, and that there was a market there. He brought the idea to Robins on one of Vistaprint's social nights out at a local bar. Robins was in. But they needed more—and so they called over Liberman, known for his technical expertise (and the only one with an extra room to use as an office) and brought him in on the plan.

Within two days, they were shocked to learn that a nascent industry already existed. But after a brief down moment, they were motivated—realizing that meant the idea was sound. They resolved to push forward with the plan. They claimed Liberman's spare bedroom as their headquarters, adding a whiteboard and repurposing three beer pong tables from his basement to serve as their desk space.

Now they just needed a name.

"It's funny how we came to the name DraftKings," Liberman recalled. "We were just looking for an open URL on GoDaddy. We tried typing in like a million different combinations. We liked the word *draft*, because we thought it was explanatory. We're like, okay, Draft, and a whole bunch of things. Then we tried *kings*. And we're like, cool. Kings. That's pretty regal."

They worked on the concept for DraftKings for a year, starting in early 2011, and finally left their Vistaprint jobs in early 2012, after receiving $1.4 million in seed funding from Atlas Ventures. The site debuted on Liberman's birthday, April 27, 2012. There were seventeen users and $400 in entry fees on that first day—mostly from family and friends. But they were live.

With the industry growing and the field getting crowded, one company after another began bulking up in an effort to challenge FanDuel's dominance—DraftStreet brought in fantasy guru Matthew Berry and

StarStreet made a deal with *Playboy* to hold live events at the Playboy Mansion. But no partnership was more important than the deal DraftKings made with Major League Baseball in 2013.

Bob Bowman, the head of MLB's innovative and profitable technology media arm, Major League Baseball Advanced Media, was one of the first mainstream sports executives to take an interest in Daily Fantasy Sports. I've been told that baseball hired an outside firm and spent roughly two years vetting the legality of DFS, finding it safe to engage with. Bowman met with FanDuel executives in 2013, wanting to do a deal, one that would cost the company $1 million and allow FanDuel to be listed in MLB's fantasy section on its website. But it came with conditions: FanDuel couldn't announce the deal, and couldn't put MLB logos anywhere on its own site—so the industry leader turned it down. DraftKings, however, was eager to fill that void. Through mutual contacts, Robins got a meeting with Bowman, according to the *Washington Post*'s Adam Kilgore. Bowman and his staff were ready to do a deal immediately, Robins told Kilgore.

"I sat down, and in the first five minutes of the meeting, [they were] like, 'Oh, yeah. [We] know what you guys do. Are you interested in doing a deal with us?'" Robins said. "I was blown away. It was awesome. I thought I was going to have this lengthy education process, and they were ready to go."

Even though DraftKings couldn't announce the deal publicly, it could tout its existence to investors, further validating its product and its future. With MLB's support—and purchase of a small stake in the company, according to Kilgore—DraftKings was legitimized and began to grow rapidly. The MLB deal wasn't the only thing that made DraftKings different. The company also dreamed bigger than its competitors, and believed that exponential growth was not just possible, but attainable. DraftKings aggressively courted the poker crowd, which had long ignored DFS because the prize pools were so small; in November 2013 it signed a partnership agreement with the World Poker Tour. It built the first truly successful DFS mobile app, allowing players to take the sweat experience wherever they went. And importantly, DraftKings didn't just try to attract elite, high-volume DFS players, as, for instance, StarStreet did—it went after everyone, offering stunningly large prize pools for a start-up, plus tantalizing offers for new customers. Thus began the first phase of a marketing push that would eventually culminate in the massive ad blitz before the 2015 football season, increasing the company's user base, capital, and importance. In July 2014, flush with cash, DraftKings purchased DraftStreet, combining the second- and third-largest DFS sites to create a true second option behind FanDuel.

Over at StarStreet, Jeremy Levine looked at DraftKings' aggressive strategies, and at how fast it was growing, and realized two things at once: his company was done for, and DFS would never be the same.

"The first time I really understood their approach, I grabbed my team. I said, these guys are suicide bombers. They may figure it out on their way down, but no matter what, they're going to blow things up, and change things," Levine said.

He sold his DFS business to DraftKings that August.

By the start of the 2014 football season, the rise of DraftKings had created a duopoly in the industry, but FanDuel was still the far larger company. To bridge the gap, DraftKings needed more partners. FanDuel needed to keep them away. Fresh off new fund-raising rounds that saw DraftKings raise $41 million and FanDuel $70 million, both companies started throwing money at leagues and teams hungry for revenue. FanDuel laid out obscene amounts of cash, locking up the NBA as its exclusive partner and giving the league an equity stake. DraftKings eagerly spent more.

To secure the MSG group—which owns the Knicks and Rangers—as a partner, New York–based FanDuel offered what it believed was an aggressive deal, a million dollars a year. An industry source says DraftKings blew that out of the water with $5 million per year for five years, a deal that got the company's name atop the jerseys of the women's basketball team the New York Liberty, among other marketing perks.

DraftKings was continually more aggressive, and more cavalier, confident that bigger payouts would win the day. A person who was in the room said that at one of DraftKings' meetings with the NHL, the DraftKings representative came into the meeting in shorts, claiming to have a hangover after having been out with Twitter employees the night before. It didn't matter. FanDuel offered the NHL a million dollars per year; DraftKings offered four times that. The NHL went with DraftKings.

DraftKings' stellar fund-raising and forceful partnership tactics had grown the company from a tiny start-up to well-established second banana as 2014 closed, but it was still far smaller than FanDuel. Convincing existing customers to leave the comfort of FanDuel for a new product, with different rules and an unfamiliar interface, continued to be a challenge.* DraftKings was making inroads advertising to the poker crowd and was drawing in DFS naïfs via television ads, but the gap remained large thanks to FanDuel's established status as trusted market leader. So at the end of that year, DraftKings approached FanDuel about a merger.

FanDuel reps were hesitant, people with knowledge of the discussions said, even though an initial DraftKings proposal had FanDuel taking a majority stake in the new company, roughly 60 percent. That wasn't enough; as the larger company, FanDuel wanted it to be an acquisition, one done by unit economics—each side presents its numbers, and the merger is done by relative share. DraftKings, still far smaller, balked at that. FanDuel returned with an adjusted list of demands: first, appoint a banker; second, share numbers; and third, the two companies' boards would work together to approve a management team. That too proved problematic. DraftKings wanted to have the respective heads of each

---

* Virtually every high-level player I know prefers the experience on DraftKings, even though FanDuel is considered the easier site to win on. I found the same, loving the astute player pricing, late swap, and general responsiveness the site offered, and played roughly 90 percent of my action on DraftKings. As a company, DraftKings was always more aggressive, and it's debatable if that was a good idea. But when it came to building the better product, their innovation versus FanDuel's conservatism was no contest.

company sit down together to decide who was going to be in charge. DraftKings declined the terms.

In the aftermath, FanDuel execs thought they had made the smart choice. At the time, they were bigger, and antitrust issues would have made a merger difficult anyway.

"The only reason our guys would do it is that if we acquired them, they wouldn't be out there doing crazy shit," a FanDuel higher-up said in late 2015. "It would be a defensive acquisition."

The merger talks died, though that wouldn't be the last heard of them. Instead, DraftKings returned to plan B—raise even more money, and use it to kill FanDuel. DraftKings locked up the UFC and NASCAR, forged a marketing partnership with the WWE, and in April 2015 expanded its partnership with MLB to become the league's official partner. Momentum was clearly on the side of the challenger, but DraftKings still entered the summer of 2015 as the smaller of the two sites. It needed more if it was going to unseat FanDuel by football season, and FanDuel needed more to hold off its hungry competitor. Both sites began aggressively courting investors, to great effect. With the advertising plans already on the drawing boards, Robins and Eccles made the rounds, building their war chests. DraftKings raised $300 million, with $160 million coming from Fox. FanDuel raised $275 million, with KKR & Company, Time Warner Investments, and Google Capital among the investors. Both companies locked in enormous media buys for the start of the football season, with FanDuel preparing to spend upward of $20 million and DraftKings willing to pay more than four times that.

Yet amid this bonanza were warning signs, hints that Daily Fantasy was on shakier footing than it seemed, despite these mountains of cash. In April 2015, word leaked that Walt Disney Company was planning to invest $250 million in DraftKings, in return for an ad buy spend of half a billion on ESPN's platforms in coming years. But Disney abandoned that deal months later amid concerns that DraftKings was a little too close to gambling for their family-friendly brand.

And the deals the companies were able to make weren't exactly on favorable terms for the Daily Fantasy giants. The DraftKings-Fox deal, for instance, contained similar terms to the failed deal with Disney; as part of Fox's $160 million deal to take its 11 percent ownership stake, DraftKings agreed to spend $250 million over three years on advertising on Fox's sports properties, according to a filing with the Securities and Exchange Commission.

"We were offered those deals. I think those were very bad deals," Eccles told the *Wall Street Journal*.

They may not have been worthwhile, long term. But those deals gave DraftKings the ammunition it needed to wage its advertising war against FanDuel. FanDuel fought back, and both companies fired off commercials at a pace that made them national leaders, a national topic, and then, finally, national targets.

08

The porn star Ron Jeremy slithers through the lobby of the JW Marriott in Los Angeles surrounded by hundreds of women in matching purple outfits who have no idea of his fame, and a few dozen men wearing DraftKings nameplates who know exactly who he is.

The DraftKings staffers track his every move, angling for a little face time with the man himself. I join their effort, we lions stalking this well-hung antelope around the vast lobby bar. We wait, patiently, for our time to strike, hanging back as he creeps from one social group to the next.

Finally, he is alone. One of the DraftKings employees pounces.

"Mr. Jeremy, could we get a picture?"

He nods his weary assent as I crowd in with the DraftKings posse, all smiles as we pose for the shot.

The DraftKings crew is here for the much-anticipated live final to their $15 million football challenge, with its biggest-ever, $5 million first prize on the line. I'm attending as a guest of pro DFS player Underjones, one of the ten finalists who made it out of the two-hundred-man semi-final in San Diego a month before.

The women in purple crowding the lobby are here for a confer-ence: they are the minions of makeup giant Mary Kay. The direct-sales cosmetic company is holding a major event at the hotel this week, and legions of fortyish midwestern women in matching purple skirt suits throng the lobby, sipping furiously at their mimosas and gin martinis.

Ron Jeremy is here for the after party to the XBiz awards, one of the porn industry's largest award shows. XBiz is the unofficial kickoff to porn's awards week, which will culminate a few days later with the AVN Awards in Las Vegas.

The awards show had just let out from one of the ballrooms upstairs, and the porn group entered en masse, whooping and hollering, tatted-up women spilling out of their dresses as gigantic, overly chiseled men loomed over them. The Mary Kay ladies were both overwhelmed and titillated, clearly unsure how to handle this invasion of the body sculptors. To my surprise, the DFS crew doesn't seem overly excited by all the porn starlets, who one might think would draw rapt attention from a group of drunk males in their mid-twenties.

But in a world where most of these guys have been to the Playboy Mansion more than once, a few semifamous porn stars don't move the needle anymore. Except, of course, for Ron Jeremy. Ron Jeremy is special. Ron Jeremy has crossover fame, his hedgehog looks and stunning longevity making him a comic phenomenon well beyond his body of work, like Abe Vigoda with a monster penis.

He's an average-looking guy—well below average, really—who managed to live the everyman dream of having sex with thousands of the most beautiful women in the world, making a storied career out of a leisure pursuit. It isn't hard to see why DFS players would identify with someone like that.

The Ron Jeremy picture captured for all eternity, I pull out my own phone. I've got business to attend to.

The next day, Underjones will begin the two-day battle with the nine other finalists over the $5 million first prize—not to mention the $2 million second-place bounty, the $1 million third-place pot, and so on—and so he and nearly all the other finalists are sequestered in their hotel rooms, tweaking lineups. As one of the five members of his team (DraftKings even made us "Team Underjones" nameplates), I'm technically supposed to be helping him prepare. I have a vested interest in his success: through Beep, for $565, I'd bought 0.25 percent of Underjones's seat, and that means a five-figure payout if he lands first place. But the reality is that I'm pretty useless. Underjones knows more about this weekend's NFL games than I ever could, even though I'd been helping the *Wall Street Journal* cover the New York Giants for much of December. He's got a pair of finance quants with him to help run statistical analyses on the best tactics. He has Beep with him to talk game theory, and to analyze whom our opponents might pick. What am I supposed to do, write the team newsletter?

So as I take out my phone and open up the DraftKings app, I'm not concerned with football. I'm far more focused on another qualifying process, for a totally different live final: hockey.

In March, in San Diego, DraftKings will hold its hockey live final, a forty-seat event with $500,000 in total prizes, including $100,000 to first place. While those numbers might not seem like much when compared to the ludicrous $5 million football top spot, it's by far the biggest final in the history of DFS hockey. And I want in. This is what Beep has been training me for—this is my chance to hold up one of those big checks and take my spot among the best of the best. But to get there, I need to qualify. And that isn't going to be easy.

Qualifiers are the equivalent of throwing your money into a paper shredder and then lighting the shredded bills on fire. Most of the forty seats to the hockey final will be acquired in the same way: by winner-take-all twenty-four-man competitions with a $1,000 buy-in. First place wins the seat. Second place gets his money back. Third place on down? They get nothing and like it!

For this reason, qualifiers are largely the domain of well-funded pros. They are serious contests with tough fields and few, if any, mistakes made. Each player can win up to three of the forty total seats, and each seat brings with it a $5,000 minimum payout, so the best players try to max out, winning as many entries as DraftKings will allow. The hockey qualifier process has just begun, with the first two seats awarded earlier in the week, but I hadn't entered those first ones. I wanted to feel the whole thing out a little more before dropping $1,000 on what was almost a sure loss.

And $1,000 isn't exactly money I have to burn—though finally, I hope, I've reached something of a turning point. The numbers on my phone look good; my hockey lineups for the night are actually doing pretty well, and I'm up a few hundred dollars. I'm finally starting to notch a few quality wins, and man, do I ever need them. Over the stretch from mid-December through mid-January, my losses had continued to mount. I was betting on hockey every day, hundreds of dollars at a time, and usually I was losing. Beep kept telling me that things would turn, and that he noticed my lineups improving day by day, but frankly I couldn't see it. Not long after the new year, I hit a low point of $6,500-plus in losses since the start of my efforts in DFS last spring. It was a number I would shy away from mentioning when anyone would ask how I was doing; when Amalie would gingerly inquire, I'd respond with a curt "I'm still down," and generally leave it at that, feeling bad that it was affecting my mood and my relationship with her. But it was.

I give her a lot of credit for accepting this crazy plan of mine despite how harebrained it all is. She hates gambling anyway, and she's generally pretty frugal—so seeing me throwing around thousands makes her cringe. Because she's on the road much of the time with the Bruins, she doesn't have to see all the day-to-day of my winning and (mostly) losing, and that's probably a good thing—it would make her even crazier than it's making me. She tries not to ask too much about it, but it naturally comes up. We'll talk, often on the phone, about what stories she's working on, and that talk will turn to how I'm doing, how much money I'm wagering that night—I'm almost embarrassed to admit it at times, it all seems so foolish. I'm sure it's a lot of fun telling her mid-thirties friends, with their stable families and new babies, that her insane husband just quit his prestigious, secure job to become a professional gambler. But against her own natural impulses, she's continued to support my deci-sion to quit and pursue this dubious undertaking—even acting excited when I win—and I appreciate that tremendously. It makes me feel even worse that I'm losing, though. Like I'm letting her down, too.

But really, that's just what I've been doing—and throwing away our savings, to boot. On top of just being a chump, a now-longtime fish, the money itself (or lack thereof) started to gnaw at me. Everything in my day-to-day life that cost anything suddenly seemed that much more costly. My $50 monthly gym membership? Unnecessary. A $100 dinner out with Amalie? An extravagance. It ceased to feel like a $100 dinner—it felt like a $6,600 dinner. Meanwhile, click, click, click, bet another $500 on hockey that day. Hope to get at least $350 of it back. DFS was threatening to become another of those life-leeches that sucked up time and energy and money and never really gave much back, like guitar les-sons and grad school.

Still, promising slivers of profitability are peeking through these clouds of bankruptcy. In the months following my first training session with Beep, DraftKings and FanDuel have changed their rules, respond-ing to public criticism about the dominance of the multi-entry sharks, and to regulations proposed by Attorney General Maura Healey of Mas-sachusetts. Now there are entry caps on the larger tournaments, pre-venting pros from putting hundreds of entries into contests where that would give them 10 percent of the field. The industry is moving toward a consistent entry cap of 3 percent or 150 entries in nearly all tourna-ments. They have also improved site-wide caps and low-stakes limits on the number of total contests a single user can enter, which means the biggest pros aren't gobbling up every head-to-head game at the lower dollar levels. The changes are a great start. I've seen fewer and fewer mass multi-entry trains crushing me in the larger tournaments, and co-incidence or not, my results have been improving. Beep, who disliked playing that "brute force" style of hundreds of correlated lineups, says the new rules have made him change his tactics already—the entry lim-its make those kinds of strategies far less effective. Now, refreshed, he's focusing on creating six to ten good lineups, and he's winning even more than before.

"I'm actually enjoying it a lot more," he says. "I guess it's good to be forced to change sometimes."

Other than, y'know, the losing-money part, I'm enjoying it, too. In the two months since I started playing DFS hockey with Beep, I've become something of an obsessive. I'll start working on lineups around 3:30 p.m., putting in hours of research and lineup building, leading up to the 7 p.m. lineup lock. His training, and my study, are paying off: my hockey knowledge has expanded to the point where I can really begin to incorporate advanced statistics and apply them to specific situations—which team's CORSI value* means they'd dominate possession and keep the puck in the offensive zone against a weak goalie, which ill-disciplined teams concede too many penalties, making them vulnerable against clubs with strong special teams units. I'm finally fluent in which players are on which lines, allowing me to make late swaps when needed and exchange scratched players for quality replacements moments before games start. I've even developed a pretty good game-watching routine: after puck drop at 7 p.m., I'll stay updated on any late changes through the start of the 7:30 and 8 p.m. games, and then head to the gym—where I frantically check my phone for scoring updates between sets. With my routine in place, my knowledge improved, I've started to chip away at that $6,500 deficit, and I think good things are coming.

Amazingly, so does Beep. The DraftKings final marks the first time I've seen Beep in person since December, and when we reconnect he looks at me like a proud papa, thrilled at what he sees from my lineups. He looks through my well-correlated lineups most days, and has begun to really compliment me on my tactics: my focus on hockey inputs like opportunity, minutes, and shot attempts rather than outcome stats like

---

* A basic measurement of shot differential, enabling one to determine which hockey teams and players have possession more than others.

goals and assists; my ever-improving ability to make changes at the last minute; my decision to use some of my salary base for high-priced, high-scoring defenders, when many DFS hockey players ignore them in tournament formats. Thanks to my "success," he has a proposal for me.

"You've progressed far enough that I think we can start swapping and selling your action," he tells me.

This is a big step, I assume, even though I have no idea what it means.

What it means is that Beep wants a piece of my bets every day—that despite my results, he thinks I'm actually getting pretty good at this, and is willing to risk his money on me to prove it. It's similar to my onetime buy-in of Underjones's action, except a more formalized and regular relationship, where we'd literally trade percentages of our action to one another each day, and he'd regularly cover huge portions of my buy-ins on bigger contests.

"You're a winning player, I trust you," he told me. I feel like I should get business cards made up: "Daniel Barbarisi: Winning Player. You can trust me."

The upshot is that I can start playing those $1,000, twenty-four-man, winner-take-all hockey qualifiers because Beep is willing to cover much of my buy-ins—and my potential losses—in exchange for the chance at what I might win. He planned to enter the first twenty-four-man qualifier twice, at $1,000 per entry. I would enter it once. We decided that I would sell him 85 percent of my qualifier entry—meaning he would cover 85 percent of the cost of entering, and in return, 85 percent of the winnings would be his. He would also sell me a portion of each of his entries. So, in effect, for about $300 per qualifier, I would own 15 percent of my one entry and 8 percent of each of his. It allows me to actually take a shot at this thing without totally destroying my savings, and gives Beep a chance at additional profit in a contest he thinks is winnable—if, of course, I ever prove good enough to win it.

Earlier that Friday night, Beep and I built our lineups for that night's qualifier. We adhered to strict rules—even though he was backing me financially, it would be collusion* for us to know anything about one another's lineups in such a small contest, and we took that seriously. We discussed who we thought might be the most highly owned players that night, but otherwise we drafted in silence.

I expected a big night from the Pittsburgh Penguins against the Tampa Bay Lightning and ran some numbers on the history of Pittsburgh winger Chris Kunitz, like me a creaky gent in his mid-thirties. In exploring how he played after two days off, I found a pattern where he shot significantly more often on two or more days of rest, with a much higher percentage of those shots going in. Feeling every bit of my thirty-six years after my cross-country flight from Boston that day, I could relate! Rest matters. With the Penguins coming off two rest days in a row, I grabbed Pittsburgh's top line with Kunitz and star Sidney Crosby, and paired them with the second line of the Anaheim Ducks, who were facing the defensively porous Dallas Stars.

Now, looking at the scores on my phone in the Marriott's lobby bar, I'm annoyed to see that I'm not some first-time phenom, qualifying for a hockey final seat on my maiden attempt. I was right about one thing: Chris Kunitz had shot a lot, and scored. I was wrong about everything else. I'm mired in the middle of the pack.

Beep, however, is surging ahead. He had also picked Pittsburgh, but went with their second line instead, led by Evgeni Malkin—and that group is dominating. My heart beats faster—it's not my lineup, but if he wins the seat, with its $5,000 minimum payout and $19,000 "value," I'll get some cash back myself. That would help pull me a little closer to my break-even point.

Even though it's only 11 p.m., Beep has already gone to bed. He's

---

* At the time, there was very little policing of collusion or syndicate play, but later on the sites would toughen their rules and ban players who were suspected of colluding. Many suspected brothers Martin and Tom Crowley, known as PapaGates and ChipotleAddict, of colluding late in 2016, and though there was an investigation, they were subsequently cleared.

misguidedly trying to break himself of his 5 a.m. bedtimes by reversing course completely and getting into bed by 10 p.m. So it's up to me to sweat this for him. At the moment, though, the prospect of winning money is superseded by the incredible scene on the dance floor, where porn stars and Mary Kay ladies and a few DraftKings contestants are doing the Dougie. Not even constant scoring updates can top that.

As I sip a Johnnie Walker Black on the rocks and take it all in, Beep's Pittsburgh/Boston group extends its lead. His win, and his final seat, are all but guaranteed now, making him the third person to claim one of the forty spots. My qualifier team is dead in the water, and my lineups in other contests have fallen out of the money, too. Depressing. Still, I'm going to clear a little money off Beep's win, offsetting some of my own losses. Celly? Nah. The dance floor is still in full swing, but Team Underjones has a big day ahead, so I say my good-byes and head off to sleep.

The first Daily Fantasy live final was more of a PR stunt than anything else. It was the fall of 2010, and DFS was in its relative infancy. There was no community to speak of, no big-name players, just a few sites, a little bit of cash, and some budding experts loosely connected via Internet message boards. Tournaments didn't even exist—Daily Fantasy consisted only of head-to-heads and five- and ten-person table games.

By this time, FanDuel had grown larger than its rivals, outpacing SnapDraft and becoming the clear industry leader. But the company needed something to make the larger world take notice. The perception—correctly, mind you—of Daily Fantasy was of a loner's activity, a geek in a basement turning over lineups and hoping to make a little spending cash. Nigel Eccles wanted to bring it all out into the light, and maybe get a headline or two doing it.

"We needed something to put ourselves on the map," Eccles said. "We knew football was really important. So we thought, what's newsworthy? What's PR-worthy? Somebody winning a tournament on a site is just not PR-worthy. What if we did an event where we had finalists and brought them in?"

They drew up a plan: a qualifier-only tournament, complete with satellites, where ten players would win their spots from a much larger field and then compete for what at the time were massive top prizes. They would fly contestants out to Las Vegas, rent out a room at the Venetian's sumptuous sports bar, Lagasse's Stadium, and bring everyone together for one giant football sweat. They'd interview the contestants, make them feel like celebrities—like athletes in their own right. From the qualifier-satellite format to the ten-man final, much of it was modeled after a poker tournament, attempting to give Daily Fantasy the same tense vibe that can come with a big-money poker final table, where players stare one another down through their sunglasses.

RotoGrinders founder Cal Spears was one of the original ten finalists.

"They ran ten qualifiers to get into this thing, and I hit one of the qualifiers with a Matt Cassel–Dwayne Bowe stack. Kansas City. The prize pools felt so big at the time—first place was $25K, second was $15K, third was $10K, and the other seven people didn't win anything, you just got the trip to Vegas," Spears said.

Until it was over, Eccles didn't know if the entire venture would be a success or a failure; would it be remembered as a symbol of a young DFS industry overreaching? It turned out to be the opposite. The first live final was a transformative moment.

"It was enormously stressful, trying to put this thing on. But when we got it together and we met our finalists, that was probably the moment where I realized that this, that DFS in general, was going to be big," Eccles said. "Up until that moment, we didn't know if we had a niche product. When we met our finalists, we were going to find out if they were all very similar—supergeeky. The kind where you'd look at them and think, I don't think there's more than a couple thousand people like this in the U.S."

Instead, Eccles met a surprising cross section of players—not just math nerds, but true sports nuts. The kind you could build an industry around.

"That being the case, I started thinking that fundamentally this is a better form of fantasy sports. It was really only that trip where I realized, this could be mass-marketed. We can start talking to the fifty million people who play fantasy sports," Eccles said.

For players, making a live final became the ultimate badge of honor. Winning money in a midweek tournament? That's nice. But only the best of the best make it to live finals and beat the toughest competition in a closed, controlled environment. No mass multi-entry tactics here; just top players facing off, hoping to hold up the big check at the end of the day.

The winner at the first final was a player named GeneralV, who is still active today. Spears came in seventh. The money involved seemed huge back then, but in the world of modern Daily Fantasy, it's peanuts.

"It's so funny: the guy who came in third in that wins less than the guy who now comes in last," Eccles marveled.

Five years later, Daily Fantasy's live finals have come to represent the industry's best and worst. They are a multiday orgy of excess, complete with models brandishing trophies, off-hours trips to strip clubs, enormous side bets, and of course, piles and piles of money at stake. They are also a remarkably human event at times, as when normal guys like Roman win the $3 million FanDuel top prize and see their lives change. And there truly is a sense of community there—the regulars look forward to the live finals as social events. Daily Fantasy is normally a solitary, lonely pastime. At these events, hard-core players finally lay eyes on the people they compete against nightly over the Internet. They put faces to usernames, talking over bad beats past, discussing strategy. Friendships are forged, and the camaraderie is real. It's like a convention, but with a really, really big door prize. The sharps who don't make it lament the feeling of being left out. That's part of why everyone wants to qualify for these live finals, even though the qualifier process is an unforgiving money sink.

All those years of events reach their natural climax in this $15 million football final, to be held over two days at the Conga Room nightclub in the L.A. Live complex. L.A. Live is the site of the Staples Center, home of the NHL's Kings and the NBA's Clippers, and of the Novo by Microsoft theater, host of the Grammy Awards. This weekend, it also welcomes 1990s R&B act Tony! Toni! Toné!, which makes me briefly consider buying a walk-up ticket, before remembering that I really know only one of the group's songs, and it should probably stay that way.

With the final looming for Saturday and Sunday, Underjones spent much of Friday doing a series of awkward interviews with a Fox Sports crew on scene. Originally, ESPN was ticketed to cover the event, as part of its marketing arrangement with DraftKings. But that deal is slowly falling apart, as DraftKings looks to save money, and ESPN is no longer televising the final.* In the meantime, the company needed a fallback plan to cover the event; in stepped Fox, one of the investors in DraftKings, keen to prop up its struggling investment any way it could. Fox had bought an 11 percent stake in the company, worth roughly $160 million, less than a year earlier.†

So as part of the deal to step in and replace ESPN, DraftKings gave Fox exclusive access to televise the event; all other media was barred. That leaves Fox with the unenviable task of turning this crew into viable, relatable characters, the kind you can root for. In that they have a little help from the DraftKings internal video staff, who produce a series of videos called "Contenders," highlighting the personalities of each of the final players. They're actually quite well done, if a little overdramatic, especially considering that most of these guys are generic gamblers or mid-twenties math geeks with little in the way of on-camera charisma.

---

* Shortly after the final, it would be revealed that DraftKings had ended its expensive, exclusive marketing deal with the Worldwide Leader.

† In mid-February, Fox would reduce its valuation of that stake by $95 million, representing a loss in value of 60 percent. It was one of the first official acknowledgments of what everyone intuitively realized by now: The DFS market isn't what everyone thought it would be, Haskell or no. The companies—and their big venture capital backers—had overreached.

Just from watching the videos, it's easy to see that most of the ten finalists fall into one of a few easy categories. There are the regular guys who got lucky, and probably won their way in through one of the smaller satellite tournaments. This includes pleasant midwesterner Huggins8168, big football fan Stuckcee, L.A. pretty boy Danny1234, Kentucky hick Cory318, and some guy who goes by Box_97. I haven't laid eyes on him yet.

The most interesting of the regular guys, though, is an ex-con from Baltimore who goes by the handle RockenRaven. RockenRaven is a former heroin addict who served three years of a ten-year sentence for armed robbery and then turned his life around with the aid of a program that pairs inmates with horses, emerging as the program's star pupil and garnering some press in the Baltimore papers. RockenRaven, real name Edward Rybolt, seems like a good enough guy—he says he's going to use any winnings to get his daughter a needed eye operation. He's also legitimately pretty funny, and even has a catchphrase, "Hell yeahhhhhhhhhh!" which he shouts at the top of his lungs whenever . . . anything happens. Like, really, pretty much anything.

Then there are the professionals: Underjones, a heavyset pro who goes by DandyDon, and a former poker pro called Aejones, who arrived trailing a posse that included some of the top current poker players in the world. These guys are dangerous. It's no surprise that most smart people are picking all three to finish in the top half.

But virtually no one is picking them to finish first. Because the tenth and final contestant is the biggest, fiercest shark of all, and he comes in brandishing a thirty-point lead over everyone else after dominating the December semifinal.

Condia.

Condia isn't just another Daily Fantasy pro. He is *the* Daily Fantasy pro, for good and ill. Saahil may be the best now, but Condia is probably regarded as the best of all time. His methods are . . . well, cutthroat would be a nice way of describing them. Numerous players have recounted to me the feeling of posting a head-to-head game, say in 2013 or 2014, when they thought they were hot stuff, and watching Condia instantly challenge them before a lesser player could take the game, a tactic known as "scooping." Then he would win much, much more often than not. Condia became notorious for scooping the games of anyone whom he deemed a threat and seeking to immediately quash them, especially if they sought to raise the dollar amounts they played. He didn't want to dominate the ecosystem; he wanted to be the ecosystem.

On DraftKings' Contenders series, Condia explains—with what sounds like it might be a slight tinge of remorse, maybe?—that he long sought to be the *only* Daily Fantasy pro.

"I felt like everyone was an enemy," Condia says. "I had a mission, to beat everyone. To be the one and only professional Daily Fantasy player. I used to take every game on every website."

It's pretty easy to see why Condia represents all that I both feared and resented from the moment I entered Daily Fantasy Sports. He drove, and publicized his driving of, exotic cars bought with everyone else's entry fees. He posted faceless pictures of his abdominal muscles on Twitter (dude, seriously?). He leveraged his bankroll and his skill to beat everyone, from the newest rookie to the toughest pro. And he played in tandem with another strong pro called 1ucror, pooling their resources and minds to win.

"I really don't care what people think about me. Some people are going to not like you, and some people will admire you," Condia says into the camera.

He went out of his way to avoid meeting any other DFS players, because he didn't want to have to think of them as human beings, just usernames he could crush. When I was out with Cal and Jonathan Bales, a strong player and tout,* I heard a story that for years the only high-level player Condia had really met in the industry was a fellow Colorado-

---

* A tout is a DFS player who seeks to leverage his expertise into a media profile, offering picks and strategy advice, and Bales is one of the best. He has written a series of books on DFS strategy, and with CSURAM founded the excellent tools and projections site FantasyLabs. Many others tout with varying degrees of success.

based pro, CSURAM, who at long last convinced Condia to meet for sushi. Condia was so affected by seeing another pro in person—by how nice CSURAM was, by how bad he'd feel taking CSURAM's money in the future—that afterward, he long refused to meet with any other players for fear of going soft.

To most players, Condia remained so mysterious that many believed "Condia" was actually an acronym for some sort of a computer program, built by a group of developers—a myth that was only, finally, laid to rest when Condia made his first public appearance at the DraftKings semifinal in December.

"I used to hear that I was a robot," he says. "That I worked for the big Daily Fantasy companies, and that they would keep my winnings."

(The name "Condia," by the way, is actually a combination of the name of two of his favorite bands, "Condition" and "Lydia.")

Condia's tendencies, and his ruthless playing style, are one of the reasons longtime players didn't hate Saahil and his reign of dominance so much. When Saahil rose to prominence, he directly challenged Condia, playing him wherever he could—$10,000 head-to-heads, small three-and-five-man competitions, everything. After twenty nights of high-stakes combat, it was no contest. Saahil had routed Condia in incredible fashion. On the twenty-first day, Saahil says, he went to look for Condia's games—and the all-time great simply wasn't there. Saahil had beaten him so badly that Condia just gave up; he had chased him out of DFS entirely for the summer of 2015.

"I'm not ashamed to admit that MaxDalury has seven figures of my money," Condia says into the camera.

In person—perhaps unsurprisingly—Condia is the antithesis of the swaggering, take-all-comers pro. He's a quiet, fit, golf pro wannabe named Charles Chon. I'm not sure if his real-life shyness makes his Internet arrogance better or worse—but I know I want Underjones to beat this guy.

Because DraftKings combined the point totals from the semifinal and the final, Condia enters this weekend with a significant advantage, his semifinal score of 219.2 bringing him into the ten-man final nearly thirty points ahead of the nearest challenger. As we built our lineup, we contemplated the best ways to chase him. Yet as kickoff neared on that Saturday morning, Twitter turned out to be the real arbiter of how we built our team. Originally, Underjones was planning a big Patriots stack, with Tom Brady, Rob Gronkowski, Julian Edelman, and more. But during pregame warm-ups, *Sports Illustrated* reporter Greg Bedard tweeted that Gronkowski, coming off an injury, seemed like he might be used only in the team's third-down packages.

"Judging off warmups, he'll mostly be limited to third downs and red zone. But I'm not sure," Bedard tweeted.

It was incomplete information, hedged, based on the practice tendencies of an NFL coach in Bill Belichick who delighted in trying to deceive his opponents with pregame disinformation. But it was still too much of a threat to ignore. Underjones switched to an Aaron Rodgers–Randall Cobb–Richard Rodgers grouping, emphasizing the Packers QB-WR-TE trio and keeping only a few Patriots.

Kickoff looms, and I make my way from the hotel over to the Conga Room to join the rest of Team Underjones to watch the games. Walking up the stairs and entering the club, I'm greeted by a pair of models as tall as giraffes, standing guard over the DraftKings Fantasy Football Championship Belt, a heavy gold and black monstrosity meant to mimic those given to boxing champions. They ask if I want to pose for a picture with it. I quickly decline—hey, I'm not going to win the thing—and move into the nightclub itself. The staff has set up the room with ten clusters of DraftKings' signature white couches, each group of the two-seaters surrounding a table overflowing with power outlets and USB ports. DraftKings knows its audience. The couches look out on a pair of giant television screens showing football games, and these screens themselves are surrounded by smaller boards showing the DFS standings. A few minutes in, nothing has changed—Condia is of course on top, followed by DandyDon and Box_97, with Underjones in the low middle of the pack.

The four games on the slate this weekend, the NFL's divisional play-off round, are New England Patriots–Kansas City Chiefs and Green Bay Packers–Arizona Cardinals on Saturday, followed by Seattle Seahawks–Carolina Panthers on Sunday afternoon, and finally Denver Broncos–Pittsburgh Steelers Sunday night.

Sitting down with Underjones and his quants, Ilya and Vivek—Beep, despite his new bedtime, still hasn't managed to wake up—it's easy to see that my compatriots are in a somber mood. The Patriots are off to a hot start, and worst of all, Gronkowski is leading the charge. Belichick had been trying to deceive the Chiefs, after all—Gronk is healthy and gobbling up yards like they're Bud Lights.

Making matters worse? No one else has rostered Tom Brady as their quarterback. If Underjones had stuck with the Patriots' Brady-Gronkowski pairing, it could have been a winner.

As we watch the Patriots rack up points, Vivek balls up his fists and rubs his eyes, as if it's hard for him to watch what's transpiring. It had been his job to pay attention to late-breaking news; his focus on the Bedard tweet was what swung our lineup from Patriots to Packers.

"This is my fault," Vivek moans. "I feel terrible about it, Mike."

Underjones doesn't hold a grudge. He changed the lineup based on what he believed to be the best information, and besides, as a full-time pro wagering hundreds of thousands each NFL weekend, he knows the swings of the game as well as anyone.

"It's okay. It's early," he says, before going outside to get some air, leaving me to survey the room. Early on in this two-day slog, it's pretty low-key—boring, really. Most of the teams aren't even in the room yet—especially the pros. They know there's a lot of football still to be watched.

Our group, however, is slowly growing. Beep shows up, and not long after we're joined by JeffElJefe, the shaggy, Californian DFS pro who bunked with us at the Mission Beach house a month before. Once they see how well the Patriots are doing, they join us in sulking about what could have been.

As the first game leads into the next, Packers-Cardinals, most of the finalists watch in relative silence—most, that is, except RockenRaven. In the quiet room, the ex-con is a raspy one-man cheering section, seemingly rooting for everything and everyone. Whenever a big play is completed, he stands, looks around, then unleashes a "Hell YEAHHHHHHHHH," or chants the results of the play—"intentional grounding, intentional grounding." At first it's funny. Then it's incongruous in the silent nightclub. Then, finally, it's kinda annoying.

As Cardinals-Packers wears on, we get another bit of bad news: our top receiver, the Packers' Randall Cobb, is hurt trying for a leaping catch near the end of the first quarter. The Rodgers-to-Cobb connection was going to be our ticket to success. Losing Cobb hurts Condia, too, but at this point, that hardly matters. We're headed for a bottom-five finish. My visions of grabbing the $12,000 that my .25 percent stake of $5 million would entitle me to are evaporating, to say nothing of Underjones's dreams of multimillions.

Downtrodden and feeling beaten, we jump at the chance for a change of scenery when DraftKings cofounder Matt Kalish wanders over and asks if we'll be their guests at tonight's L.A. Clippers–Sacramento Kings game, next door at the Staples Center. Thanks to its outrageous spending on team and league partnerships, DraftKings has use of a series of luxury suites at arenas around the country. Sounds good to me.

The misery of football gambling behind us, our group makes its way across the crowded L.A. Live complex and into the Staples Center. I join up with Kalish, to bend his ear about the state of his embattled company and industry. Kalish, one of the three DraftKings founders, is a Columbia alum in his early thirties, married with two young daughters who sometimes join him at these live final events. His horn-rimmed glasses sit perched on a large round head bearing a friendly face and a scruffy beard. He's a genuinely nice guy, relatable, and fantasy-obsessed, and so it's little surprise that of DraftKings' triumvirate, he's the one who spends his time dealing with player issues.

As the Kings and Clippers players bounce and leap their way through warm-ups below, Kalish tells me that these live final events have long been money losers for the companies, but they've become so important to the brand itself that they've become grander and grander as time has gone on.

But it's not the live events that are sucking out so much cash for the big two now. Instead, it's the two new realities of the modern DFS world: compliance, and lawyers. To get into compliance with a nation-wide map of DFS legality that looks more and more like a checkerboard every day—some states legal, others barred—the companies are pouring money into new geolocating and geotracking software, to ensure that customers aren't logging on from barred locations.

It's the lawyers, though, who are really straining DraftKings' re-sources. David Boies and Company don't come cheap—and the litigator reportedly has a team of eighteen lawyers on this case, all paid top dol-lar. DraftKings' legal fees have risen to more than $1 million a week at times. Compared to that, comping a night at an NBA game is nothing.

"I wish we had zero lawyers, and the world was a little different, but if we have to spend a little more to get in the right place, then okay," Kalish says with a shrug as the Clippers and Kings tip off beneath us.

When I tell him my honest belief that the changes the companies have made to level the playing field (multi-entry limits, slate-wide entry caps, more single-entry, more beginner contests, etc.) are making a dif-ference in fixing a lot of the situations that put them in the crosshairs in the first place, he bristles at the idea that those changes came in response to outside pressure.

"I swear to God, it's a hundred percent true—over half the stuff that people talk about, in terms of regulations, or different protections, are things that we wanted to do," Kalish says.

Well then, the obvious question: why didn't they implement them earlier? If they understood that there were problems, why leave them-selves so open to disaster? And more important, leave the casual players so open to exploitation?

"There's a lot of things at this stage in the industry that are very clear, that are clear with experience, but that it's hard to foresee," Kalish says. "It's not like there's some template you can pull from. You have to figure out what makes sense.

"Like, it doesn't make sense to let somebody take a thousand one-dollar games," Kalish says. "That's some bullshit. It's almost a process of learning that hey, there's actually a guy who wants to take a thousand one-dollar games? That guy's kinda a dick. But they're going to profit by it. Then you realize, oh, that's an exploit."

Makes sense, then, that one of the first steps DraftKings took to address these kind of problems was to limit the number of $1 and $2 games a single player could take to roughly forty.

Expanding on this idea when we revisit the subject later, Kalish says the rapid growth of the industry at the start of the 2015 NFL season pushed a whole new set of ecosystem problems on them in an instant, and they needed to figure out how to deal with them.

"We grew really fast, and adjustments need to be made to the product to deal with the new reality of the company," Kalish says. "We went from hundreds of thousands of users to millions of users very fast—in a month."

When Kalish and I are done talking, we turn to see that most of the other finalist groups have spilled into the suite by now, and even though there's a live basketball game taking place right in front of our eyes, nearly everyone has their backs to the on-court action. Instead, they're focusing on the small, flat-screen television hanging in the rear of the suite, playing the final quarter of the Packers-Cardinals game.

"We came all the way to an NBA arena to watch an NFL game," Underjones says, marveling at the scene.

In the time since I'd last paid attention, Aaron Rodgers and the Packers had come to life. The Packers held a 13–10 lead heading into the fourth quarter, but the Cardinals answered with a Carson Palmer touchdown, and then a field goal to extend their lead to 20–13. Yet now Rodgers and the Packers are driving themselves, reaching midfield, and setting up for a few last-ditch shots at the end zone. A Hail Mary touchdown would tie the game. I ask Underjones how we're doing; he seems a little more buoyant than earlier, but still reserved. He knows the Packers will probably lose, largely ending our chance at real money, even with the second day of the final still to come tomorrow.

"We're alive, I guess, but I'm not getting too excited," Underjones says. "They're at the forty-one-yard line, there's like five seconds left. It should be over."

As I digest this, we look up at the screen as Rodgers takes the snap in the shotgun formation. He backpedals, turning and rolling to his left, stalked by Arizona defenders. As time expires, the quarterback sets his feet and launches a ball high in the air toward the end zone, where receiver Jeff Janis is streaking under it.

All thirty men in the suite, dreaming of millions of dollars, keep their backs to the basketball game and their eyes trained on the television as the ball reaches the peak of its parabola and begins its long journey downward. We let out a collective "ohhhhhhhh" as it comes down, down, down . . . into Janis's hands. He caught it. He caught it!

We explode with a sound that I guarantee was heard on the court itself, jumping up and down, slamming hands on backs and heads alike. I look around to see half the arena staring at our raucous celebration, wondering what the heck we're cheering when the action on the court is so tepid. Even the reserved Underjones is into it, slapping fives and smiling broadly, knowing he's suddenly a candidate for multiple millions, if Rodgers can just win this game in overtime with another touchdown pass.

As OT begins, DandyDon sits in an armchair in front, surrounded by his family, all of us then ringing them in a vast, fingers-crossed circle. Not all of us have our fingers crossed for the same things, however. Both the Underjones crew and the DandyDon posse are rooting for Rodgers and the Packers. Several other groups are cheering on Palmer and the Cardinals. If Rodgers can only pull this off . . . I can't help myself, I start dreaming of $12,000 in my pocket. It may not seem like a massive windfall, but $12,000 would basically mean that this whole DFS enterprise couldn't possibly be a loser. I'd be up close to $10K overall—that's hard to lose, even for me. I'd buy a new suit, maybe, and I'd prove to my wife I wasn't a lousy gambler—or, at least, even if I was, that I'd picked the right friends.

Except then the Packers lose the coin toss. Two passes from Palmer to Larry Fitzgerald later, the Cardinals are winners, and my crazy dreams go poof. DandyDon slams his palms on the chair's armrest, stands up, and storms out of the suite. His family scurry after him, their eyes glued to the floor. I guess that's what losing millions looks like.

We aren't nearly as traumatized. DandyDon had started the day in second place. We'd begun it in sixth, so really, what did we have to lose? Other groups are busy celebrating—the Palmer-to-Fitzgerald score vaults poker pro Aejones into first, ahead of Condia, and some other teams move up as well. Just not us. We turn our attention away from football, collectively noticing that there's a basketball game being played right in front of us. Ooh, and free crudités!

JeffElJefe and I settle into seats in the front of the box to watch a little of the game itself. Jeff is a good person to watch a basketball game with; as a basketball pro, wagering thousands a night, he really knows his stuff. He gives me the full breakdown of everyone on the court, essentially quintupling my NBA knowledge in five minutes, dragging it out of the Kevin Garnett Big Three era and into the days of Steph Curry.

NBA DFS, he explains, is all about what happens in the ten minutes before games tip off. There are late scratches all the time, and the game favors those who can react, employing viable options to replace their departed players. Information is king. NBA regs frantically check Twitter in the half hour before tip-off, desperate for knowledge of who is in and who is out. A few minutes' edge makes all the difference in DFS, so Jeff has a question for me, knowing my background.

"Do you think I could hire a couple reporters, beat writers, to get me information on scratches before everyone else? Like as soon as they might know?" Jeff asks me.

My first reaction is to recoil in horror and lecture him about the in-dependence of journalists, and how we're not simply guns for hire, for sale to whichever professional gambler wants to pay the most. We're there to do a job, a great and noble profession, be the voice of the people and a conduit of impartial information, etc., etc. And that's all true.

But sad as it makes me to think about it, the line is pretty blurry already. As a reporter, I remember realizing that the spike in people de-manding that we post lineups and instantly inform them of scratches via Twitter coincided directly and exactly with the rise of DFS. And most reporters have become incredibly responsive to that demand, rushing to offer this data first. They may not realize exactly who is asking for it—only that they get more Twitter followers by being Johnny-on-the-spot with the lineups and the scratches. But really, who beyond the most in-sane and ardent of fan is going to care forty-five minutes before first pitch that a fourth-outfielder type like Slade Heathcott is now batting ninth and playing right field, instead of the equally unimportant Mason Williams? That's gambling info. We're an integral, if unwitting, part of the long wink-wink-nudge-nudge relationship that continues to exist between the leagues and the gamblers. Not to mention the scores of re-porters I've seen gambling on everything from DFS to baseball to football to horse and dog racing, and certainly on sports they actively cover—or the fears I have that someday an official scorer, usually a job filled by a reporter, could be accused of improperly influencing DFS outcomes on judgment-call events like shots-on-goal, or hits and errors.*

So, no, as I quickly tell Jeff, you can't hire reporters. They wouldn't do it, and they'd probably be fired for being on the payroll of an outside interest—certainly one blatantly using their information to gain an edge in gambling. But I don't feel as high-and-mighty about it as I badly want to be, and as I absolutely would have been not six months ago.

---

* MLB would deal with the Daily Fantasy end of this just before the 2016 baseball sea-son; I obtained a copy of a memo barring all MLB on-staff reporters—not to mention players, umps, staff, almost everyone—from playing DraftKings or FanDuel fantasy baseball for money.

The basketball game wraps up, and I'm honestly not even sure who won. Spoiled brat that I am, neither my heart nor my head is in it. My hockey lineups have lost again, Underjones is going to end up in ninth or tenth, and DFS is even making me feel bad about my long-loved, long-defended profession. I should get my rest, so that we can play out the string on Sunday. Ah, but I'm dumb, so I join the group for a few more drinks at the hotel bar anyway. Sleep when you're dead, right?

On Sunday evening, DraftKings will hand out the biggest prize in the history of fantasy sports, one that rivals any poker tournament, one that offers massive legitimacy to an upstart industry in terms of prize pools and dollars in play. Someone, or more likely a group of someones, is going to get very, very rich.

But it isn't going to be us, so I wake up late.

By the third day of a Daily Fantasy live final, a persistent fatigue has set in, the fallout from the late nights and the blaring sports and the all-day intravenous drip of Miller Lites and Vodka Red Bulls. The voice is hoarse from talking over the music and the high-volume television commentary, the body sore from bruises that seem to have no specific origin. And for most, the adrenaline that constantly pumps through the body at the thought of winning big money has started to fade, leaving a drained shell behind. That's me as we start the third day—really, it's all of Team Underjones. As I arrive at the Conga Room, midway through the first game, only Ilya, one of our quants, is on scene, lonely and forlorn on one of the bright white couches as he watches our only active player, Seattle receiver Doug Baldwin, run routes and snag passes.

"Baldwin's having a pretty good game for us, but it probably won't matter," he reports with a sigh.

Yup. We're probably headed for a seventh- or eighth-place finish, and no money beyond the min-cash payment Underjones had already received for winning the final seat. My dreams of winning are giving way to the reality that I will be lucky to just lose half my small investment.

So I decide to eat my way back to even, settling in to chow down on the Conga Room's spread. Years of training as a baseball writer has honed my ability to locate and dominate any available free food, and the DFS crew are minnows to my ravenous shark when it comes to munching on the plentiful supply of DraftKings shrimp.

The room is quiet, with several of the top players not in attendance yet. There are a few pros about, though. In one corner, Assani Fisher, a bearded, fit, bespectacled former poker pro, is actively hitting on several of the leggy models hired to be there as eye candy. The genial Assani—also his DFS username—had been a middling poker player at best. But in the world of DFS, he's a star. Assani took a $600 deposit and turned it into a half-million-dollar bankroll in a little over a year, and this weekend he's flying high with a 10 percent stake in his pal Aejones, the current leader. If Aejones wins, Assani's bankroll could climb to more than $1 million. Not bad. I'm not sure whether the models know this, or if he's really just that charming, but they sit crowded around him in the back of the room, hanging on his every word.

"It's the same girls at every event," Assani explains, so he's gotten to know them.

The models, the booze, the backslapping, the strip clubs, the gambling, the boxing-style prize belts—hell, even the Ron Jeremy sightings!—it all drives home the sheer maleness of it all, this *Mad Men* time warp where the XY chromosome is still blissfully the center of everything. Outside this bubble, debates rage about sexism and modern feminism and the hatefulness and misogyny of Donald Trump and whether the late David Bowie was a predatory rapist or merely a rock star. Inside the Conga Room, the man is still king, or at least the man-boy. Regular-sized men in ill-fitting sports jerseys watch events featuring other, impossibly large men in tight-fitting uniforms doing gladiatorial things, and we regular types wager dollar bills on the outcome. Typically, almost no women play. If they do, they're laughed off as cute stories like the lady at the FanDuel final who picked her players by how handsome they were.

I'll admit, though, that the number of nonmodel women in this room is actually surprising. Thirty to 40 percent, maybe. None of them contestants, but most of these guys are married or have girlfriends, and unlike a few years ago the WAGs now seem to want to come along—to keep a watchful eye, perhaps? DraftKings has hired a DJ to play thumping hip-hop during commercial breaks and halftime, and the women of Condia's crew delight in getting up for impromptu dance parties, grinding on one another and setting tongues wagging.

Even though his posse is the biggest and loudest, Condia himself is nowhere to be seen. He doesn't have any players in the early game, but I wonder if that's all there is to it. Condia clearly thinks about how he can strike fear in his opponents—hence his longtime scorched-earth tactics for quashing other potential pros. Showing up with the day halfway over, then making a grand entrance at the moment your players all take the field? It's what a Tiger Woods would do, and if anyone in DFS is Tiger, it's Condia.

He's still technically an underdog, however, sitting in third place, behind poker pro Aejones and L.A. slickster Danny1234. A big day by Condia's guys in the late game could vault him into first, but failing that, Aejones will probably hold on and win the $5 million.

Our only player in the early game, Baldwin, delivers a decent 16.2-point performance, which isn't bad on a low-scoring weekend. It is, at least, enough to make me put down the shrimp and pay attention as the weekend's final game, Broncos versus Steelers, kicks off. We have two players active: Broncos running back C. J. Anderson and Steelers wide receiver Martavis Bryant. Both are low-owned, so if the pair explode for big points, we've got the chance to maybe make a little money.

Applause and shouts break out from the other side of the room. Ah, the king has arrived; Condia walks in, greeting his adoring followers. Not bad when people literally cheer as you enter a room.

Beep, too, finally drags himself out of bed and arrives (we do not applaud), resplendent in his usual outfit of T-shirt, sweatpants, and crooked baseball cap. He quickly engages in his favorite pastime: gauging the odds, handicapping our chances of landing the $300,000 fifth-place prize or the $200,000 sixth-place pot.

"I think we've got a five percent shot at fifth place," he muses. "A little higher at sixth, obviously. Maybe fifteen percent, twenty percent."

Turns out that our luck is better than Beep's math. Over the first half of Broncos-Steelers, our players—Bryant, the receiver, and Anderson, the running back—deliver strong performances. Bryant, in particular, eats up yardage, even running a forty-yard reverse play for big points. Everyone else's players? Nothing. Even Beep has to admit that we close halftime with a strong shot at landing either fifth or sixth place, and we soon start to dream even bigger. Ahead of us, in fourth, is RockenRaven. RockenRaven is now standing at all times, his gravelly cheers and chants accompanying every play as he edges closer and closer to the $500,000 fourth prize.

"Hell YEAHHHHHHHHHH" he shouts as he tosses soft, DraftKings-branded footballs around the room, which occasionally bounce off the backs of his unsuspecting receivers. As the third quarter kicks off, we rise out of our seats as well, and when Martavis Bryant hauls in a catch and stretches it for fifty-two yards, we offer a few cheers and chants of our own as a fourth-place finish enters our minds. By now, every member of the ten teams is on his feet, each group packed into its own little fortress of white couches, living and dying with each play. With so much money at stake, the pressure weighs on Underjones and he excuses himself to head outside, saying he feels claustrophobic. Beep, who never, ever watches the games, looks almost as tense.

"Man, it's draining watching sports," he remarks.

Perhaps it's because I've got so little money involved here, but I'm not stressed at all. This is a blast—cheering on football players whom I could hardly have named a few days ago, spitting venom at players owned by other DFS teams, caring not one bit about the final score of the actual game.

With the fourth quarter under way and the Broncos driving downfield, my brain is hard at work trying to calculate my potential payouts. If winning the $5 million first prize would have netted me $12,000 with my paltry 0.25 percent stake, then it stands to reason that landing the $500,000 fourth prize would be worth $1,200. Even I can do that math. And that kind of a win might finally drag me back to near even on the whole DFS experience. Still, we probably aren't going to get fourth place. We're likely too far behind for anything but fifth.

But as Anderson and the Broncos push downfield, a pair of unlikely partners approach with an intriguing business proposition that might get us some of that fourth-place money after all.

In poker tournaments, players at a big-money final table will often forge clandestine agreements to chop up the winnings. Usually media outlets frown on the practice because it undercuts the televised drama of one man winning the mountain of cash, and most are conducted quietly. It seems that Daily Fantasy has borrowed yet another custom from the poker world.

In fourth place, just ahead of us, sits RockenRaven. He shuffles over to us, along with his DFS advisor, a whip-smart, ADHD-addled graduate student—and top DFS shark—named Jeff Gopez, aka 00_Oreo_00. Oreo had met RockenRaven at the football semifinal and helped guide the fortunate amateur through the final process. RockenRaven and Oreo have an offer for us: they want to cut a deal, splitting up the fourth- and fifth-place prizes. I'm immediately wary.

Oreo is, by his own admission, always working an angle, like one of those scrappy street urchins in a newsboy cap romanticized in old movies about New York City. When not playing Daily Fantasy, or working on his chemical engineering PhD, the twenty-eight-year-old is part of a subculture that makes gobs of cash buying goods on the cheap, then reselling them on Amazon. His MO is to try to find deals on improperly priced merchandise or predict which items will blow up around the holiday season.

"I'd find a DVD on sale for ten dollars, and I was able to get a hundred to a thousand copies, and eventually they go back in price to twenty-three dollars," Oreo explains. "After Amazon fees and shipping, on a ten-dollar item I might make five dollars. I would try to project which Christmas items would be the big sellers for that year. My older sister told me to get these dolls that my niece wanted and had to overpay for. They're called Monster High dolls. They're like Barbie dolls, but they're monsters. I bought them for fourteen dollars, resold them for ninety dollars. Not bad."

He's tried to help me out, too, telling me that I was a sucker for not setting up a second DFS account using my wife's information and Boston address, referring it from my original account, and playing under her username so that I could get referral cash from DraftKings and FanDuel. I passed.

"I do so much shady shit," Oreo says during one of our chats, shaking his head.

When he discovered DFS, Oreo quickly found a few new angles no one else had yet thought to exploit. Not only did he realize he could be good and make money right away despite knowing near nothing about sports; he also figured out how to lure the biggest fish to him, after only the first day: with a username guaranteed to sit at the very top of FanDuel's head-to-head lobby. He changed his username to something starting with two zeroes: "00_Oreo_00." Forget bumhunting, the nasty practice of targeting new and inferior players—Oreo had found a situation where the bums hunted him.

"That put me at the top of the FanDuel lobby. Because of that, I've never been the type of person to scoop cash games; I've never bumhunted. I didn't need to. I was at the top of the lobby. I posted my games, people came to me," Oreo says.

Other players tried to follow his "00" convention, one going so far as to create a username that was simply fifteen straight zeroes—"000000000000000." FanDuel quickly banned all the imitators, realizing the exploit at play. Oreo protested, citing the value he'd built in his burgeoning brand, and was allowed to keep his name, eventually becoming known and feared throughout the DFS world.

He built numerous computer scripts to help himself succeed, writing one, for instance, that let him pull his teams out of contests late before he is auto-matched against other dangerous pros. But soon Oreo realized that there was an even bigger business opportunity out there than using scripts for his own play: he founded a company called FantasyCruncher, which brought the kind of advanced DFS tools Saahil built for quickly building mass multi-entry lineups to the common player. It fast became the industry leader.

Now Oreo is coming at us with another of his business proposals. RockenRaven, his charge, is in fourth, looking at $500,000 in winnings. We're in fifth, staring at $300,000. But we're gaining, and the Steelers are driving, and Martavis Bryant is having a helluva game. Some mathematical models might even give us the better chance to claim fourth. So Oreo and RockenRaven are offering to "chop": to split the pot between fourth and fifth. They propose a split of $450,000 to whoever comes in fourth—likely RockenRaven—and $350,000 to the team in fifth.

"This way, everyone wins," Oreo says, giving it the hard sell.

Beep, Ilya, and I stand behind Underjones, acting like the world's least intimidating street gang as the two pros talk it over. Four hundred and fifty thousand is obviously an opening offer, and Underjones treats it as such: no deal, he says, asking for a better percentage to the team that finishes in fifth—likely us. As they haggle, the Denver Broncos keep driving downfield on the screens in front of us. Negotiations are put on hold as we watch to see what unfolds.

"I'm not saying no," Underjones says. "But let's see what happens."

At the goal line, the Broncos try to stuff the ball in time after time, and we're forced to watch in disgust as Peyton Manning hands the ball off to Denver's other running back, Ronnie Hillman, on a pair of red zone carries. Yet Hillman can't get the job done, and the Broncos line up for another shot at goal as we strain our eyes to see which Denver running back is in the backfield.

"Is that Anderson?" I shout.

"I can't tell," says a frantic Underjones.

Manning hands the ball to some Denver running back. The back scampers forward, hurtling into the end zone. We start yelling, demanding a closer view from the cameramen a thousand miles away in Denver. Which player was it?

They pan in to show our guy C. J. Anderson celebrating his touchdown. We exult, jumping all over the white DraftKings couches and marring them with our shoeprints. Who cares? We've got a real shot at fourth place, $500,000. Bill me later.

Moments after the touchdown improved our bargaining position, RockenRaven and Oreo come back to the negotiating table. They're still leading, but now they offer a better split. As Martavis Bryant hauls in another catch, this time for eighteen yards, the deal comes closer to reality: $425,000 for fourth, $375,000 for fifth. There are only minutes left in the game, and the odds are constantly shifting with each play. We do mental math as best we can to determine what the right chop would be.

"I'd be willing to chop, but I don't know what the math is, on the right split," Beep says, his words coming rapid fire. "It's whatever you're comfortable with. I can't do the math on this one now."

Another Bryant catch. For three yards. We're closing in. Now it's clear that either team could win. RockenRaven, breathing hard, says he needs every cent he can get for his children. What if both just took $400,000, no matter who finished ahead? Underjones turns to us, his team of advisors.

Beep says that sounds fair. I agree.

"Take even money," I say, blatantly misusing a blackjack term. What the hell do I know? It's all happening so fast.

They shake hands. The deal is done. Whichever one lands in fourth, it'll be that person's responsibility to pay the other one $100,000, based solely on that handshake.

They walk off to discuss it with others and solidify the details of the chop—RockenRaven, understandably, wants to know about the tax implications. I'm just relieved it's over. For the first time all day, I'm genuinely tense. Having even the slightest hand in negotiating a transaction over that much money has my heart racing. And I'm not the only one. In the front of the room, the Aejones crew—also Martavis Bryant owners—are coming to grips with the fact that they're about to win $5 million. They're whooping it up like mad. Across from them, Condia's group sits, morose, in third place. They're about to win a million dollars—and they're acting like they're headed for last.

Just then, Underjones and RockenRaven return, and the conversation is heated. Something's wrong.

"RockenRaven reneged on the deal," Oreo explains. "He shook his hand on even money. And then they went away to go talk to the DraftKings people. And then when they were explaining it a little bit more, [RockenRaven] said even money wasn't right. RockenRaven wanted the winner to get more money. When I was there, [Beep] was there, you were there, they agreed to even money. They agreed to fifty-fifty, so each of them would get $400K. Then they walked away, after the handshake, and somewhere along the line, RockenRaven was like, this is not what I wanted. This isn't the deal I want."

You've gotta be kidding me. The Steelers are driving downfield. The final two-plus minutes of the game are upon us. Voices are rising, and tempers with them. A broken deal, with this amount of money at stake, is no small thing. Our crew meets, RockenRaven and Oreo only a few feet away, to hash out whether a chop is still the right idea, as the Broncos take the field for the next drive.

Beep is nervous. Mathematically, a deal might still be the right move. But who are we dealing with? All we know about this guy is a few salient facts: He's an admitted ex–heroin addict who was arrested for armed robbery, served three years in jail, and now has apparently turned his life around. He says he has kids with health problems and that he badly needs the money. He's loud. He seems friendly. But most of this is atmospheric, or hearsay. The one thing we do know, for certain? He's already broken one handshake deal.

Underjones is not happy. The former finance man is all business now and the situation is starting to feel a little too tense, a little too keyed up.

The Broncos kick a field goal to extend their lead, and hand the ball to the Steelers with the score 23–13. The Steelers set up for the final drive of the game. Either Bryant will haul in two catches and we'll take fourth place, or he'll go catchless and we'll end up in fifth. The odds still seem to favor RockenRaven. Time is running out to craft a deal.

"What about $415,000–$385,000?" Oreo offers.

It's close enough. The Steelers are about to start their drive. Underjones takes a deep breath, shakes RockenRaven's hand again, and takes the deal. If Bryant goes catchless, at $385,000 he'll end up with $85,000 more than he'd have had otherwise. If Bryant snags two balls? Well then, $415,000 is even nicer, though it's no half million.

Our team stands shoulder to shoulder as we watch. With less than a minute left in the game, the drive begins with quarterback Ben Roethlisberger firing an incomplete pass—but there's a penalty flag, putting the Steelers closer to the end zone. Roethlisberger takes the next snap, cocks, and fires—right to Bryant. Seven yards. Another catch and we'll claim fourth place.

"We just want one more catch," Underjones says. "We don't even want the touchdown. If it goes to overtime, all the teams with Broncos players will probably pass us."

Ask, and ye shall be paid. Roethlisberger drops back, looks in the direction of a racing Bryant, and hits him for twenty-two yards. We break out in a joyful, elaborate man-dance of high-fives and bro hugs as we move into fourth place. The clock winds down as the Steelers settle for a field goal and fail to recover the onside kick. It's over. Five hundred thousand dollars—or, rather, $415,000 now—is ours.

I grab Underjones by both shoulders.

"Dude!" I say, ever the portrait of eloquence.

"I know." He smiles wanly, obviously exhausted, perhaps now regretting making the deal. "I didn't think we had a chance to pull that off."

Our back-of-the-room celebration is nothing compared to what's going on in the front. Aejones is the $5 million winner, and his poker posse is going crazy, leaping all over one another. In the middle of the room, second-place finisher Danny1234's massive gaggle of L.A. bros is slamming into one another in a weird button-down mosh pit, collectively $2 million richer.

Waitstaff bring champagne flutes around the room as we pose for pictures, and the three finalists take to the stage to give speeches. Condia, clearly depressed at his mere $1 million win—he had been the odds-on favorite—congratulates his opposition, and still manages to lead his crew (which we join) to a sushi dinner and then a hot tub party on the roof of the Ritz-Carlton. Danny1234, newly rich, reaches into his now-deep pocket and books a private jet to take his crew to Las Vegas for the night, so they won't be hampered by California's early closing times. The Aejones poker squad begins a long night of celebratory partying.

Fourth place? Not bad, but no one in our group is over the moon like the top three finishers. In the end, because of a series of factors Beep explains but I hardly understand, my take somehow amounts to less than $600, which seems ludicrous in the light of a $415,000 win. But I trust Beep, so that's what it is. Better than nothing—one small step closer to DFS-even, which is only a few thousand away now.

After the speeches conclude, RockenRaven comes by to talk to Underjones, thanking him for making the deal and explaining how much it would help his family. He lays the praise on thick, complimenting Underjones on his win, and on his qualities as a man.

"You seem like a really good guy, a real trustworthy guy, a man of his word," RockenRaven says. The words themselves are kind, but I wonder about the subtext. Are they meant to probe? To intimidate? To menace, in the event that Underjones doesn't honor the deal?

Underjones does pay up, eventually sending RockenRaven $85,000 to honor the arrangement after the tournament concludes. If the roles had been reversed? We'll never know.

"I'm pretty sure RockenRaven would have paid. I'm ninety percent sure. Actually, maybe eighty percent sure," Oreo says. Then he corrects himself again. "My confidence level is maybe eighty-five percent that he would have paid out. He seems like a nice guy—the kind of person who would value his handshake. But you don't know until it comes down to it.

"I don't know." He pauses. "You just never know."

09

A pair of cardboard boxes and a glass door marked with blue construction tape greet me as I pass through the recently completed foyer of FanDuel's midtown Manhattan headquarters. Once inside, I receive a more formal welcome, from FanDuel PR assistant Emily Bass.

"Pardon all that, we're still getting settled," she says, welcoming me into the company's new home, a two-story office in the city's booming Flatiron District.

Bass is one of hundreds of new employees brought on in the mass hirings of the past year, when it still seemed like the company would take over the world. She brings me past the main desk, into an airy, open-floor-plan office filled with men and women in their twenties and thirties quietly working away at computer terminals.

"Can I get you anything?" she asks. "Water? Soda? Beer? We've got a pretty good selection, actually."

I grab a water and an apple.

After many months of observing this world from the outside, I'm finally getting a peek at the inner workings of DFS, as FanDuel has allowed me to spend a few days inside the company, talking with employees and executives and seeing how day-to-day life actually unfolds. It's a rare chance to pull back the curtain, understand these much-maligned companies, and maybe even pick up an insider tip or two on how to play better. I mean, that's what Ethan Haskell was thinking, right?

My guide through much of this is Justine Sacco, FanDuel's director of communications. It's possible that name might mean something to you: Justine was already famous—or infamous—before she came to work at FanDuel full-time, perhaps the most well-known example of a person eaten up by the Internet's outrage industry, and the pervasive culture of public shaming that grew alongside Twitter.

At the end of 2013, the thirty-year-old PR professional was on her way to visit family in South Africa and tossed a few tweets into the ether as she made her way from New York to Cape Town, via London. She tweeted about the BO of a man sitting near her. She tweeted about the English weather. She had only 170 Twitter followers, so it wasn't a surprise when the last tweet she issued before leaving Heathrow didn't register at all at first.

"Going to Africa. Hope I don't get AIDS. Just kidding. I'm white!"

She then turned her phone off for the eleven-hour flight and upon landing found out she had become the most hated person on the Internet.

She insists that she was mocking the bubble that privileged white Americans live in. Whether she was or not, the Internet took it literally, and the tweet spread around the world. The hashtag #HasJustineLandedYet? became a phenomenon all its own as a hungry, out-for-blood Web waited for her to touch down and learn that her job was in jeopardy and that her life was about to change.

There were a few facts that didn't help matters. Sacco is a pretty blonde, and was also a PR professional, working in corporate communications at InterActiveCorp, which made the misstep even more delicious.

Sacco was fired from her job at IAC and went into a deep depression, her life forever altered by the tweet, which she refuses to talk about today. But FanDuel had been a client while at IAC, and after a few jobs in between, she came on as the company's PR director. I've found her to be sharp and highly competent at navigating the full-time maelstrom that is DFS—which isn't the case for all in her position. I often wonder if that's a direct result of having already gone through the worst the Internet has to offer, and coming out the other side.

"There was always going to come a point in time when there were going to be regulatory issues that we were going to have to deal with," she says. "And there were going to be questions of legality. You knew that was something you were going to go through, and you understood. If you're going to be a spokesman for a company, you have to know what's coming down the line.

"It happened at a much quicker pace, and at a much greater magnitude than I had originally expected. But we're here, and we're getting through it."

Nigel Eccles swings in to greet me, all energy and rapid-fire patter. He's coming from an investor meeting, and he's got another one in an hour. Eccles splits his time between the company's office in New York and its outpost in Scotland, and when he's in the States, he tries to cram in as many meetings as possible.

"I'm sorry, it's just crazy around here. How have you been?" he says as we shake hands.

Eccles takes me on a tour of his offices, showing where he sits, out in the bullpen with the rest of his staff. Touring FanDuel, I'm struck by the notion that this office wouldn't be out of place in Silicon Valley. There are young people everywhere, not to mention open floor plans, a lack of executive offices, video games, pop-a-shot, and that steady supply of craft beer as needed. It all calls to mind a tech company, and that's no accident.

Really, that's one of the major disconnects between the public and the DFS companies themselves. The general public sees FanDuel and DraftKings as gambling companies. The companies see themselves as tech start-ups. Yet there are a few key differences between the offices of these two companies and most tech start-ups. The first is color. At DFS companies, it's impossible to escape the one color they care about most: green. That lush, light green of E Pluribus Unum—it's the dominant color in both offices. When I toured DraftKings' Boston office last year, I noted that the green was offset with orange. In FanDuel's new headquarters it's paired with wood.

The other physical feature that sets them apart is the focus on sports: walls are adorned with quotes by Vince Lombardi and Michael Jordan, pictures of various stars, high-priced memorabilia like jerseys and signed balls. Eccles guides us toward conference rooms named for prominent sportsmen. We sit down in the Mario Lemieux room; he pronounces it Lee-muh, as if the former Pittsburgh Penguins star and current co-owner were the capital city of Peru.

Both companies have rapidly expanded their offices in recent years to account for their spectacular growth. FanDuel's staff grew nearly fivefold in less than two years. DraftKings did much the same. As it grew, FanDuel consolidated its two small New York offices into this new one, kept its Edinburgh site, and added outposts in Glasgow, Los Angeles, and Orlando. DraftKings expanded by chomping up whole new floors in its Summer Street office building in Boston, and added a London office.

"We're at four hundred people today, overall," Eccles says. "A year and a half ago, we were at eighty people. It's been explosive growth. Every day it's like, here are ten new people. Welcome."

Since the Haskell scandal, however, FanDuel has shrunk somewhat, laying off several dozen employees at an Orlando office it acquired to work on mobile gaming. The New York office is full and lively, though, and remains so all day and largely all night. Because games start at all times, from soccer in Eastern Europe to baseball on the West Coast, these are truly around-the-clock operations. There are divisions managing customer service, marketing, brand relationships, event planning, technology engineering—all the hallmarks of a modern start-up. There are also VIP relationship officers—the equivalent of brick-and-mortar casino hosts—whose job it is to cater to the big-time players and make sure their needs are met.

But it's the work on DFS itself that defines these companies, and as Cal Spears says, that puzzle renews itself every day. In both DraftKings and FanDuel, it comes in the pricing of players and the setting, sizing, and pricing of contests.

Pricing players is fairly straightforward. The companies try to make sure that users can pick a few stars, but not build all-star teams; tough decisions should be a daily occurrence. Pricing is manipulated to encourage users to pick different players. Hot streaks drive prices up, cold patches drive them down. It's all based on a computer algorithm, with human tweaks coming after—and the algorithm itself is fairly straightforward.

"When you say an algorithm, people think of *Good Will Hunting* shit on a wall. It's not nearly as complicated," a FanDuel staffer says.

That said, while not necessarily complex, player pricing is at the very foundation of the game and determines how skillful it is. A high-level DraftKings employee told me that they could make the game more or less skillful by adjusting player pricing; keeping the pricing tighter reduces the number of bargains, and that dulls the edge of the best players, who rely on those bargains to win.

Building the contests themselves is less straightforward, a more intricate and complicated daily dance. It's also one that at times has created an arms race between DraftKings and FanDuel, with each one trying to force the other into money-losing situations.

It all comes down to what the industry calls overlay. According to UIGEA, the companies must lock in the sizing and pricing of tournaments before they begin. If larger, guaranteed contests don't fill, the companies are on the hook for the difference. For instance, let's say the companies announce a one hundred–person tournament with a $100 buy-in, and prizes of $5,000 to first, $3,000 to second, $1,000 to third, and they take the remainder as the "rake," or the fees they use to make money. The problems start for the companies when the tournament attracts only eighty entrants. The same prizes must still be paid out. But now the company is losing money on this contest; it must give out $9,000 in prizes, after taking in only $8,000 in entry fees. That extra $1,000 is the overlay.

Build contests that are too large and you lose money to overlay. Size them too small and they will fill too early; you've left money on the table. Being a successful DFS company means finding the correct balance and predicting the demand that will exist on a given day. At FanDuel, that falls to the revenue team, composed of close to fifteen people, many of them math whizzes, and just as many former DFS players. That's not surprising; working in these situations was alluring for potential employees. It made them better at understanding the concepts that would let them win when playing DFS on competitor sites. That led to the rise of players/employees like Boccio and Haskell, who then got the companies in trouble.

"One of the main draws of why the people we would hire were current—now former—players, was that they were like, 'Oh wait, I can get a shitty paycheck, but my job is to help me do everything I want to do anyway.' It attracted that. It wasn't like we went out and looked for active players to work here. It was a natural fit," says one FanDuel higher-up.

When building contests, FanDuel uses statistical modeling to look at similar days from past years, then projects current growth and user engagement from that baseline. They then analyze the actual matchups and upcoming games themselves to see if they will draw interest. Next, they weigh abnormal factors—holidays, for instance. The Fourth of July wreaks havoc with projection models, as do lesser holidays like Presidents' Day or Thanksgiving. Valentine's Day doesn't actually change DFS engagement too much.

Finally, a human being will go through the computer's results and make tweaks. FanDuel staffers show me screens where, through the day, red and green bars with percentage numbers track how quickly contests are filling, and project how close they will come to maxing out. If a contest isn't going to fill, the company can either offer promotions, send reminder emails, or bump certain contests up in prominence on the site in order to encourage users to join. If a contest fills too early, they'll often post another, a "special," hoping to capitalize. But late specials almost never generate the proper demand and are often prime candidates for money-losing overlay themselves.

DFS companies sometimes plan for overlay to try to bring in users, a strategy DraftKings in particular pushes early in the NFL season to promote growth. But generally, they hate when their own contests overlay—and love when the other company suffers from it. And because they control so much of a limited market, the rivals can actually push one another into overlay conditions, by when and how they size their own contests.

Much of it comes down to when the contests are released; whoever releases their contests second can exploit either the aggressiveness or conservatism of their competitor. For a long time, FanDuel employees gripe, they believe DraftKings simply copied their contest sizing and pricing. FanDuel employees tell stories of waiting up all night to release that day's contests as late as possible, forcing DraftKings to either wait indefinitely or post first. A DraftKings employee acknowledged that when they were trying to size contests, it was not uncommon for a company founder to enter the room, ask what FanDuel's contest size was, and simply tell them to size their own contests larger.

It all culminated in what the companies call "Red Tuesday," in the fall of 2015. It was September 14, the Tuesday after the first Sunday of NFL season, the biggest and most highly promoted day in DFS history. Both companies wanted to capitalize on the momentum and push new NFL users into also playing the final month of the baseball season.

"So, we were planning on launching a contest," a FanDuel employee says. "DraftKings came out first, and they [sized it at] $1.5 million. It became the prisoner's dilemma. Where you go, well, we could just size conservatively. And they'll fill, and they'll get their $1.5 million. Or, you could size ours at $1.5 million, and no one will make any money. We'll both lose. And we chose the latter. And boy, does that data point stick out on the chart."

The contests didn't come close to filling. I remember it well—I told everyone I knew playing DFS to get entries in, and upped my own as well. Then I watched from Tropicana Field as the Yankees played the Tampa Bay Rays and I actually made a little money. Both DraftKings and FanDuel, however, lost hundreds of thousands on those contests alone. That, and the Haskell scandal, largely ended the overlay wars.

Post-Haskell, the companies have mostly been too busy trying to survive to fight silly battles over market share with one another. Instead, much of their energy is now put to use on two fronts: to address what I believe is well-deserved criticism, like that in Jay Caspian Kang's widely circulated *New York Times* article, that their ecosystem is unfairly tilted to give the top players too much of an advantage; and to address what I see as less valid charges that the games are rigged, or not on the level.

To counter the first argument, both companies introduced widespread changes to the number of entries each player could have per contest, and across their sites as a whole. The main thrust of the criticism was that top players like Saahil were able to be everywhere at once: they could enter literally thousands of games on every level from $1 to $10,000 with virtually no restrictions, and they could also enter large-format tournaments and double-ups with hundreds of entries. Eccles said it was important to address these concerns, though he maintained that FanDuel was never in the business of trying to appease the sharks.

"Is there danger that the game is tilted towards the best players? Unfairly? That's something we've spent a lot of time worrying about, and considering," Eccles muses. "We built our business on casual players. We've always focused on being the most mass-market product. The accusation that we've been out trying to cater to the sharks is just completely untrue."

But the reality has long been that any whiff of changes to level the playing field used to arouse the fury of the top pros. For a long time, the companies allowed these top players to hold sway, because their business was so important to keep; if one site blunted the pro edge, the pros and the massive revenue generated by their entry fees might run to the other site. As the sites grew, the biggest pros came to wield enormous power, and it's not hard to see why. At his peak, Condia could often account for half of the total action on several smaller DFS sites, Saahil said. Piss him off, send him to your competitor, and it could be a death blow for your tiny but growing site.

There were other reasons as well to cater to the pros. People like me rail against them, but the harsh reality is that the Saahils and Condias of the world are exactly who generate the rake that keeps the prize pools as big as they are. For a long time, that's what DFS users gravitated toward: the biggest prizes. It's what fueled the rise of DraftKings, it's what brought over the poker crowd, it's what made regular people sit up and take notice when million-dollar payouts became a regular phenomenon in 2014 and 2015.

But there's a tipping point there. As the high-volume pros became more and more effective and lethal, as more new players flooded into DFS, and as the companies became large enough that they were no longer as beholden to the big pros and their big fees, it became clear that something needed to change in order to preserve the ecosystem and protect the smaller players. But until the Haskell scandal, I believe the sites were too concerned with losing high-volume pros to really make big changes. Once the scandal occurred, the companies acted—they had to, as some inside the companies now admit.

"For a long time, [the pros] were so vocal," says a top employee at one of the two major sites. "Now, we have much more of a pedestal to be like, come on. Come on. Before, we were still growing, and you might pander a little bit to it. Now it's like, guys, look what's happening here."

The changes began with FanDuel raising the number of single-entry contests, which are seen as fairer outside the community, and introducing some limits on total number of entries. In late spring, FanDuel would go further, significantly limiting the number of head-to-head games players could enter.

DraftKings introduced a number of three-entry-max contests—which I love—and limited tournament multi-entry sizes to 3 percent of the total field. They later introduced many more restrictions that went a long way toward making the contests much fairer.

Both companies have long trumpeted the fact that they offer beginner contests restricted only to new players. But to me, beginner contests are mostly a joke and don't go nearly far enough. Both companies long offered fifty beginner games per sport; those could be wiped out on the first night, following an otherwise intelligent strategy of entering twenty $1 and twenty $2 head-to-heads, and a few $3 tournaments. Suddenly it's day two, you've invested $50, and you're now forced to swim with the sharks. But beyond that, I've found that the changes the sites have made are sincere efforts to create a more balanced game, and they've made a significant difference.

The other charge they needed to fight was the contention that the games were literally not on the level, that either there was "insider trading" going on by employees of the companies or that players were using computer programs—commonly called scripting—to skirt or ignore the rules and gain an unfair edge.

They took care of the first issue relatively easily—though far too late—by banning employee play on competitor sites. Usernames and identities of DFS employees are now circulated among the sites. And if employees are found to be using opponent sites or playing through relatives' or friends' accounts, they're out of a job.

Eccles looks at his failure to ban employee play as one of his biggest mistakes—it was something he simply didn't think about until it was too late. It was part of an era when the companies were growing so fast that they hadn't realized they needed to adopt entirely new sets of standards. He now looks back on the hilarious HBO piece featuring Seth Rogen and John Oliver as a wake-up call.

"When John Oliver did the takedown on us, my reaction was, wait a minute, that's really unfair," Eccles says. "They do takedowns of big companies, like FIFA. The people who can't defend themselves. And then I thought, oh, wait a second—we are those guys. That's the thing. We thought we were the little guys. And then I realized, we're not. We're just not the little guys anymore. We raised $300 million. People don't think of us like that. To be honest, when I watched that show, that was the point where I was like, okay, that's where we went wrong.

"So yes, absolutely, I would like to go back, and there's a point where we could have spotted it. There should have been a point where we said, look, we're now a really big business, we should ban employees from playing on any site," Eccles says.

Now that employees are prohibited from playing mass-market DFS, they play internal tournaments against other employees, in fiercely contested company games.

The issue of scripting, however, remains an ongoing debate among the sites, the casual players, and the serious regs and pros. Scripting is seen by some as maximizing the tools at one's disposal, and by others as flat-out cheating.

At its most basic, scripting is writing computer code to make the site itself—meaning FanDuel or DraftKings—do what you want it to do. The site lacks a feature you want, whether that's making last-minute lineup changes en masse or providing the won-loss records of all your opponents? Then write a program that changes the way your computer interacts with the site, Kobayashi Maru–style.

"The three biggest leverage points you can get from scripting is first, mass entering into overlay [situations] without ever having to pay attention. The second is mass-editing a lineup when there's an injury. And third is to understand [opponent] player performance—if I could write a script that could download a CSV of how everybody placed at the end of a contest, I could start aggregating who's good and who's not, and use it to target people in head-to-heads," says a high-level DFS employee who works to try to crack down on scripting, banning players for weeks or months at a time if they break the rules.

After I left FanDuel, I got back in touch with DFS shark Oreo, who had brokered the deal between Underjones and RockenRaven at the DraftKings football final. As mentioned earlier, Oreo, who long made use of scripts to gain an edge, built the website FantasyCruncher to bring pro-style DFS tools to the masses. He walked me through how he built and used scripts that allowed him to alter the way FanDuel operates.

"The scripts that I used were run in JavaScript, directly on my Chrome browser," Oreo says. "They weren't very complicated. They were maybe a hundred words or less, that would do something automatic. The kind of scripts that I used before scripts were known about—so, I had a script that was maybe thirty words, that quickly canceled all my unmatched contests. This was important for me, playing head-to-heads, because FanDuel had auto-matching of head-to-heads right around lock. So I'd end up playing all the other regs."

I remember that, it's what CSURAM was apologizing to that other pro about—failing to cancel contests—when we were at the FanDuel NFL final. Oreo says running a script for that is something of a victimless crime.

"Some people would say it's cheating, but I don't think anyone would really complain about it besides FanDuel," he says.

Other types of scripts are far more nefarious. Even among the pros, there is a vast range of opinions on what kind of scripting is too much, which scripts are truly dangerous, and where the line is drawn. Many, for instance, believe scripts that allow mass lineup changes are acceptable, but find "crawlers," which gobble up the games of lousy new players posting in the lobby, and "scrapers," which collate data at the end of contests, to be predatory and going too far.

"Those are the kind of scripts that people didn't like, that they weren't sure if they existed, but they do—for instance, like a script that allows one to locate, and buy up games against, new players in the FanDuel lobby," Oreo says.

"Or a script that allows you to keep and maintain a database of player performances. There were a few sites that popped up—like FanDuel fish finder, which would tell you the win rates of cash players. You could combine that kind of thing with your head-to-head finder. I didn't need to do that, so I never wrote anything like that, but I know for a fact that these things existed."

The scripting issue lurked in the background for years but finally came to light when Saahil, then known as MaxDalury, used scripting to his great advantage in March 2015, in what became known as the Channing Frye incident. That day, late-breaking news informed NBA DFS players that Orlando Magic forward Nikola Vucevic would be out, and Frye would be taking his place. This torpedoed the lineups of many players, especially those who would suddenly need to adjust multiple entries. Saahil, who had four hundred in play, shouldn't have been able to react in time. But he had built a script that allowed him to swap Frye instantly into hundreds of lineups. Frye helped him win massively that day, landing across the top of leaderboards for hundreds of thousands in winnings. (When I asked him about how he used scripting to swap in Frye, he said, "allegedly used" with a wan smile.)

That kind of scripting was a violation of the sites' terms of use. But instead of cracking down, the sites initially responded to the uproar by changing their rules, in favor of the high-volume players. DraftKings permitted certain types of scripts, while FanDuel allowed users to submit scripts for approval. That prompted additional criticism that the sites were catering to the power users at the expense of the little guy, allowing dedicated players to essentially create their own versions of the sites while everyone else played a different—and less efficient—game.

After months of negative press following the Haskell scandal, however, the sites were spurred into action. In January and February of 2016, both DraftKings and FanDuel finally banned all outside, automated scripts and vowed to crack down on any cases of malfeasance. Since then the sites have introduced their own versions of some of these scripts, making their features accessible to all players, and that has solved some of the problems.

The vast majority of scripting behaviors are banned, but that hasn't stopped users from trying to find new ways to win; having finally crafted and decided to enforce a tough set of rules, the sites are now engaged in an arms race to try to stay ahead of cheaters. At FanDuel, an engineering team spends parts of its days monitoring pace of mouse clicks, to determine if a user is a human or a machine. And they also try to look at instances of mass late entry into high-overlay, free-entry contests—where there is limited upside to entering—to see if users are deploying overlay-seeking scripts, for instance. At DraftKings, cofounder Matt Kalish says they are far better than a year ago at catching scripting cheaters, and are now dedicating significant resources toward combating them.

"Even if you can't be completely perfect, that's not an excuse to do nothing. You still need to establish the behaviors that are appropriate, you need to establish the rules, and then you need to do everything in your power to enforce against the rules that you have," Kalish says.

But in the end, they admit they can't stop all, or even much, of the dedicated scripting; Oreo says there's no question many still use barred scripts, and that for the sites it will always be a losing battle.

"The stuff that I wrote, the only way to detect it is by looking at my click frequency," he says. "But that's something I could easily write into the code. I could slow it down to one click every ten to fifteen seconds, so it seems human. There's really no way for FanDuel to detect a skilled script or a more complicated, advanced script.

"I could still use my cancellation script," he continued. "I don't post head-to-heads anymore, but the script still works, and if I used it, I'm pretty sure FanDuel couldn't stop me."

10

In the world of traveling sportswriters, nothing matters more than status.

Not one's reputation as a writer, mind you—that kind of status only gets you so far.

No, the most important thing is *elite* status—the kind that hotels and airlines award to their most valued customers. Hotel status means room upgrades, lounge access, more points for booking future vacations, free Wi-Fi, and many other perks. Most writers are steadfastly loyal to Marriott hotels because their program best marries strong rewards with the ubiquity of their various hotel brands. Starwood is a close second, however—I always thought their hotels were better, though there weren't as many options in each city.

Airline status is even more critical. With airlines shoving fliers into smaller, tighter seats and planes booked to capacity, status is the only thing that makes frequent flying bearable. Lower-status tiers get free bags, access to slightly improved seats, and sometimes the ability to cut security lines. Higher tiers offer the Holy Grail: first-class upgrades.

I've pulled all manner of loopy tricks in order to reach higher-status tiers. Once, when I was just a few thousand miles away from reaching Platinum status (seventy-five thousand miles flown in one year) on Delta with January nearing, I called a Delta agent and asked her to find me the closest destination that would let me reach Platinum. She said I could fly from New York to either Phoenix—or Las Vegas. Well, that's the ultimate no-brainer. I bought a ticket, flew to Vegas, spent one night there (on Marriott points, of course), saw Carrot Top, walked out halfway through, lost $100 at blackjack, had too many drinks, missed my morning flight, and got to Washington, D.C., for a wedding midway through the cocktail hour. Still, Platinum status achieved! The only person I knew with higher status was Mariners and Yankees outfielder Ichiro Suzuki— he was a Diamond member, thanks to all those trips to Japan. A travel geek himself, he was suitably impressed by my achievement.

There's one thing, however, that airline status still doesn't get you, and it's infuriating: free Internet. You could be ruby-emerald-adamantium status and you'd still have to pay the absolutely exorbitant rates. Need a half hour online? That'll be $20. Want the whole flight? Fifty dollars, or even more, on a cross-country. It's highway robbery. When I was still on staff at the *Wall Street Journal*, I was able to charge the company for airplane Internet when I needed it for work. But now that I'm footing the bill myself, and still losing a little money at DFS to boot, it seems like an expense to avoid.

This January morning, I'm putting that Platinum status to work skipping the check-in and security lines at Los Angeles International Airport, on my way from the DraftKings football final to the Fantasy Sports Trade Association conference in Dallas. Dallas Mavericks owner Mark Cuban will be the conference's keynote speaker, and his address is highly anticipated—he'll be one of the most prominent voices to date to weigh in on DFS.

My mind isn't zeroed in on the conference yet, though, as I'm occupied with another problem: I won't be able to play DFS today, because I'll be in the air. I *could* buy the stupid airplane Internet and draft lineups as I fly—if I win, that more than pays for the cost of Internet. But that's not exactly a foolproof plan. The smart part of my brain points out that this sounds like something a gambling addict would think. Do I really need to spend $30 just to hastily draft some mediocre lineups? Besides, that's like letting the airlines win. Chastened, I listen to the conservative, responsible side, though it's a closer call than I'd like to admit.

There's no time to ponder my weakness, however, because it seems DFS has gone too long without a crisis. My phone suddenly starts buzzing.

"Did you see the Texas AG opinion??" says the first text.

Texas, of all places, has become the latest state to drop the hammer on DFS, on the very eve of the industry's centerpiece conference. A conference that, mind you, had been moved from Las Vegas to Dallas after Nevada declared DFS to be gambling and mandated licensure, effectively forcing the industry out of the state. Give Texas attorney general Ken Paxton credit; the man's got a sense of timing.

Paxton has issued an opinion establishing his stance that DFS is illegal gambling. He isn't going as far as Schneiderman had in New York—he's not actually issuing cease-and-desist letters. He's merely offering his take that DFS is illegal in Texas, and that if anyone challenges its status under Texas law, Paxton expects the courts to agree.

"Odds are favorable that a court would conclude that participation in daily fantasy sports leagues is illegal gambling," he wrote, "Paid daily 'fantasy sports' operators claim they can legally operate as an unregulated house, but none of their arguments square with existing Texas law. Simply put, it is prohibited gambling in Texas if you bet on the performance of a participant in a sporting event and the house takes a cut."

It's more than a half measure, though still not the Full Schneiderman. The furious responses begin pouring in from DFS Twitter, most in the vein of this gem from Al_Smizzle: "Texas, where it's legal to carry a gun on the street but not an iPhone with a DraftKings app."

Mark Cuban himself wades into the fray, firing off a series of angry tweets slamming Paxton as antibusiness and essentially clueless. For my part, I'm just glad I didn't preorder that airplane Internet—depending on how the companies respond to Paxton's declaration, DFS might be dead in Texas by the time I touch down, and I wouldn't be able to tweak or edit my lineups once I land. An even worse thought crosses my mind—I'm going to be unable to play for the entire FSTA conference. Ugh. Three days, cold turkey. I'm not sure I can handle it.

———————

The Fantasy Sports Trade Association traces its roots to fighting the first real government effort to classify fantasy sports as gambling, fending off Senator John Kyl's efforts in the late 1990s.

Now, almost two decades after its birth, the FSTA is the undisputed central authority for the fantasy sports industry, and its semiannual conferences are major events, a fantasy nerd's paradise of socializing, networking, and pitching new products. Many of the newest trends in the fantasy industry have come through the FSTA's "Elevator Pitch" sessions, where new companies get a few minutes to make their case for support and funding. FanDuel was once one of these hopefuls, Nigel Eccles up onstage pitching for a bit of the time and money of FSTA members.

That was no easy sell; fantasy sports had its own well-established culture by then, with its own stars and castes and cliques. In *Fantasyland,* my old *Wall Street Journal* boss, Sam Walker, spent a year among them, going inside the ultracompetitive fantasy baseball league Tout Wars. In the book, which Eccles said helped guide him as he was delving into fantasy, Walker describes the experts of the elite season-long fantasy world as "baseball's lunatic fringe." Those top players were the older fantasy gurus who had grown the industry from the start, and were dominant in the era when fantasy was only beginning to take over the lives of mainstream sports fans. The big names—otherwise average guys like Matthew Berry, Lawr Michaels, Larry Schechter—became celebrities in this odd little world, and the FSTA conference was their annual chance to get together and strut like the fantasy peacocks they were.

At FSTA conferences of old, the centerpiece event was the Fantasy Baseball Expert League draft, when the best of the best would congregate in a room and draft teams a full three months before opening day. This drew major crowds, as onlookers watched these geek gods make their picks.

Compared to them, the Daily Fantasy people were the weirdos, the lunatic fringe of the lunatic fringe. StarStreet founder Jeremy Levine remembers the 2011 convention, when he and the other Daily Fantasy upstarts assembled in a box at a San Francisco Giants game, bonding over how no one even at FSTA really understood what the heck they did.

"In 2011, there were five of us. That was the extent of the Daily Fantasy guys. And no one knew what Daily Fantasy was, even here," Levine says.

Those who did take an interest were wary of DFS, seeing the obvious gambling parallels. Mainstream fantasy had fought long and hard for acceptance. The lions of season-long weren't about to let their empire be jeopardized by a new and legally risky product.

"It took a while to explain," Levine says. "People saw us as threatening, and didn't understand it."

Now FanDuel and DraftKings *are* the FSTA. There has been a dramatic shift in the FSTA's outlook, mission, and role over the past few years, as it has gone from keeping Daily Fantasy at arm's length, to embracing it wholeheartedly. The reason is money, of course. Once it became apparent how much venture capital was flowing into Daily Fantasy by 2013, the piles of money were soon irresistible to fantasy industry pros who had long been grateful that they could eke out a living in fantasy sports at all. Now Daily Fantasy was promising to make them rich, and everybody wanted a piece of the pie.

"It seemed to happen all at once, too," Levine says. "It's only the last two conferences where everyone seemed to say, shit, we've got to figure this out, we've got to get on board with this."

That means the FSTA has become the lobbying arm of DraftKings and FanDuel, waging their fight for legitimacy in statehouses across America. Once Schneiderman et al came after DFS in earnest starting in November, the DFS industry responded by planning and executing a massive campaign to explicitly legalize DFS state by state.

This state-level strategy is both a tacit admission that UIGEA might not universally protect them as they'd hoped, and an acknowledgment of the harsh reality that DFS cases waged in the courts are likely to be losers. All the David Boieses in the world can't save FanDuel and DraftKings from laws that could brand them as illegal gambling in roughly half the states.

"We can't stand by and do nothing," FSTA president Paul Charchian announces in a bellicose address to open the Texas conference. "It's going to be fifty small battles. It's not going to be one big battle . . . is it a tumultuous time in the community? Yes it is. Bring it on."

After years of hoping that self-regulation, à la the video game industry, might work, the DFS industry has recognized that it's grown so big, and eroded the public trust to such a degree, that the only solution is to pass regulatory bills in as many states as possible before legislative sessions end in the summer of 2016. Three days after Schneiderman issued his cease-and-desist orders in November, Eccles, Robins, and their advisors met at the New York offices of law firm Orrick, Herrington & Sutcliffe. They engaged the firm to lead a massive and aggressive campaign to pass DFS bills in any threatened state, jointly funded by the two companies at tremendous cost.

Martino, the venture capital investor, recalls that the strategy was to make sure they didn't lose so many states that the payment processors, like Vantiv (which handles Visa and MasterCard charges) and PayPal, got spooked—which is what crushed online poker.

"It wasn't even that the federal legislation had us concerned, or even the state actions—it was all the payment processors. We've got to go win enough states that the payment processors don't go away. Those were the marching orders through the end of '15.

"Once we got comfortable with that, it was, okay, it's a fifty-state Whac-A-Mole now," Martino says. "It's going to be expensive and time-consuming, but we're not going anywhere, and we know what we need to do."

In the few months since that meeting, bills to legalize and regulate DFS have been introduced in more than thirty states, most of them backed by the FSTA and, by extension, DraftKings and FanDuel. It represents a sudden and stunning onslaught by an industry that to date had largely stayed out of the legislative game.

"This is an industry that's going from being an unregulated industry to an industry that will have clear laws, and be regulated in forty-five states within three years," Eccles says.

According to my pals at the *Wall Street Journal,* the FSTA lobbying effort involves "78 lobbyists in 34 states, up from four lobbyists a year ago, according to a person familiar with the matter. The companies are spending between $5 million and $10 million on the lobbying effort this year and are hoping to pass bills exempting fantasy sports from state gambling laws in at least six to eight states." The lobbying team would eventually top one hundred, and surpass $10 million.

Chris Grove, of Legal Sports Report, was taken aback by the unprecedented scope of the push, he told the *Journal.*

"This legislative rush in the first few weeks of the new year is unlike any on gambling that I've seen," Grove said.

What that means for the FSTA and its signature conference is that in addition to the fantasy players and businessmen, there are now huge contingents of lobbyists on scene, seeking to understand the industry they're now tasked with protecting. At the welcome party on the conference's first night, I meet Derek Hein, a DraftKings lobbyist who says that he was the sole DFS lobbyist present at the 2015 FSTA winter conference, and he felt so out of place he wasn't sure what to do with himself. A year later, he says there are about twenty lobbyists on hand for DraftKings alone, many of them from the Texas area.

One of these is a Texas lobbying veteran, familiar with the ins and outs of the state's politics, who is advising Eccles on whether to go to court and preemptively sue Texas attorney general Paxton.

"Paxton doesn't really want to go after this," the lobbyist says. "He's just got three or four big donors, real antigambling types, who are up in arms about it. So he had to placate them by doing something. But now that he's done that, he's not going to go further. [FanDuel] should let this lie—going to court is taking this down a dangerous path."

At the welcome party, Eccles tells me he still hasn't decided what he wants to do. Court action is a big step, of course, but Texas is home to 5 percent of all DFS customers, and losing it would be a major blow. He also has to weigh what DraftKings, always the more aggressive company, wants to do. Divergent legal strategies are a recipe for disaster.

Conversations about legality and lobbying and money are going on all around us in the crowded bar, where the average age is probably just under thirty. Not far away, in a brown-paneled conference room, the older men of the season-long community are still finishing the Fantasy Baseball Experts League draft. They've never seemed more like dinosaurs, trying to conduct a season-long fantasy draft while attorneys general are taking aim and the deep-pocketed upstarts at DraftKings and FanDuel are nearby feverishly planning their responses.

Understandably, not everyone loves the direction that fantasy sports, and specifically the FSTA, have taken since the DFS boom. Ron Shandler is a legendary figure in the fantasy community. In 1986, he started publishing the *Baseball Forecaster,* one of the first works to apply sabermetric analysis to fantasy baseball, and he later created Baseball HQ, an early and important website that brought the same analysis to the Internet. He was the founder, in 1997, of the famed Tout Wars league that Sam Walker dove into, and he is revered in fantasy circles as one of the industry's great players and voices.

At one point I spot Shandler, and we get to talking. It's clear Shandler is no fan of what DFS has done to his world.

"I've kept my distance [from DFS]. But the money was just so big that people wanted to get on the bandwagon. They wanted a piece of it," Shandler says. "There was so much money, oh my God there's just so much money."

Once daily began to boom, Shandler feared that it would put his season-long fantasy business in jeopardy.

"My gut reaction from the very beginning was, not only is this gambling, but this is dangerous. Eventually someone is going to recognize this for what it is, and it's going to put me in danger. And that was prophetic," Shandler says.

He was right, as he and his friends in the season-long world have been dragged into the battle over Daily Fantasy after all.

The FSTA's strategy has been to lump DFS and season-long fantasy together, and to tell its members and supporters that both are under siege. This is, to me, disingenuous at best, and a self-fulfilling prophecy at worst. At every turn, DFS opponents like New York's Schneiderman have made clear that they are specifically not going after season-long fantasy. But the FSTA has chosen to play the game that all of fantasy is under attack and could be banned if the various DFS foes get their way.

"Essentially, they are the same game," FSTA chairman Peter Schoenke argued to me. "The time frame is shorter. When you look at the risk of what's out there in the legal landscape over the past year, we've seen a lot of places that have treated them the same. Like, in Texas, the attorney general was very clear that any fantasy game of any kind that takes money is gambling."

There may be a reason to make this argument—it is, as David Boies pointed out in court, hard to separate season-long with cash prizes from daily, in a legal sense. In a practical sense, though, it makes it more likely that season-long really will be threatened, given that lawmakers already hardly understand the difference. Whenever the FSTA is asked how many people play Daily Fantasy in a given state, for instance, they nearly always offer up the number of total fantasy players—touting a figure of more than two million players in Texas for instance—when the DFS user base is usually only 10 percent of that.

"The problem is that DFS is both skill and gambling. It's a hybrid," Shandler says. "And nobody knows how to deal with it, as a hybrid. So it's better to pick one battle and fight it, rather than try to fight two different battles. The battle they've picked is that it's all fantasy. It's all the same, we've got to sell fantasy. That's troubling, because they're putting full-season up as a shield, and that's worrisome. Because if we lose, we lose everything."

The season-long fantasy companies aren't the only ones along for the ride, pulled wherever DraftKings and FanDuel take them. Smaller Daily Fantasy sites, like StarStreet founder Jeremy Levine's new venture, Draft, are swept up in their wake, too. Usually, when DraftKings and FanDuel decide to fight a legal battle to stay in a state like Texas or New York, the little companies pull out regardless, because they lack the funds to join the fight in court. More than that, they are essentially compelled to leave because their payment processors demand it. Payment processors are the grease that makes the DFS industry function. If they refuse to offer their services, a fantasy company is DOA. And they are famously risk-averse, largely because of their history with online poker. When the government wanted to crush the poker industry, via UIGEA, it went after the payment processors, their financial lifeline. Remembering that well, Vantiv tried to stop serving DraftKings customers in New York following Schneiderman's cease-and-desist order. The company continued serving the state only because DraftKings took it to court to force it to continue processing transactions. Smaller companies don't have that kind of weight.

With Attorney General Paxton's opinion now on the books, Levine is counting the minutes until the call comes from his payment processors telling him he's out of business in Texas. DraftKings and FanDuel have decided to keep operating in the state for now. Not everybody is that lucky.

"We haven't gotten it yet, but I'm expecting that'll come by the end of the day, today. We got it in Illinois. We got it in Vermont. Vermont, Illinois, Nevada, New York, and now Texas," Levine says. "It hurts."

Other smaller DFS companies are feeling the pressure, too. I'm introduced to brothers Trent and Bryan Frisina, who, with their father, Tom, founded current top-four DFS site FantasyAces. Far, far behind DraftKings and FanDuel in traffic, FantasyAces occupies the top of the next tier, alongside DraftDay, FantasyFeud, and venerable old Yahoo! I've heard they have a good product, and as a family-owned company, they're something of a different player in the DFS space. Chitchatting,

I let them know that I was playing hockey DFS pretty heavily, and they encourage me to sign up for their site.

"It's custom-built by Boggslite"—a username I knew as a strong hockey DFSer and tout—"and it combines the best parts of DraftKings and FanDuel's hockey product," Bryan tells me. He also pumps their deposit bonus, telling me it pays out at a much faster clip than the slow, painful, widely despised programs offered by DraftKings and FanDuel.

"What's the maximum the site matches?" I ask.

Two hundred and fifty dollars, he tells me. Well, usually. That's the limit for the common people, apparently. Not for me. "We'll match however much you want to put in," he says.

Ah. So that's how that works. I put in $500. More money likely to go down the drain in the name of research.

I'm hardly going to stem the tide of lost customers by my lonesome, of course, and the FantasyAces founders are bummed about the Texas news. They, too, expect to be out of business in the state within twenty-four hours, and it'll hurt them badly. Every state they lose, they say, is an ax chopping away at their bottom line. If it keeps going in this direction . . . they don't want to think about what would happen. Normally, the FSTA conference is a highlight of the year for these guys, a chance to join other like-minded entrepreneurs excited about the growth of their budding industry. This year's conference feels more like a funeral than a rally.

What they need is a pep talk.

When Mark Cuban bought the sad-sack Dallas Mavericks from businessman and former presidential candidate H. Ross Perot for $285 million in 2000, the first thing he did was make them feel good about themselves.

Nobody wanted to be a Maverick, or follow them. The Mavericks were losers. They were the team that won 24 games total over two seasons in the early 1990s, and 40 games only once that decade. The team that traded away 1994–1995 rookie of the year Jason Kidd during the 1996–1997 season. The team that went through six head coaches from 1992 to 1998.

Cuban couldn't erase that miserable history. But with new head coach Don Nelson overseeing the beginnings of a multiyear on-court renovation that eventually turned the Mavericks into a perennial NBA powerhouse, Cuban changed one thing virtually instantly: he made being a Maverick seem pretty cool.

He pampered his players to a degree unheard-of for an NBA team, overhauling their locker room facilities with personal DVD players and stereo equipment for each locker, booking them into Ritz-Carltons on the road, and offering them rides in his private jet. He bought the players new luggage, plush towels—first-class all the way. And he rebuilt the fan base from the front row, famously cheering on his team and razzing opponents and officials from his courtside seats, all while personally answering the emails of any interested fans who wanted to talk about his team.

His on-court talent was still poor. But before any free agents decided to sign with the Mavericks, and long before the team became winners, Cuban had turned around the team's vibe.

Now he's here to do the same thing for DFS.

In the three months since the commercials flooded the airwaves and the Haskell scandal broke, the players and operators of DFS have been vilified and accused of everything from running organized criminal rings to rigging games to being scam artists and predators. Some of it is justified, to be sure. But the white-hot level of hatred shocked everyone involved and put them on the permanent defensive—in the aftermath of the scandal, DraftCheat said he simply started telling acquaintances that he's unemployed rather than admit to being a full-time DFS shark. Some DraftKings and FanDuel employees began telling people they worked for "a start-up" instead of one of the two big DFS giants.

Enter Cuban. As a geek made good—able to party, rub celebrity elbows, and name-drop with the best of them—he represents the dream of every DFS player hoping to parlay his intelligence and fandom into riches and glory. Now he's here, unafraid to speak perceived truth to perceived power about how everyone has gotten it wrong about DFS.

His arrival this morning is like waiting for the pope. Fantasy players line the hallway where he's expected to enter, hoping to catch an early glimpse and snag a handshake or a pat on the back. The massive ballroom where he's scheduled to speak is packed to the brim, and wall-to-wall news cameras line the back of the room, there to cast him as the foil to Attorney General Paxton. The buzz in the room is electric. Cuban means legitimacy. Cuban means pride. Cuban means a chance to feel good about DFS, if only for a day.

Sitting in the front right corner of the room, I've got a prime seat to see Cuban somehow slip in without many noticing, casual in a gray hoodie and jeans, and wander up to the front of the room. He looks younger than his fifty-seven years, with a jet-black mop of hair and a face that may or may not have benefited from some Botox. He's like someone's cool, overgrown older brother, but with billions and a basketball team.

As more people realize that Cuban has arrived, the fantasy types stand and crane their necks for a better view, and a murmur runs through the crowd, turning to cheers as he walks up to the podium and waits through a brief introduction before taking the mic at last.

"It's been a fun couple of days, hasn't it?" Cuban opens to appreciative laughs.

Over the next hour, in a brief off-the-cuff speech and then a wide-ranging Q&A, Cuban gives the DFS industry exactly what it so desperately craves: a hug. With a populist's sneer at entrenched politicians and their motives—their "hypocrisy, stupidity, conventional wisdom that makes absolutely no sense"—Cuban explains why he had just invested more money into DFS (in Jonathan Bales and CSURAM's excellent DFS analytics and tools company, FantasyLabs) and why he sees reason for optimism in the current unrest.

"When things seem to be going against you, and everybody seems to be ganging up on you, that's typically when the best shit's about to happen. When the shit hits the fan, it tends to blow all the poop everywhere, but then it's clean," Cuban says, earning hearty chuckles. Everyone loves a good poop reference.

"When people are taking shots at you, they fire their best shot. You learn exactly what the issues are, and you get a chance to address those issues. In the end, you're going to look back at this and say thank you," Cuban says, this time to sustained cheers.

This is taking on the feel of a revival. The crowd is thrilled to be hearing that maybe there's a silver lining after all, and the hooting and hollering grows with every Cuban joke and pronouncement. Cuban isn't done, however. He's dreaming big for DFS. DFS will be taxed, regulated, and legitimized, he says, and that's a good thing. But it could someday mean more. Putting DFS on solid legal foundation could help lead to the Holy Grail for all sports gaming interests: to bring nationalized sports gambling one step closer, something Cuban has championed.

"I think the industry is ripe. I think gambling as a whole will be made legal. . . . I think there's a whole lot of upside to this industry. While this is a stepping-stone that we have to step over and on and across, I think it's going to happen, and it's going to create a foundation that's going to make fantasy sports, and Daily Fantasy Sports in particular, much, much stronger."

That prospect—the eventual legalization of sports betting—underpins many of the conversations happening at this conference, and throughout my time in DFS. It's fairly obvious that DFS appeals to the same people who bet on sports, or would if it were legal and easy. (A 2010 FanDuel pitch to investors described its target market as male sports fans "who cannot gamble online legally.") Many believe that this battle over DFS is something of a first skirmish in a larger campaign that will eventually lead to the legalization of nationalized sports betting.

It makes sense. Many of the traditional barriers to sports betting are falling. All types of gambling are expanding nationwide, and sports betting thrives on the shadier corners of the Internet. Meanwhile, one barrier is gradually coming down: the sports leagues. The leagues have long opposed legalized gambling because of the prospect of games being fixed; but that stance has been slowly weakening, and in the near future two pro teams are expected to take up residence in Las Vegas. The rise of Daily Fantasy Sports has contributed to pushing that conversation. It's no coincidence that right around the same time the NBA's Adam Silver became the first league commissioner to publicly endorse the legalization of sports betting, his league partnered up with FanDuel.

The sports leagues have every reason to embrace sports betting right now, as viewership is down, and many fear that the sports-entertainment bubble is ready to pop. For years, the leagues could count on enormous payments for their television rights from CBS, NBC, ESPN, and others. That era is ending as viewers cut the cord.

What could ensure that viewers stay engaged with sports? Gambling. That's why I agree with Cuban completely—legalized sports betting is the future, and DFS is the tip of the sports betting spear, forcing tough conversations and getting people more used to the idea that this is coming. Sara Rayme, spokesperson for the leading gambling lobby, the American Gaming Association, makes the case very clear: "Daily Fantasy Sports has been the gift that keeps on giving for us," she told *Bleacher Report*. "It has mainstreamed the business." *

After Cuban leaves the stage to thunderous applause, I trail him out to the lobby, where he's meeting with local media, trying to explain to them why DFS isn't so bad, why he wants to be involved.

I join the group, because I want to talk to him a little bit more—specifically about some comments from his remarks on his concerns about multi-entry, scripting, and the DFS ecosystem, and what he thinks needs to change in order to help DFS survive and thrive. But it's hard to

---

* In October 2016, Congress officially began a review of federal sports betting laws with an eye toward amending or removing the twenty-five-year-old ban on sports betting; the committee's ranking Democrat, Frank Pallone—a vocal proponent of legalizing sports betting—told ESPN that addressing DFS would be part of their effort.

get a word in edgewise. Not because of other reporters, mind you, but because Cuban is constantly under siege by conferencegoers.

Every time he stops speaking to take a breath, another would-be entrepreneur shoves a business card, a double-spaced piece of paper, or a manila envelope in his direction and launches into the fastest elevator pitch I've ever heard, most of which go something like this:

"MrCubanhere'smyproposalit'sreallynewanddifferentIthinkyou'llbe impressedI'mabigfanofyouandeverythingyou'vedonethanksforbeing here-GoMavs."

It's like being live on an episode of *Shark Tank*. Cuban accepts most of the handouts and passes them off to assistants or shoves them in a pocket, while generally speaking over most of the interruptions. It's an impressive display, honed over what I assume is years of randoms coming up and hoping he'll throw some investment capital and entrepreneurial pixie dust their way.

Finally, I manage to outpace one of the pitchmen and talk to Cuban a little more about his dislike for mass multi-entry. "Like anything else that's automated, there's ways to win with volume that I didn't like. And the [companies] are trying to accommodate dealing with scripts. But I think things are going in a good direction," Cuban says, pointing to the multi-entry limits starting to arrive across the major sites, and pros being forced to change their strategies as they're no longer able to cover large parts of the board. We're certainly in agreement on that—I honestly believe those changes are a big reason for my recent success.*

Leaving Cuban to the pitchmen, I head back up to my hotel room.

---

* Even the biggest multi-entry pros believe the practice needs to be restricted for the good of the ecosystem. Saahil thinks a cap of between 3 to 5 percent of a contest is wisest. He resents when people think he's good simply because he utilizes mass multi-entry—and to me, it's silly for anyone to think that—but multi-entry certainly allows him to leverage his skill to an extent that we agree is bad for all. "Obviously, there's an advantage to it, or I wouldn't do it," he says. "If you're good, multi-entry allows you to leverage that edge and make more money. If you're bad, though, it just means you lose more money faster."

I'm not concerned with multiple lineups right now. I'm focused on building a few really good ones. I've got a qualifier to win.

———

My original plan was to spend much of that Wednesday night following Cuban's speech researching and working ahead on lineups to submit in Thursday's $1,000-entry hockey-final qualifier. But I've never been one for willpower, so I ended up at a Dallas Mavericks game talking DFS with Oreo, and then out late at the bars for drinks with the famed TommyG1979. A high-level player and Sirius fantasy radio host, Tommy Gelati delights in playing the bad boy role, happily stoking flames, arguing contrarian positions (he was a loud and unabashed Trump supporter before there were any), and basically living and promoting the dream life of the New York–centric mid-thirties bro: booze, gambling, expensive cars, day trading, one-night stands, no apologies. So many in the industry run from the perception that DFS is about any of those things. TommyG embraces it all, lovingly so. He's also highly intelligent, has made live finals in all four major sports, and routinely speaks out against mass multi-entry. I'm a fan.

Unfortunately, spending a night in the TommyG zone means I wake up Thursday morning with a throbbing head and no lineups built for tonight's qualifiers. I throw my bags together, hop into a cab, and rush to the airport for my late-morning flight out of Dallas. I'll be in the air all day, with no time to land and then hastily cobble together lineups. That's probably just as well—building two hungover lineups in a hurry sounds like a good way to throw away $2,000. So, I'll probably have to sit out tonight's qualifiers entirely, which may be a blessing considering that all I've done so far is lose my and Beep's money. Beep is still offering to buy or swap three-quarters of my action, though, and the last time I'd managed to finish fourth out of twenty-four, a marked improvement. Only the top spot matters, of course, but maybe it's a sign of progress? Still, it's probably good that I stay away.

But waiting on the jetway to board my flight, I can feel it start to gnaw at me. There is a solution, albeit a painful one. Airplane Internet. Sigh. I swallow my Platinum-member pride and sign up.

Once we reach ten thousand feet and are steadily cruising back toward Boston, I start delving into stats at ultraslow speeds for $30. I want the top line of the high-scoring Dallas Stars—Jamie Benn, Tyler Seguin, Patrick Sharp—but those guys are budget busters. Grouping them together is possible only if they can be paired with a line that's dirt cheap, but has potential.

The New Jersey Devils, a defensively strong but offensively anemic team, are playing the Ottawa Senators, a club that scores in bunches but doesn't play defense. On the surface, it looks like a situation where Ottawa would spend the night attacking and New Jersey would try to fend them off, and then hope to score on the counterattack. But looking deeper into the numbers, I see something interesting: Ottawa is a heavily penalized team, and their penalty kill can't stop other teams from scoring. New Jersey is actually pretty efficient on the power play. If a situation develops where Ottawa takes some ill-advised, sloppy penalties, and New Jersey takes advantage . . . maybe I've got something there. The New Jersey second line also plays together in power play situations, making for a strong correlation effect. The Vegas data predicts a low-scoring game there, so I can safely predict that ownership will be low on the New Jersey players, meaning that even if I pair them with chalky Dallas, I'll still have a unique lineup. I put the cheap New Jersey second line with the expensive Dallas group and go to work on my second lineup as we hurtle toward Boston.

We touch down less than an hour before the games are scheduled to get under way, and as I collect my bags, I constantly refresh Twitter to make sure there are no last-minute scratches or line changes. Walking outside into the January chill, I flag a cab and head back to our apartment on the Allston-Brighton line. Amalie is covering a Bruins game tonight, so I'll be sweating this qualifier alone, which is fine because following along and living and dying by these games generally makes me into a crazy person. Just before 7 p.m., I swing through the apartment door, dump my bags in the hallway, flip open my laptop, and fire up the NHL.com game stream in time for puck drop.

Six minutes in, the Ottawa Senators take their first penalty, a holding call on Chris Wideman. A few seconds later, one of my players, the Devils' Joseph Blandisi, fires in the game's first goal, with an assist from another of my guys, Travis Zajac. Even better, a look at everyone else's lineups shows that I was the only one of the twenty-four players to pick that Devils line. So these are my points, and mine alone, and such an early goal means I'm actually winning the qualifier, however briefly. Seeing that "$19,000" next to my name sure looks cool.

Then something weird happens. The Devils score again—the full second line, *my* second line—Kyle Palmieri, from Blandisi and Zajac. I get a text from Amalie saying that my lineup is looking pretty good. Four minutes later, the Senators take another penalty, this time a high-sticking call on forward Mark Stone. The Devils go on the attack. They score. Again. Palmieri, with an assist from Zajac. I instinctively throw my arms in the air. Holy shit.

The Skype messages start coming in from Beep.

"Holy crap wtf," "This is nuts," "Glglgl." They pour in, as the points pile up.

"I think I need to run out and buy a Devils sweater," I tell him.

That's confirmed a minute later, when Zajac scores again to put the Devils up 4–0 in the first period. I've got 26 points, which on some nights is a decent final score—and we're only twenty minutes into the first game. I've got the Dallas top line, the highest-scoring group in hockey, queued up to play later, and my nearest challenger has 6 points, a full 20 points behind me. It's as good a spot as I've ever been in.

My heart's racing, and I start pacing the room. I couldn't possibly sit still. As the night wears on, my lead stays solid, and when my Dallas grouping starts to play, they make it even larger: a Jamie Benn goal with an assist from Sharp. I can't stay in the apartment, by myself. I've got to get out and celebrate, even if no one else understands why. It's the night of the annual dinner of the Boston chapter of the Baseball Writers' Association of America, an event I'd attended for years. Since I'd quit, there was no reason for me to go this year. But some of the writers asked me to attend the after party, so I venture out to the Copley Marriott to join them, frantically checking the scores to make sure no opponents are catching up to me. My lineup finishes with 48 points, a big number on an otherwise low-scoring night. The next-closest competitor is 10 points away, but with a few games remaining, anything is possible. Amalie meets me at the Marriott hotel bar after the Bruins game ends, and we try to remain calm and have normal conversations about baseball and writing and other things not nearly as profitable or exciting as Internet gambling. I fight the urge to check my phone every fourteen seconds. I'm trying not to draw any weird attention to myself, as I already feel like an outsider in the baseball world. The reporters I'd spent years flying around the country with are talking about new players on the Red Sox, changes among the reporters on the beat, differences in the Fenway front office—it's so alien to me. I can't relate. My life is in the gambler's world now, one that no one here understands. I'll ponder whether that's good or bad later. In the meantime, I check my phone again just to make sure the scores haven't changed.

At last, it goes final. The seat is locked in, and Amalie and I raise our glasses in a giddy toast. It's all I can do to keep it together—I'm brimming with excitement. I show her my phone again, the winnings listed at more than $20,000 because I'd done so well in other contests, too.

"I can't believe it," she says, laughing as we look at the number together.

I can't, either. I get a message from Beep congratulating me, and telling me it's time to "celly," which he should be doing, too, seeing as I had to pay him more than half of that $20,000. I didn't mind a bit.

I'm a finalist. I'm in the black at last. And DraftKings is going to fly me and my wife to San Diego to compete against the best DFS hockey players for $500,000 in prizes.

Thank God for airplane Internet.

INTERLUDE

Author's Note: It is highly recommended that for maximum effect, this next section be read with musical accompaniment, as befits any success/ training montage scene. Some personal suggestions include "You're the Best," from The Karate Kid, *"Hearts on Fire" from* Rocky IV, *or the aptly titled "Playing with the Boys," Kenny Loggins's sterling effort to back the* Top Gun *volleyball scene.*

But really, "Push It to the Limit," from Scarface, *may be the most apt. After all, this is a world complete with FBI investigations, private jets, parties with hot models, and above all, mountains and mountains of cash falling from the sky. Tony Montana would have felt right at home in DFS.*

Professional athletes strive to reach the point where they're "in the zone"—where they're no longer thinking and planning every move. Instead, a perfect blend of ability, skill, experience, technique, and confidence takes shape to make their actions feel effortless and automatic.

From the moment I win that first seat, I'm in that zone.

My hockey knowledge has finally reached elite levels, and I'm exploring finer points like how early into the third periods opposing teams pull their goalies, in order to achieve the greatest possible number of empty-net goals. Beep and I continue to refine our correlation strategies and look for new ways to combine players—situationally using full-stack power play lines instead of regular lines, for instance, or stacking six players from the same team in rare but important cases—to achieve the best results. I begin to delve into truly advanced statistics, using goal prediction formulas like ixG60* to weave in a number of inputs and anticipate player performance. Beep and I begin

---

* Individual expected goals per sixty minutes of ice time. It's complex. Trust me.

implementing advanced midgame strategies, utilizing DraftKings' late-swap feature to rebuild my lineups while games are already under way, pivoting to riskier or safer combinations depending on my point totals through the first half of the night. I treat all of it like a full-time job, spending a minimum of five or six hours a day building lineups, and at long last, it's working. It's like I suddenly turned on a faucet; money starts flowing in.

Emboldened, I start playing $1,000 to $2,000 per day, taking on the top hockey pros in the highest-value contests—and doing more than just holding my own. I'm winning. I start crushing one tournament after another—$2,000, $3,000, $4,000, $6,000 wins. I'm not just good at this, I'm suddenly and surprisingly great. I'm betting so much, and so regularly, that DraftKings invites me into their VIP program, and I start getting the high-roller benefits that the big whales get; tickets to sporting events, special event offers, private contests. I'm even earning the respect and trust of the other top pros, becoming part of their cadre. Saahil and I become unlikely friends, and go to grab beers and watch soccer at bars in downtown Boston from time to time; one afternoon, he loses $100,000 while we're sitting there for an hour and doesn't seem to notice. Nice guy that I am, I pay the bar tab.

That afternoon, like nearly every other, just feels like so much prelude to 7 p.m., when lineups lock. I win my second hockey final seat only two weeks after I won my first. Beep is buying into my action, and I'm making him money hand over fist.

As a way to thank me for the tens of thousands I'd already won him, Beep invites me to be his guest at a FanDuel party at the Playboy Mansion. We fly out to California—the two of us, his friend Quinn, his dad, and his uncle Warren—and draft lineups by the hotel pool. There's another hockey final qualifier that night, and Beep encourages me to up my bets, even though it would mean I'm putting $4,500 in play, the most I've ever wagered at any one time. It's terrifying, but I push the button and enter, and we head upstairs to get changed for FanDuel's pool party that night.

Six hours later, I'm excitedly showing my phone to Assani, to DraftCheat, to JeffElJefe, to Saahil—to anyone I can find. How could I not? Because when that night's hockey contests go final, my phone's screen says I have $35,000 in winnings. Thirty-five thousand dollars! That's more than I'd made in each of my first two years as a reporter, just out of college. Between winning my third hockey final seat, and taking the win in several other big tournaments, it's my biggest day ever, by far. I have to give roughly half of it to Beep, but so what? It feels like half of infinity.

Where better to celebrate my huge win but at the Playboy Mansion? Flush off my stellar night, we hit the drinks hard the next day, and by nightfall I'm living it up in Hugh Hefner's famous grotto amid a gingham-and-backward-hat sea of DFS bros, a few topless girls, and an endless supply of vodka tonics. There are women everywhere—some of them the "professionally pretty" models hired to be there, some of them actual Playmates. More are the Eastern European types CSURAM had mentioned, plucked out of clubs and told they could come party at the Playboy Mansion with a bunch of rich nerds. The DFS guys, most of them veterans of these kinds of events, hang back and let the women come to them. And come they do. The scene blows my mind—hundreds of women in various states of undress, hammered, hanging all over DFS bros and geeks in the Playboy Mansion's grounds and pools, while peacocks walk the grounds and monkeys shriek from Hefner's backyard zoo. There's high-stakes beer pong being played, a dance floor under way—it's a bacchanal straight out of an eighth-grade fantasy, one littered with nooks and crannies for quasi-discreetly having sex. Go to the bathroom? There's a bed in there, in case you need it. And yet it's all nothing, numerous players say, compared to the DFS mansion parties of only a few years ago, both by Levine's StarStreet and by FanDuel once they took over the license. One of the men who helped organize those, a current FanDuel employee, says that it used to be routine for small groups to head inside the mansion's "game room" late in the party—where off to the sides are mirrored alcoves popular for semi-public hijinks. Then they'd rent a house nearby for the after party—complete with stripper's pole, which was put to good use.

But in the modern DFS climate, and with *Playboy* magazine itself removing nude photos from its pages, this is much more of an R-rated event, not XXX. I learn that firsthand in the grotto—a few topless girls come to hang out, late in the evening, with everyone good and soused. Then one of the girls decides to go bottomless, and security comes in and boots us all out. I didn't understand—aren't fully naked girls the whole idea? I guess even the Playboy Mansion ain't what it used to be.

After hitting the hotel bar for more drinks, the DFS crew, maybe twenty in all, head out to an L.A. strip club called the Body Shop, since clearly the Playboy Mansion wasn't enough T&A for us. I'm pretty cooked, and spend the night leaning up against a wall, talking to Oreo. We hang back, shooing away strippers, a pair of boring married guys doing nothing—until, that is, someone walks by whom I recognize: a tall, young-looking kid in a suit, with a little acne and unmistakable curly hair.

"That's Jack Eichel," I blurt out to Oreo. He doesn't know who that is, but I sure do—this nineteen-year-old is the Buffalo Sabres' star young center, and I've bet thousands on him in countless hockey lineups. He's followed inside by numerous Sabres teammates; they had played the Los Angeles Kings earlier in the night, on the end of a long road trip. Oreo and I end up hanging with several of them, using my newfound hockey knowledge to kinda-sorta join their free-spending posse briefly, before we finally and wearily head home.

The saddest part? Even though I knew the Sabres were out until 4 a.m. and then had to fly cross-country back to Buffalo, I still bet on them—Eichel, specifically—in their next game. Where, predictably, they got mashed. Talk about wasting insider information.

But it hardly matters. In less than four months' time, I've bet more than $200,000 and racked up close to $60,000 in profits, including the value of three seats to the hockey final, where I'll get a shot at $100,000 more. A lot of that goes to Beep—and let's not even talk about how much I'll have to give the government in taxes yet—but I'm a winner, and a dangerous one. By March I've become one of the scariest names you could come across in any hockey contest. I'm what I'd most hated when I'd started on this journey.

I'm a shark.

11

As Daily Fantasy consumes my world, turning it into one constant adrenaline rush of winning and losing, I sometimes find myself wondering if I've gone a little too far.

When the games are finally over, every bit of dead time begins to seem like so much prelude until they start again. The moment the last game finishes, around 2 a.m., until the instant the next day's slate begins is just one long, boring wait.

It stays with me, though; when I finally get to sleep every night—and that takes a while—I dream about lineups. I literally see the DraftKings home page in my sleep, the numbers rising up off the screen at me: point totals, winnings, dollar signs, and floating, gloating zeroes taunting my bad decisions. When I awake the next day, my moods are often directly tied to the results of the previous night's games. If I won, I'm on a high for the whole day. If I lost, I'm just a little more irritable. The swings aren't dramatic, but they're there, and they're consistent.

With DFS occupying so much of my brain, I'm way, way less interested in anything else in my life. Nothing seems to hold the same interest—books, television shows, video games, it all pales in comparison to hockey, and by that I mean hockey with money on it.

There are times in my life when I've toed the line between living on the edge and going over it into addictive behavior with alcohol. I can usually pull back before it's too bad, but that feeling, that beckoning, that desire to cross the line and stay there grabs at me.

My late father, a wonderful man, struggled with alcoholism much of his life, and there's a lot of him in me. I've never drank the way he did—that constant flow, most nights—but when I do go out and drink, I generally drink too much. Often way too much. I get good and drunk, and I'm the life of the party, and it's great fun. Why stop? For most, this wouldn't require much of a thought, wouldn't prompt any soul-searching. It's just something that happens, not a cause for concern beyond the hangover or the extra recycling to take out.

Yet I'm my father's son in so many ways, and as much as I love being that, I know it's something I also have to guard against—the compulsive part, the addictive part, the part that can't quite stop and usually doesn't want to. My dad—who passed away in 2013—never quite could, and it hounds me, gnaws at me, tries to overtake me. I feel that part growing stronger with every day I play high-stakes DFS hockey, every day I get deeper into this. Because with every passing slate, I feel more and more obsessed.

When I'd first started training, Beep had warned me not to watch the games, telling me that it would make me crazy, sink me too deeply into it. No true pros can survive sweating all the games, he'd cautioned.

But I can't help it. I routinely, blatantly, enthusiastically violate that rule. Pretty much every day. For about seven hours a night. Once my lineups are in, I have to watch the games. When they're on television, and my players are scoring points, it becomes the most important thing in my world. I can't concentrate on anything else, no matter how hard I try. I'll be out at dinner with Amalie, and I have to fight so hard against the urge to pull out the phone and look at my scores, just to watch the points slowly rise. Even if I know the games are between periods, I need to see it. In a way, it makes a certain kind of twisted sense. What could be happening at that dinner that's more important than the $3,000 I have riding on that night's games?

I've started to think that I should probably be playing less, and doing some other things with my time. I've played almost every day on one site or another for ten months beginning last May, with a few chunky breaks around October and in early November. Since November I've had some sort of action in almost every single day, as long as I was in a state that permitted it. There would be mornings when I'd resolve not to play— and then by the afternoon I'd cave and throw in a few lineups anyway. And then since I had those lineups built, I'd put $1,000 on them. I mean, they were going to be good lineups, probably. I shouldn't waste them, right? And what's the point of betting $25, $50 anyway? You can't win anything meaningful that way. Not unless you get really, really lucky.

Could I have stopped if I wanted to? Sure. Even though I'm clearly obsessed, no part of me thinks I'm actually addicted. I just don't see a logical reason to quit. When making these kinds of profits, why would I let a night of hockey go by without playing it? I'm good at this, and it takes this kind of total commitment to be this good, I keep telling my-self. Besides, you can't be a "problem gambler" when you're this good at it, right?

The truth is, though, I know that not everybody is good at this. And not everybody can stop.

Fyodor Dostoevsky wrote his 1867 novel, *The Gambler*, in just over three weeks because he owed money. Desperate to satisfy a gambling debt, he drew on what he knew: the love for roulette that had tortured and sustained him as he traveled Europe several years earlier. It's not considered one of his major works. But it's one of the author's most visceral—his emotion coming through in his protagonist, who is quite real and fully nuanced to anyone who has lived and died with the swings of luck and emotion that torment the true gambler.

When sports gambling was restricted to visiting sports books in Las Vegas or Atlantic City, or actually knowing a flesh-and-blood bookie, there was a limit to how many people would end up as Dostoevsky did, addicted and indebted. But with the accessibility and ubiquity of DFS, it's easier than ever to feel that rush. And that can come at a cost. While the "click your mouse and lose your house" doomsday scenario of Internet gambling never came true, there are certainly isolated cases of people who have become addicted and blown tens of thousands of dollars they couldn't afford to lose playing DFS. The *New York Times* profiled a gambling addict, Josh Adams, who lost $20,000 playing DFS. A Tennessee woman, Erica Miller, sued FanDuel to try to recover $545,000 her husband, Kenneth, lost on FanDuel in 2015 and 2016, and then sued DraftKings to try to recover $46,400 her husband lost on the site in just over four months in 2015, according to court records.* The sharks couldn't exist if the fish didn't.

Problem-gambling support organizations are only beginning to understand that they have a new issue on their hands in DFS, and they're now trying to grapple with it. To learn what they're doing, I signed up for the Massachusetts Council on Compulsive Gambling's annual conference, outside Boston. The conference features a segment specifically on the rise of DFS, intended to help the clinicians and social workers who made up the MCCG's membership understand how to deal with this new type of game, one that is suddenly sending them clients just like those who used to come in talking about poker—smart, savvy mid-twenties males.

The organization has rented out space in a nondescript Four Points Sheraton in Norwood, just under an hour from DraftKings' main office, for the two-day conference. They've brought in experts on a number of topics, but there's really only one I'm here to see: the keynote speaker, Keith Whyte.

Whyte is the executive director of the National Council on Problem Gambling and is considered one of the foremost authorities on gambling addiction nationwide. Whyte also has the distinction of being one of the very first in the world of problem gambling to recognize how DFS was likely to grow, boom, and create issues similar to those fostered by

---

* Separately, Kenneth Miller, an officer at First Tennessee Bank, was charged with theft by a bank officer or employee for embezzling roughly $1 million from bank customers in order to feed his DFS habit. He reached a plea agreement with prosecutors in November 2016, according to the *Greeneville Sun*.

online poker. But he is no nattering nabob, throwing shade from the sidelines; he's engaged with the companies to confront the problem head-on, actively working with both DraftKings and FanDuel to introduce safeguards against problem behavior on the sites themselves, and working at the legislative level to build consumer protections into the DFS bills being pushed through the state legislatures.

Whyte delivers his keynote, delving into a lot of basic DFS issues and concerns, and afterward I flag him down and introduce myself. He's instantly interested in my evolution from fish to shark, and we get to talking about his first encounters with DFS.

Whyte, a gregarious, fast-talking Virginian, has been running the NCPG since 1998, and in that time, he's come to know traditional, season-long fantasy sports as a nonissue. There are a few rare cases of men—always men—who had run into problems, usually in Wall Street leagues with six figures on the line, for instance. But those instances of players getting "jammed up," as he calls it, are so abnormal that they're clear extreme examples. The duration of the contest is so long that addictive behavior simply isn't a widespread problem.

When Whyte first encountered Daily Fantasy, however, he immediately knew he was dealing with something different. It had all the hallmarks of an addictive product: quick turnover, high payouts, frequent contests, appealing to men in their twenties in search of action. In DFS, he quickly realized he had come upon a mutant strain of fantasy that was likely to go viral.

"Every so often, we'd run into someone who got jammed up in season-long," Whyte said. "But it's always been a fairly minor problem. But as the amount wagered goes up, and the event frequency decreased, we predicted we'd see a lot more, and we weren't wrong."

Whyte contacted Nigel Eccles at the end of 2011 to offer assistance and share his expectation that problem gambling was going to become an issue for DFS sites.

"Basically said, great meeting you, you might want to get on top of this responsible gaming thing," Whyte recalls. "Because even then, we said, look, the demographics of your players are going to be at higher risk than the general public for addiction. Young, male, sports fans, a lot of poker crossover.

"And two, we know from forty years of research into gambling, the structural characteristics of these games: high speed of play, rapid, frequent rewards—it's all associated with addiction. So just based off those two things, we said, you might want to get on this."

With Daily Fantasy booming, and FanDuel fending off new challengers like DraftKings, there were always other things to deal with. Nothing came of those early conversations. Meanwhile, DFS continued to grow.

"By 2014, we were starting to have clinical reports coming in. People calling the help line, clinicians telling us about this. We were having clinical cases of people who were losing five figures in small amounts of time," Whyte said.

One of the problems with the hoops that DraftKings and FanDuel jump through in pretending that they're not gambling operations is that it prevents them from fully engaging with entities that want to help problem gamblers—who are undoubtedly among their user base. Organizations like the NCPG don't care about the skill-versus-chance debate, or the practical definition of gambling versus the legal definition of gambling. They care only that people are responding in the same way and experiencing the same problem-gambling issues they see with poker, or blackjack.

If all this "we're not gambling!" rhetoric were truly just a wink-wink nod-nod relationship, conducted so that FanDuel and DraftKings could avoid further legal entanglements when they could least afford it, and if they were willing to quietly acknowledge what they really are in order to protect customers from problem-gambling issues and help those in trouble get the assistance they need, that would be fine. But some people at the sites appear to have drank their own Kool-Aid.

"I remember talking with a developer at FanDuel who will remain nameless. He's like, 'I'm really glad to be working here, because our product is not dangerous to people and no one can develop a gambling problem,'" Whyte recalls, with obvious incredulity.

"He said, 'The event frequency is too long,'" Whyte continues. "'The contest locks on Wednesday, but the game's not until Sunday, and I know from sports betting, that's too long.' And I said A) that interval doesn't seem to hinder sports bettors. And B), if you're doing five hundred line-ups, you work on those the whole time until the games start. But that's the perception—if it's not slots, it's not gambling. That's a risk factor that was known, and everyone else already knew it except this doofus."

I certainly knew it. Everything I've been feeling lately—the way DFS consumes me—vies with the fact that I was making money whenever I think about whether I'm too deep into DFS. I ask him the question that nags at me.

"What if you're really, actually good," I ask. "Can you have a gambling problem even if you're making money at it? Don't you have to have a certain level of obsession to succeed?"

Whyte laughs. He's encountered this before. And there's no easy answer.

"One of the difficulties we have is how you distinguish a heavy recreational player from a problem gambler," he explains.

Those tests online, the ones that promise to determine if you have a gambling problem? They're basically useless—the equivalent of those silly screening tests they give to college students that warn that you have a serious drinking problem because you consumed more than five beers in one night this weekend.

"Our screening criteria don't distinguish. It's very possible to be a highly successful professional gambler. But our screening criteria would say that you're just a stone-cold, pathological gambler," Whyte says. "So the hallmark of it is being able to set a limit, and stick to it. Maybe your limit is a million dollars. You've got a million dollars in play a day, and it's not letting yourself go on tilt."

I've experienced that tilted feeling many times—chasing losses, pushing hard to try to get back what I'd lost, betting more and more. Feeling that self-destructive part, the compulsive part, rear up and start to take over. I usually win again before it gets too bad, and in the glow of that victory, everything feels good again; the chasing, the desperation, is forgotten. It's the gambler's roller coaster.

The problem comes when you ride that roller coaster too many times. And when your brain gets used to riding it. It adjusts. Then it needs a bigger and bigger coaster.

The reason gambling is so addictive has to do with the way our brains are wired, and with a chemical messenger known as dopamine. Dopamine is the cookie in the brain's rewards system. When we do something that the brain perceives as beneficial—activities that keep us alive, help us procreate, help us advance our standing among our peers—the brain shoots out a squirt of dopamine, which makes us feel good. It's a reward, but also a reminder to keep doing more of whatever it is you just did.

Addictive drugs—cocaine or amphetamines, for instance—stimulate the brain to fire out more than ten times the normal amounts of dopamine. It's why doing drugs makes you feel good. The problem comes in what that does to the brain. Addictive drugs cause the brain to pump out so much dopamine that it eventually becomes less responsive to its effects, and more dopamine is required to keep that good feeling going. In common parlance, you've built up a tolerance.

Gambling stimulates the brain in much the same way.

The brains of pathological gamblers and cocaine addicts are functionally the same, the same regions dead, the same regions activated. The rewards system is the same, even though there's no substance involved.

"It's an injection of dopamine every five seconds into the brain, every five seconds," Whyte said, explaining that long gambling binges produce a kind of sustained high. "It's the longer you can stay in action—from a neurochemical basis, it's shooting cocaine into your brain every three to five seconds for fifteen hours straight, and never overdosing."

Sports gambling and, by extension, DFS are perfect for this. From the moment the games start until they finally conclude at the end of a long night, you're engaged. It's why I can't pull away from it. It takes hold, and every check of that phone at dinner fires a shot of dopamine into the right receptors. Anything that doesn't offer that perfect shot seems second-rate.

"That's why addicts report that everything else is kinda gray—their receptors have improved to need more and more dopamine to achieve that high, because they get filled," Whyte says. "The other receptors get deadened away. That's why it's addiction. Because tolerance is a bitch. If only you could spend five dollars and keep getting that level of excitement. But you can't."

This is something Beep had actually explained to me when we'd first started training. His explanation had started tongue-in-cheek.

"I was not always this hardened veteran you see today," he said, clearly half kidding. "I was a cheerful kid when I was younger."

Then the smile disappeared, and his words got considerably darker, as he talked about the ways betting has dampened how he sees the world.

"Now I have moments where I'm low energy, things don't get me excited. It's a legit thing. Dopamine is the thing that gets you excited about things. Now, if I find a five-dollar bill, it's not like I get excited about that anymore. It's like, cool—five bucks—I just lost twenty-five hundred dollars today."

"That week when we were talking in Miami," he said, referencing our first meeting at the NFL kickoff party, "I think I lost thirty thousand dollars. That sucks, but at the same time, you're used to it. But a lot of things don't get you as excited."

Beep is no gambling addict. He is one of the most stable gamblers I've met in this world, always hedging, thinking long term, not chasing the big score. Yet it's clear it has a pull on him, even as he suffers from DFS fatigue. Every few months he says he wants out of DFS for good. At the end of the hockey regular season, just before baseball begins, he pins a note to the top of his Twitter account saying that he's getting out of DFS. He tells me he's retiring to work on building a board game full-time.

Less than a week later, I see him back in hockey playoffs contests; what gives, I ask? He says he figures he might as well just finish the hockey season, playoffs included. A week after that, he admits he's diving back into baseball—just to win a few baseball finals seats, he says (which of course is a massive undertaking). Even for someone as smart, and as in control, as Beep, DFS is a hard thing to quit cold turkey.

Whyte goes on to explain that there are two kinds of addictive gamblers: action gamblers and escape gamblers. Studies show that the action gamblers tend to be male, playing skill games like poker (or DFS), and they use the action for the high. Escape gamblers tend to be female, playing games like slots or the lottery, and they do it in order to lose track of time, and to dull pain. Both are desperate for the rush of dopamine, though they're using it for different reasons and in different ways.

I'm clearly an action gambler. Slots or the lottery hold no appeal for me whatsoever. So many of the little things Whyte says he sees in problem gamblers resonate with me, from the need for more games and higher buy-ins to odder tendencies, like how action gamblers develop bladder problems because they can't pull themselves from the television when their action is in play.*

As he talks about permanent changes to the brain, I can feel my heart speed up, a hot, sickly wave of nausea washing over me, the kind that comes when you worry you may have done yourself some lasting damage.

I tell Whyte about some of the things I'd started to feel nightly—the preoccupation, the compulsion to check scores, the inability to focus on anything else during the six to seven hours that the games are on. I don't mention my family history, but I say that sometimes I feel it pulling at me, more than I would like. At the same time, to do this at a high level, I have to be all in on it.

---

* For the record, I never peed myself. But man, sometimes I come down from watching a big stretch in some games and realize it's closer than it should be.

Whyte has heard this before. That's the tightrope so many walk, he says—being so heavily invested while maintaining control.

"Preoccupation is a bitch," he says. "You have to be preoccupied. To learn how to do it. Maybe even a little bit compulsive. But is it obsession? That's the question. It goes preoccupation—compulsion—obsession."

"Where is the line? How do you know when you've crossed it?" I ask. "There are definitely times when I feel like I'm a little beyond it."

"Most gamblers experience a loss of control at some point," he says. "A loss of control is very common in gambling. It's a little like—I had one extra beer. I'm not an alcoholic. You hear that from almost everybody. Then you pull yourself back. It's not pathological at all, until it gets to where that's better than sex. And you've changed your brain permanently. You can burn those receptors out."

Well, I haven't reached that point. But I've definitely thought about DFS during sex at times (sorry, honey), and I've talked to other serious DFS players, like one of Underjones's quants, who've said that focusing on DFS massively dampened their desire for sex. It replaces it.

Sensing my discomfort, Whyte reassures me that permanent changes, really burning out those receptors, takes thousands, tens of thousands, even hundreds of thousands of hours. Even a few problematic episodes, or a string of preoccupied nights, don't mean that the brain has been permanently altered—at least not in a major way.

I just need to be more careful, and maybe take a few days off from time to time. Even if it's just to prove to myself that I can. Maybe try to force myself not to watch the games, when possible. DFS is like anything else—even when you're doing it full-time, everything in moderation.

But there's really no way to know yet. We assume that DFS will affect people in the same way that online poker does, but there's virtually no scholarship or study about how exactly Daily Fantasy Sports impacts the brain, or those with a predilection toward problem gambling. To learn more about it, I reach out to Dr. Marc Potenza, a PhD and MD who runs the Problem Gambling Clinic at Yale University. He helped the NCPG craft its early response to the rise of DFS, but he thinks far more research and scholarship are needed before we really understand how people are responding to this new type of game.

"With Daily Fantasy Sports I don't think we know very much at all about what's going on in the brain," Potenza said.

Yet he does not expect some sort of epidemic of DFS addiction, or that its inception will cause a measurable spike in the number of problem-gambling cases nationwide.

"The data suggests that the prevalent estimates do not change substantially over time. There may be a slight change after the introduction of a form of gambling. But if there is a bump, it quickly goes back to the baseline level," Potenza said.

That doesn't mean that the people who have gambling problems or a propensity toward them should be ignored, or that DFS isn't a new danger for them. For those people, fortunately, more safeguards are in place than ever before. In the past two years, to the sites' credit, Whyte says they have taken steps to deal with this looming problem. They've adopted the NCPG's "responsible play amendments," incorporating consumer protections, age and identity verification, tips for understanding the games and how to manage a bankroll, and tools for self-exclusion.

There are still concerns, however, that many of these changes are for show. Marlene Warner, the head of the MCCG, tried hard to get a representative from DraftKings to attend this conference, to help explain their product to clinicians in their home state.

No show. This is consistent with all her dealings with the company, she says.

"We wanted them here. All I wanted them to do was come in and explain how the games work. Because we told them, clinicians don't know," she said.

Whyte is more measured, saying that he's generally happy with where things stand now and the progress that has been made. But he looks back with chagrin at how long it took DraftKings and FanDuel to see that there was a problem here.

"That's probably what I regret the most—we weren't effective, we didn't make a coherent enough case for why they needed to make changes, and we probably lost a couple years, and a couple people probably got jammed up because of it.

"We're there now. It's good. But it could have been better. We've been engaging with them for a long time." Whyte shakes his head.

With our conversation winding down, I look at my phone and realize that if I'm going to beat traffic on Route 128 back to Boston, I have to get moving.

"I've got a bunch of tickets* for tonight's hockey contests, and if I don't use them, I lose them. So I've got to get home and draft lineups." I grin sheepishly. Whyte chuckles in response.

That night, I turn an $8,600 profit.

I try not to think about whom exactly I'm winning that money from, and whether or not they can afford it.

---

* Most of the time, when you win, you win money. Sometimes you win a ticket to a future DFS contest instead. Keep 'em coming back for more. . . .

12

It's in here somewhere, I know it is. Rooting around in the bag of DraftKings swag waiting for me at the San Diego Hard Rock Hotel, I finally find what I'm looking for: a black, metallic DraftKings nameplate.

On it is my username, etched in silver: "Pimpbotlove." That nameplate represents my ascent from terrified fish to feared quasi-shark, at least in my own mind. I set out on this journey ten months ago, hopeful that someday I might at least be able to break even at DFS. Now, here at the mid-March DraftKings hockey final, I've somehow evolved into much more than that. I won the maximum three finalist seats with three weeks to go in the qualifying process, and was able to sit back and relax. Only Beep and Rob Lokken—the Vancouver pro who goes by "I_Slewfoot_U" on DraftKings and "3Putts" on FanDuel—maxed out their seats before me. Entering the hockey final, I'm up around $60,000—some of that owed to Beep—which seems like an insane amount of money considering that only a few months before I'd been more than $5,000 in the hole.

Five days in San Diego lie ahead, a chance to hobnob with the pros and regs there for the respective NBA and NHL live finals, which DraftKings is holding on consecutive nights. Basketball comes Friday, and then, on Saturday, my main event: the Fantasy Hockey World Championship, with its $100,000 first prize and $500,000 in total prizes to split among the forty finalist seats. I'd spent all day flying out to San Diego, and the trip—airfare, five nights at the Hard Rock, free food and drink throughout—is part of the package you win when landing a final seat, valued at more than $4,000. As part of that, every finalist also receives a goodie bag, with a DraftKings hoodie, a DraftKings hockey jersey, some PowerBars, and assorted knickknacks like a DraftKings-branded hockey puck. I change shirts to shake off the funk of a cross-country flight, snap on my nameplate, and head down to the hotel bar, where a welcome party is under way.

Nerves bite at me, which is a bit of a surprise. I guess it makes sense; this entire experience feels so different from the finals I'd attended before—different, and a little scary. At those I was an observer, tagging along with Beep or whomever, hanging back in the shadows and watching. Now, suddenly, I'm fully a part of this odd world.

Wandering into the bar, I order a drink off the list of complimentary options, mostly beer and wine—this isn't 2014, and DraftKings is no longer sufficiently flush with venture capitalist cash to let us order high-end whiskies all night. Venturing onto the patio and into the cool San Diego night, I immediately run into a group of men whose nameplates bear usernames that I half recognize, like JetJaded and JBO2727. I introduce myself as Dan, which means nothing to them, of course. Then their gazes slide down to my own nameplate. JBO's eyes light up with recognition—and something else in there, too.

"Wait, you're Pimpbotlove?" JBO2727 says. "Oh man, you're nasty! I hate when you're in my contests."

That's almost exactly what I had told CSURAM when I first met him, I remember with a start.

"You maxed out your seats pretty fast. That was impressive," JetJaded says. "I've looked at your lineups to see what you've been doing, they're really strong."

Not only do these guys know who I am, but they crib off my lineups? Like any other competitive venture, DFS is a copycat game. Over the course of the season, I'd seen more and more players copying what Beep and I do—stacking full hockey lines instead of individuals or pairings—and now many of the players at the final were line stacking. But I hadn't fully realized that they look at me as a trendsetter. And they know how early I landed my seats? I feel the entire tone of the interaction shift as it becomes clear I'm the alpha dog here, the known shark. Puffing out my chest a little, I ask them a few questions, learning that they're regular guys who happened to win seats. A third guy asks if I'm a full-time pro.

"Uh, I'm not sure how to answer that," I stammer. "I guess I am, at this point, yeah? But honestly, I hadn't even played hockey DFS until this season started. I just had good teachers, and I've been running hot."

They look at me skeptically, unsure if I'm just doing a poor job of trying to be modest or if I'm actually serious. Before it gets awkward, I'm rescued by Jason Green, the Nashville software engineer who goes by the handle IHaveAReputation. Way back in November, we'd hung out at the RotoGrinders conference and at the Schneiderman protest.

Actually, I'd been hoping to run into him—I have a business proposition for him. Beep, ever cautious, suggested that I swap and sell as much of my finals action as I can—hedging against a series of poor finishes by taking guaranteed payouts and swaps in exchange for a percentage of my potential winnings. I didn't really want to sell much, figuring that I was confident in my chances. But I could see there was some logic to it. I figured I'd swap with Beep, but I needed to diversify further. IHaveAReputation has one hockey final seat, and I have three, and I trust him. With that in mind, I offer up a 3-for-1 swap: I would own 15 percent of his one seat, and he would own 5 percent of each of mine.

"To me, it's a good way for both of us to hedge. You increase your chance at cashing, I increase my chance at a big score. Floor for you, ceiling for me," I say, thinking that sounds basically right.

IHaveAReputation purses his lips, clearly into the idea, and says he'll think it over. I move away realizing that Beep would be so proud to see me initiating deals, sounding like I have some clue. Beep isn't downstairs yet—he'd flown in with Mike McDonald, aka Timex, and in classic Beep fashion, the airline had lost his bag on his layover in Chicago. So he's busy outfitting himself in the free DraftKings gear that came in the swag bag—because that's all he has.

I guess I shouldn't be too surprised that people want to meet me at this event. I want to meet them, too, and not just out of curiosity. I need to do some scouting. Of the finalists, there are perhaps ten who strike me as genuine threats to win the championship. I need to learn all I can about them.

Chief among these is Slewfoot, whom I spot across the room. There's no doubt in my mind that Slewfoot is the best of the best at DFS hockey. He helped me learn about both DFS and hockey basics when I was just starting out, and I consider us friends. But we're both wary of each other now that we're fighting it out for the big money—circling, jabbing, and feinting like prizefighters as we vie for information.

"So, who you going to pick?" he immediately opens, hoping to catch me off guard. I chuckle and say "San Jose," a team that isn't on the slate, and we quickly move on. But others tell me that Slewfoot is trying this approach with everyone all week, and some chumps actually offer up information. Morons! The lineup espionage game is going to be fierce for the next few days; I have to be careful not to get drunk and sloppy and give anything away. Gotta avoid the hard liquor at live finals, like CSURAM said.

Beep is nearly as dangerous a player as Slewfoot, of course, but I know him and his tactics as well as anyone. I have a pretty good guess at who he's going to pick—free-shooting Columbus, to start with. Besides, I've got a piece of his winnings via swaps, so I don't consider him a threat in the same way. No, my main rivals, beyond Slewfoot, are a group of four players whom I face in the $300 and $1,000 entry contests most nights: JayWilly83, Draftcharts, Dirky, and Bluish27. I don't know much about them except that JayWilly finished second in last year's final, and Dirky's lineups continually piss me off—he gets lucky last-minute goals at every turn. But at a certain point, it's clearly not luck, and I've got to be wary of him.

A few other big names had won hockey seats, but they don't scare me. Assani, for instance, is an all-time great basketball DFSer, but I consider the fact that he scored two hockey finals spots to be mostly luck, and he doesn't disagree.

Beep wanders through the door at last, clad practically head to toe in DraftKings gear. It's good to see him, but I'm a lot more excited that Amalie has finally arrived, direct from covering the Bruins in San Jose. It's funny to see some of the hockey pros do double takes as they recognize her—they follow her on Twitter, because they need her Bruins lineup updates and info. I drag her off into a corner for a little privacy.

"This is so surreal," I tell her. "Most of them are more afraid of me than I am of them. We might really have a shot here."

Only a few months earlier, I'd been awful at this. Now I was on scene, swinging deals and feeling out competitors for lineup info. Others talk of hitting a late-night club, but the cross-country flight and the free drinks are adding up to make me light-headed. There will be more than enough time to schmooze with the enemy over the next few days. For now, time to rest up, because some actual physical activity is on tap for tomorrow.

It's only after I've arrived at the hockey final that I realize being American is a huge disadvantage.

I have a certain amount of Canada envy to begin with. How can anyone not? I mean, they're all so darn nice, they have an absolutely killer national anthem, and their accents are hilarious.

They're also completely obsessed with hockey. I'm pretty sure Canadian kids grow up with hockey sticks in their hands, skates on their feet. Even Beep—who cares not a whit about sports—had played some growing up.

So when DraftKings announces that they'll be holding a hockey "skills challenge" that day, with impressive prizes given to the winners, I have a clear and distinct goal in front of me: don't finish last. There's an accuracy competition, a hardest-shot competition, and a stickhandling challenge, and I expect the Canadians to sweep. At the hockey final, roughly half of the forty seats are held by Canadians—Slewfoot, Beep, JayWilly, JetJaded, Draftcharts, and others I'm just now meeting, like a pleasant thirtysomething who goes by Booooourns on DraftKings.

Seeing Booooourns at the competition, bearded and hockey-jerseyed and Canadian looking as hell, I ask him if he played much hockey growing up.

"I played a little, but that was a long time ago," Booooourns says.

This seems dubious. I check with Draftcharts to see if he gives the same answer.

"You know, here and there, but I'm old now," Draftcharts demurs.

As soon as Draftcharts walks away, another of the Canadians points toward him. "You know he played in the OHL, right?"

The OHL, the Ontario Hockey League, is about two steps below the NHL. It's probably the hockey equivalent of Double-A baseball. It means that at one point, you were fantastically good at hockey. Even twenty years past his peak, the fortyish Draftcharts, real name Marc Borg, is essentially a hockey god. (Oh, and he plays in a men's league now, so that "here and there" routine? Yeah, um, no. Damn lying Canucks!) Standing around with fellow American IHaveAReputation, it is suddenly crystal clear that one of us is going to be last, the other second to last.

As a crowd of more than fifty look on, Draftcharts effortlessly fires pucks at a set of five targets, hitting them all (I hit two). JetJaded puts up a slap shot that borders on 75 mph (I shoot 42 mph). Slewfoot weaves around obstacles to finish the stickhandling course in roughly fifteen seconds (I take forty-five). They're all remarkably pleasant and humble in victory. Canadians truly are the nicest people in America.

It's too bad I suck, actually, because once I see some of the prizes, a pang of jealousy shoots through me. Thanks to DraftKings' partnership with the NHL, they get access to some premium loot, like signed jerseys and sticks. One of them in particular makes me wish I had played a little better during gym class hockey: a St. Louis Blues jersey, autographed by star defenseman Kevin Shattenkirk.

As I'd started following hockey, Shattenkirk quickly became my favorite player, favorite in the way that people who have no real affiliations latch on to what's familiar. The twenty-seven-year-old defender and I ran on seemingly parallel tracks through life, so I'd adopted him as my de facto guy. He was born in Greenwich, Connecticut, in the same hospital as my sister, a few miles from where I grew up in neighboring Rye Brook, New York. He then spent his formative years in New Rochelle, New York, where my dad grew up, and where I lived from 2010 to 2015 when I was covering the Yankees. He went to Greenwich's Brunswick School, where I had many friends, as it was the closest school to my alma mater, Rye Brook's Blind Brook High School. And he went to Boston University, not far from my collegiate stomping grounds at Tufts, and literally down the street from where I live now. He's also funny—going by the Twitter handle "Shattdeuces," for his jersey number, 22, and, well, you know—and intelligent. His critiques of opposing defensemen on the *Player's Tribune* are some of the sharpest player-on-player analysis I've read in any sport. So, when I started betting on hockey full-time, I rooted on Shattenkirk with particular gusto.

Unfortunately, I had zero shot at winning the sweater, which went to Boooooourns for finishing second in one of the competitions. Good thing I actually came prepared. One of the only other hockey players I'd followed in my pre-betting days was San Jose's Joe Thornton, the former captain of the Boston Bruins. "Jumbo Joe," as he's known, was born July 2, 1979, the exact same day I was. So I watched his career with interest—and when Amalie was doing a story in Sault Ste. Marie, Ontario, where Thornton had starred for the SSM Greyhounds of the OHL, I asked her to pick me up a Thornton minor-league jersey so I could rock it at the final.

That's not my only piece of lucky finals clothing, however. Amalie had ordered up a pair of shirts online for me and Beep to wear—cat shirts, of course—Featuring Felix the Cat, the old 1920s cartoon character. We figured it was a new take on Beep's normal cat theme. I planned to wear mine (a "Felix the Thundercat" variant referencing the 1980s cartoon) under my jersey so as not to totally steal his style, while still making sure he knew I was firmly on Team Beep.

As it turns out, the Felix the Cat shirt is now sorely needed, with Beep having no clothes to wear thanks to the airline snafu. He and Timex have skipped the skills competition to go shopping for some replacement duds. Of course, always looking for an edge, the pair are considering reporting to the airline that the only things in the lost bag were a group of Armani suits—estimating them to be worth more than $5,000—so they can claim the maximum reimbursement for lost luggage.

"Go big or go home, right?" Beep says. "Everyone tries to claim like two thousand dollars' worth, and the maximum is thirty-three hundred, so if we go way over that, we should get the maximum."

Though they never follow through with it, I have to admit there's a certain flair to the plan.

———————

Hockey DFS is just what Daily Fantasy Sports should be.

Very few players use algorithms—hockey stats are so scarce, and of such dubious utility, that the sport doesn't lend itself to rigorous statistical solutions in the way baseball does. The money is so relatively small— it's hard to make more than $35,000 on even the best of nights—that the sharpest pros and syndicates don't really bother. Multi-entry is not as effective, or as prevalent, and it's exceedingly rare to see a 100–200 lineup multi-entry train in a contest. The midsize tournaments—the $27, the $50, the $100, even the $300 entry contests—are small, usually ranging from 120 players in the $300 to a few thousand in the $27, so a player with three to four well-built lineups can and will succeed.

Put that together with the fact that half the players are constitutionally pleasant Canadians and are, nearly to a man, playing because they are massive hockey fans and it creates a different vibe than the one fostered by the other sports, which are more about money and automation. This is driven home on Friday afternoon, as the DraftKings NBA final unfolds in the main watch room.

NBA DFS is the domain of the big-name, big-time, big-entry pros, of Saahil and Underjones and Assani and many other names rightly feared within this community, like EHafner and Empiremaker. With the games starting around 4 p.m. Pacific, I figure I'll come down to watch the show as these sharks sweat their lineups, with the $1 million first prize on the line. But even with nearly one hundred finalists, the room is sedate around lineup lock. The big names are all up in their rooms, working on teams for nonfinal lineups. They're missing out; DraftKings did its usual plush, posh setup, with the now-familiar white couches, massive television screens, and uplit walls illuminated with splashes of DraftKings green. Out in the hallway is a bar area and a buffet, flanked by extras like pop-a-shot and old-school arcade games. Across the hall are two other rooms with basketball hoops and hockey goals set up for the skills competitions, plus a few Ping-Pong tables—a vast labyrinth of male arrested development. Sadly, hardly anyone is around to enjoy it. Actually, most of those hanging around look to me like hockey DFSers, there simply to watch basketball and hang out with other Canadians. I clearly need to move to Toronto and start listening to the Tragically Hip.

Still, my hockey foes should probably be spending their time more constructively. Not long before, DraftKings released the salary information for Saturday's hockey slate. Armed with the salary data, it's finally possible to build some test lineups. With the basketball room so dead, there's no better time to get to work in pursuit of $100,000. The elevator whisks me back up to my room, where I splay onto the bed and open my computer.

Since I won three seats, I have three individual lineups to build and submit, each one giving me a single shot at winning the grand prize. Technically, I could fill out my nine-man lineups by mixing and matching players from nine different teams all across the NHL. But that's poor strategy; Beep taught me to build DFS lineups by stacking full, well-correlated hockey lines (pick a center and two wings from a given team for my first line, follow up with another C-W-W combo from a second team, add a defenseman and a goalie who correlate with one of my

two lines, then add another, random defenseman) and that's what got
me here, so I'd be crazy to change now. Because it's about selecting and
stacking full three-man lines and not individual players, success begins
with picking which teams I think will score. The first step in that is game
analysis.

There are eight games on the Saturday night slate, and to me, it's
smart to divide them up into three categories. First there are the lopsided matchups: Tampa-Arizona and St. Louis–Vancouver, with the
first team in each pairing likely to win big. That makes St. Louis and
Tampa likely chalk picks. Next are the even games between bad teams:
Toronto-Buffalo, Columbus–New Jersey, Carolina-Minnesota, and
Montreal-Ottawa. These are also probably going to be chalky picks, because my opponents will hope that, especially in the Toronto-Buffalo
and Montreal-Ottawa contests, the games could devolve into 5–4 shoot-
outs.

Then there are even games, between quality teams: Detroit-Florida,
Boston–Los Angeles, and New York Islanders–Dallas. These games
might be opportunities to get low-owned, high-quality players who go
underpicked because they're facing strong opposition in what are likely
low-scoring games.

I've done a lot of thinking on how to play this and have decided I'm
not afraid of chalk picks—as long as they're paired with an unconven-
tional counterpart. Having studied what happens at the live finals I'd
attended, and discussed it with Beep, I believe finalists overthink it and
try to be too contrarian. That leaves some of the most obvious plays
underutilized. With three lineups, I can afford to diversify in ways other
teams can't. It's an edge, and I'm going to use it.

With this in mind, I click on the chalky top line for St. Louis (Vladimir Tarasenko, Jori Lehtera, Jaden Schwartz). With my opponents casting about in search of unique options, I figure St. Louis ownership won't
much exceed 20–25 percent. I'm into Detroit, and I like the Islanders'
top line (John Tavares, Kyle Okposo, Josh Bailey) for my third "base
line" against defensively suspect Dallas.

The foundations of half my lineups are in place. Now who to pair them with? Columbus and its free-shooting top line is attractive—but that's exactly the kind of pseudo-contrarian pick that ends up being too chalky in the end. I think Beep and Slewfoot, my top two threats, will be on them as well. I've got to distinguish my lineups by staying away. Cross off Columbus. Ditto Buffalo-Toronto. Neither team plays defense, both have a few scoring threats—that's the kind of game that my opponents would stack.

Instead, I check out that Montreal-Ottawa game. Montreal and Ottawa don't play any defense, either, but they have players who can score. Montreal's top players—especially Max Pacioretty and Alex Galchenyuk—might be picked by a few teams, but Ottawa will almost certainly fly under the radar, making them a good group to put with either St. Louis or Dallas. Messing around with the salary, their top line of Zack Smith, Mark Stone, and Jean-Gabriel Pageau fits nicely with the St. Louis Tarasenko line. That's one lineup built. Two to go.

That Detroit-Florida game is calling to me. As an even matchup between good teams, it's going to be almost totally ignored by other players, and looking through recent stats, both Aleksander Barkov–Jaromir Jagr's Florida line and Henrik Zetterberg's Detroit group have been clicking, and shooting a ton. I load up on Florida and Montreal, and pair Detroit with my Islanders stack.

Slamming my computer shut, I drag Amalie back down to the basketball final to see how it's shaping up. Entering the giant watch room, I'm disappointed: turns out, it's still dead. There's less than an hour left, but no one is hooting or hollering. They're just sitting on their couches, sipping beers, watching the points pile up, the numbers gradually creeping higher.

As the final minutes tick away, a player named Pwnasaurus hangs in first, and looks like he'll remain there. He's about to win a million dollars, and he and his group are excited, but not overly so. The rest of the room is worse—no energy. Even second-place Underjones, about to win $400,000 for the second time in a few months, seems happy but not thrilled. When the time comes, he gets up onstage, accepts champagne, smiles dutifully. But where is the elation? Is this the beginning of DFS fatigue, even among the top players? Have the regular prize pools grown so big, with the top pros winning and losing so much money every day and week, that even a half-million-dollar prize fails to really move the needle for these guys? Is this how it's going to be for our hockey final?

After Underjones comes off the stage, I shake his hand and congratulate him on his windfall regardless.

"How are you going to celebrate?" I ask.

"Oh, I don't know. DraftKings takes you to a club if you're a top finisher, or a dinner if you want, at a really expensive place, like Nobu," he says, referring to the famed—and famously expensive—sushi restaurant on the ground floor of the Hard Rock Hotel. Underjones is picking the club. Beep will be joining him. I have a hard time imagining this crew crushing a pulsating dance floor in Underjones's high-waisted khakis and Beep's sweatpants, but I'll give them the benefit of the doubt. They ask if we want to join, but we pass, instead heading to the nearby open bar DraftKings set up, arriving to see that most of the hockey finalists have beaten us there.

With the hockey final less than twenty-four hours away, the bar quickly evolves into a scene of amateur spycraft straight out of Cold War Berlin, as well-lubricated foes try to unearth scraps of knowledge while spreading disinformation about their own choices. Slewfoot strolls the room brazenly using his "Who you playing?" opener. Other finalists take a more roundabout approach, probing about which players might be due for a big game, who might be high-owned. One player, "NdeJonge," tries a trick I've never seen before: he marches around the room showing other finalists his planned lineup, from top to bottom.

"This is who I'm using. I swear to you. Montreal and Dallas. This is it right here," he says, flashing me his phone.

"Let's say I believe you," I ask. "Why let everyone know who you're picking?"

"Easy, man. If people know I'm on them, maybe that'll make them less likely to pick them themselves," he says.

Maybe. I'm trying to be as tight-lipped as I can about the work I've already done, saying only that I have one lineup I'm really happy with, and two that are probably suspect. Still, as the drinks flow and the entire group ventures up to the rooftop bar to keep the party going, it's getting harder to avoid conversations about who the smart picks are, even with Slewfoot, my most dangerous adversary.

With him, the dynamic feels especially fraught, partially because there's a part of me that wants him to be ally, not foe. Beep had suggested I try to get him to swap action and thus get a piece of his potential winnings. Slewfoot is the best, we all know it, and I'm pretty good. If he, Beep, and I all swap action, our little cabal will have a pretty good chance of placing someone in that group at the top of the field. But how do I ask him if he wants my action? Is it like asking for a date? It feels that way. I dance around the subject and then say the hell with it, just go for it.

"Beep's suggesting I try to swap with as many good players as possible. Are you swapping with anybody?" I say, lobbing that grenade out there.

He pauses, then politely lets me down easy.

"No—it just doesn't make a ton of sense for me, you know?" The DFS version of "it's not you, it's me." We settle on a different kind of arrangement: a dinner swap. If one of us wins, we'll take the other, and a guest, to the swanky DraftKings-funded celebration dinner. Good enough for me.

That business venture resolved, I look around for IHaveAReputation, to see if he's considered our 5 percent/15 percent swap further. He and his wife, Katrina, Michigan State alums both, had been mourning the loss of their top-seeded team in the NCAA tournament the day before. But he's found time to think it over, and when I ask again as the night winds down, he tells me he's ready to make the deal. That's 5 percent of my action swapped. My best friend from college, Eric, also wants in—he's followed along on my DFS journey and has gotten pretty into it. He asked if he could buy 2 percent. Despite Beep's warnings against selling to civilians, I'll make an exception here. Beep suggested I sell far more—upward of 50 percent—but I hate that idea. It's the smart approach, the conservative approach—the boring approach. I feel like it's me once again selling myself short. As I'd improved as a player, through February and early March, I'd sold so much of my action to Beep that he was taking about half of my winnings at nearly all times, through a semi-permanent staking relationship. It cost me thousands and thousands. I was fine with it, because he took me on when I hadn't yet blossomed, on the chance that I'd improve. If I hadn't? It could have cost him a lot. But having improved so much, and not fully benefited, I'm still smarting from the deal in a petty and irrational way. Now even risk-averse Amalie is egging me on to keep more of my own action and sell less. I'm torn.

By the end of the night I come to a middle ground, and decide to sell Beep 12 percent at a 1.05 percent markup, and swap him another 15 percent. With the 7 percent I've already sold to IHaveAReputation and my friend Eric, I can still keep two-thirds of any winnings, while hedging against disaster by selling that 34 percent. With that settled and the bar shutting down, I collect my lovely, wine-soaked wife and we drag ourselves upstairs, limping together into the biggest gambling day of my life.

I wake up the next morning surprisingly refreshed, one of those beautiful freebie days where you might deserve a hangover but didn't actually receive it. My body must know there's a real chance I might fall asleep tonight $100,000 richer. I let myself dream on that for a minute—popping bottles of Dom Pérignon, splurging on something silly, tooling around town in a ridiculous Aston Martin rocking an ascot and conspicuously blasting Sir Mix-a-Lot—before remembering that I can't think that way. How many times have I stuck a recorder in Derek Jeter's face and listened to him monotone that he doesn't think about the results, buddy, that he only thinks about the process? Today I will be Jeterian. In that, I mean I will date models and spout platitudes. No, screw that—I vow that my postgame interview will be far more colorful than his ever were. But I *will* focus on process.

There are five hours left until lineups lock here on the West Coast, and morning skate information is already out—at morning skate, teams usually reveal their goalkeepers and their likely lines, allowing gamblers like me to know which players are skating together. Nothing too shocking so far, except that, annoyingly, I can't find lines for Dallas, which held an optional skate. Bulling forward, I lock in my goalie picks to go with the Detroit-Islanders, Montreal-Florida, and St. Louis–Ottawa pairings I'd crafted yesterday. Right now I'm rolling with Blues goalie Brian Elliott, Canadiens goalie Mike Condon, and Red Wings goalie Jimmy Howard.

Finalizing the defensemen, I'm faced with a tough decision on my St. Louis–Ottawa lineup. The smart, conventional play would be to pick all-world Ottawa defenseman Erik Karlsson to pair with my Senators. What worries me is that it's too traditional a pick—and that if anyone else decides to go with a St. Louis–Ottawa grouping, I'll overlap too heavily. On top of that, digging through Karlsson's stats, he's been playing ridiculously heavy minutes of late, close to thirty a game. I see a mild but noticeable drop-off in his production, indicating that perhaps the massive workload is wearing him down so late in the season.

I'm intrigued instead by St. Louis's duo of attacking defenders, Alex Pietrangelo and Kevin Shattenkirk. Against weak Vancouver, they're both canny options whom few other players would use, and each is far cheaper than Karlsson, giving me more money to use elsewhere. It's a toss-up as far as stats go—so, obviously, I've got to go with my heart. Shattenkirk is my guy.

Lineups well in hand, I nudge at Amalie until she fights through her hangover and gets up. We need some healthy food and fresh air—we're not going to get much of either once the games start. Stopping by the watch room on our way out, we see Assani's cadre of leggy models, now decked out in bulky hockey sweaters, standing around a glass case. Inside is the hockey championship belt, all leather and gold silliness. I want it.

"Hey, Pimp!" I look around to see Draftcharts beckoning me over. The fortyish ex–hockey player is seated with Bluish27 and a few of the other younger finalists, kids in their twenties, all of them around a laptop showing some kind of video.

"They were asking what your username, Pimpbotlove, was from, and so I was showing them old Pimpbot videos," Draftcharts tells me.

It's a little bit touching, this group exploring 1990s culture in my name—though they look befuddled at what they're seeing. With the wizened bearing of an old campfire storyteller, I explain to them exactly what the heck a Pimpbot is.

"As you can see, the Pimpbot 5000 is a robotic pimp. It's an old Conan O'Brien sketch that came out when I was in high school—and I thought it was about the funniest thing in the world at the time. Pimpbot comes on, dressed in furs and crazy hats, and routinely tells Conan he'll cut him, and touts his sartorial flair," I begin.

"The-bitches-respects-a-man-who-dresses-himself-fine," the Pimpbot 5000 chimes in from the laptop below.

"In 1996 or so, I needed a name for some email address or early Internet sign-up or something. The lightbulb went off: Pimpbot! But that was actually already taken. So, I figured, what matters most to a Pimpbot? Lovvvvvve."

"I-gots-a-score-to-settle-with-you, white-bread. I'm-a-gonna-stick-you-like-a-pig," the Pimpbot 5000 tells Conan as the video clip runs on.

"So Pimpbotlove became my go-to username for when I needed a log-on for something I didn't really care about—like, say, Yahoo! fantasy baseball around the year 2000," I say. "I admit I didn't expect that almost twenty years later, I'd end up with people actually calling me 'Pimp' as a result."

It strikes me that that's basically what Saahil once told me about taking the MaxDalury name. I mean, it's different, because I took the name

from a robotic pimp and not a Tufts squash player—but it's a little unnerving to think about. I should go check my lineups.

———————

There's less than an hour until the final begins and everything feels
pretty good. Lying on the bed in our hotel room, messing around on the
computer, I can't think of a thing I'd change. At this point, all that's left
to do is check for late-breaking information—scratches or line changes
or similar. Why can't the damn thing just start already?

Nervous energy courses through me. I get off the bed and start aimlessly walking around the room.

"What are you doing?" Amalie asks.

"I'm pacing. I don't know," I respond, coming back to my computer
to click aimlessly at more news updates.

There I find something alarming. The in-house Islanders reporter
for the MSG network has just posted something about new Islanders
lines. My grouping of Bailey, Okposo, and Tavares? Toast, replaced by
players I don't want to use. Shit. What was that about trusting the process? I have to shift into rebuild mode, immediately.

What about high-scoring Dallas? I'd have to guess at which players would be grouped together, but the fact that the Stars lines hadn't
been announced would keep other players off them, and a recent injury
to star Tyler Seguin adds more uncertainty. Scanning last year's numbers, team captain Jamie Benn's production spiked when Seguin was
out. That's good. He'll probably be paired with center Cody Eakin and
winger Patrick Sharp. That line could be pretty fierce together, a passing center with two deadly wingers. A click here, a click there—swap
out Detroit's Howard for Dallas goalie Kari Lehtonen, an underrated
netminder. . . .

"This just might work," I say to Amalie as I click to submit the lineup.

There are twenty minutes left before puck drop. Time to dress for
battle. I pull my light blue cat shirt over my head, and soon Felix the
Thundercat proudly smiles from my chest. The red Sault Ste. Marie

Greyhounds jersey goes on top of that, like armor over a doublet. Finally, I clip on my DraftKings name tag. There it is, on my chest: "Pimpbotlove." I'm ready.

———————

The way live final prize pools work is comically lopsided. So much money is tied up in first place that the drop-off from first to second is massive—$100,000 to $60,000 in this case—and falling out of the top five is disastrous, with the payouts dipping to four figures almost immediately. If I'm going to win anything real today—real, in my new and admittedly twisted worldview, being five figures—I'm going to have to sneak into that top five, with its prizes of $20,000 and above.

There are fifteen minutes until puck drop, and I enter the watch room to find it still mostly empty, with the other finalists probably tweaking their lineups from their rooms. So much the better. There's valuable real estate to be had.

Amalie and I claim a group of three couches in the center-rear of the room and set up our command center, plugging in our two laptops and my iPad to ensure that information comes from all sides in these final ten minutes before the games begin. She seems overwhelmed by all of this, from the plastic glitz of the watch room to the pressure of trying to build and adjust all these lineups as the clock ticks down. I can't blame her.

A familiar voice chimes in behind us.

"Any scratches?" It's IHaveAReputation, who has 5 percent of my action.

"Nope, all quiet," I report—since I own 15 percent of his seat, I'm glad he's paying attention. I ask if he'd like to join us for the night, and he thus becomes the third member of the Pimpbot Couch Squad. Cal Spears wanders in soon after, and is anointed our fourth. A good group, so far.

As I look for scratches, another finalist, Brent21, an older Canadian here with his wife and teenage daughter, comes by with laptop in hand.

"Hey, Pimp, have you seen the rankings? The odds are out," he says, showing me his computer screen.

I imagine the confusion on my face is obvious.

"What rankings?"

Cal Spears joins us.

"For these finals, an oddsmaker will put up power rankings and betting odds, so people can bet on who's going to win," Cal says. "There's one guy who does it who used to be an actual Vegas odds guy, so he really knows what he's doing. But I don't think these are by him."

I start scanning the list from the bottom up, looking for my name. It isn't there. Wait, holy crap, it is there—at the top. I'm ranked second! Slewfoot is first, and Beep third. Ha! Maybe I shouldn't be so proud to be ranked ahead of my mentor—but I am. Dirky is fourth, followed by jeld33, JayWilly, Bluish27, and Draftcharts. All the guys I'm afraid of. A smart list, it seems—one put together by, of all people, Colin Drew, the whistle-blower from the Haskell incident.

"You're telling me that people bet on us, so they're betting on the bettors?" I ask Cal. "That's pretty meta."

It's not just meta, it turns out—it's big business. The bored basketball pros clearly don't have enough to bet on, so they start betting on us. And betting heavy. Over the next five minutes, one tweet after another pops up with people seeking action on the hockey final. Timex tweets that he's looking to bet on Beep and me and is seeking takers. Assani and Beep make a side bet for five figures, with Beep first betting on me, then switching to Slewfoot to win the whole thing. (Thanks for the show of faith, teach!) Big-time pro Empiremaker tweets, "Somehow have 6 figures riding on a fantasy hockey championship I'm not playing in." A pro who goes by TheSeige (misspelling apparently intentional) comes by to tell me he'd just bet on me at terrible odds. Thanks, I guess? As if there isn't enough pressure already.

Following all that side betting is a welcome distraction from the final ten minutes of tension, and I look down to realize that I hadn't even noticed it hit 7 p.m.—lineups are locked. In the front of the room, Draftcharts and a few others have congregated in front of the monitor showing the standings and everyone's lineups. Now that lineups have locked, the ownership percentages are visible. I go over to join them, hoping that all that espionage work was worth something.

Scanning the board, I see that I'd correctly predicted that Tampa Bay and St. Louis would be at about 20–30 percent ownership. More people went with my Ottawa pick than I expected, and fewer with Montreal—maybe NdeJonge's strategy of showing other players his Montreal-based lineup had really worked? My Benn-Eakin-Sharp Dallas line is hardly owned at all, and I'm the only one who has Dallas's Lehtonen in goal. My Detroit pick is similarly rare. And it looks like going with Kevin Shattenkirk over Erik Karlsson as my defenseman in my St. Louis–Ottawa lineup was the smart play—Karlsson is heavily owned, while Shattenkirk is at a mere 7.5 percent.

As I expected, Beep and Slewfoot both used Columbus. The more I look around, the more Columbus I see, actually. Looks like I'll be rooting hard against the Blue Jackets tonight, hoping the New Jersey Devils can shut them down.

The games are under way. I've got no control anymore, but my heart is still pounding out of my chest. Other players are beginning to file into the room, and despite hockey having not even half the number of finalists, the energy in here already exceeds the NBA final. About half the entrants, myself included, are sporting hockey jerseys, from a sweet Anaheim Mighty Ducks throwback to Boooooourns in the autographed Shattenkirk jersey he'd won in the skills competition.

Beep, predictably, hasn't arrived yet, but his players sure have. Columbus scores its first goal eight minutes into the first period, and any dreams I had of jumping out to an early lead are dead. Slewfoot, Beep, et al leap to the top of the leaderboard with roughly eight points apiece. They move up further when Columbus drops in its second goal a few minutes later. My teams are all zeroes.

Damn.

With his team in first, Beep makes his not-so-grand entrance. Resplendent in his Felix the Cat shirt, a pair of black shorts, and a dark blue hat, Beep looks out of it, rattled, bleary-eyed as he joins our crew.

"Helluva start!" I offer. "I totally knew you were going to pick Columbus. They're looking nasty."

Shaking his head, Beep replies something that would seem impossible for anyone else, and yet is perfectly in character for him: "I didn't mean to play that lineup at all—I wasn't going to use it. I fell asleep an hour before lineups locked and I didn't get around to switching it out. It was a total accident," he says.

Man. If he wins this thing on an accidental lineup—well, at least I have 15 percent of him, I guess?

The next few hours pass in a panoramic blur of hockey, the massive screens that ring the room showing action from all over the country. The room maintains a low hum; every once in a while it spikes with cheers from one couch grouping or another, as someone's players score. My eyes try to follow my players, and those of my chief competitors, but it's impossible to keep it all straight. Columbus keeps scoring, and Beep, Slewfoot, Draftcharts, and JayWilly keep rising with them. Right now I'm in the middle of the pack with two of my lineups, while the third one, built around Montreal and Tampa, lags behind. Still, even all that Columbus scoring hasn't helped any one team too much; the leaders have point totals in the low twenties. My best lineup, Dallas-Detroit, is in the high teens, not too far back, really, when I think about it.

"It's still too early to really know anything," I remind Amalie, and myself. "Well, except that my Montreal lineup is probably fucked."

I'm snapping my nameplate on and off, on and off, like I have a nervous tic. The odd mix of boredom and tension must be getting to me. Excusing myself to get a drink, I head out to the bar in the hallway area. Saahil is out there—he's come down to check in on us hockey small-timers.

"How's it going?" he asks.

"Not bad, but not great. I'm mid-pack," I say, just before hearing a roar from inside the watch room.

Amalie comes running out into the hall, spotting me immediately.

"Eakin. From Sharp," she says, nearly frantic. "You're in first. Oh, hi, Saahil!"

I bound back into the room, hoping to catch a glimpse of myself atop the leaderboard—but it's too late. Someone's already overtaken me, by a smidge. I missed my chance. Still, second place—$60,000!—doesn't look too bad up there, and my Dallas-Detroit lineup has a ton of minutes left. Our little white-couch fortress is suddenly abuzz with energy, and I plop back into the center of it, surrounded by Cal, IHaveAReputation, Amalie, Beep, and now DraftKings cofounder Kalish, who brings his wife and young daughters over.

"How did you build your lineups?" Kalish asks. "Did you try to go contrarian, or be more chalky?"

"I think people overthink how unique they need to be at these finals," I say. "What I basically did was pair one chalky grouping with one contrarian grouping. Chalk is the new contrarian."

He agrees, but before we can say anything more, shouts rise from the other side of the room. In the final minutes of the Detroit game, aged Russian Pavel Datsyuk has scored an empty-net goal to ice the Red Wings 5–3 win—and one of my players, Justin Abdelkader, notched the assist. The other few teams with Detroit players keep up their cheering, but I clap louder than any of them—that assist jumps me back into first place, and this time I'm actually there to witness my name atop the leaderboard, with "$100,000" written underneath it.

"Quick," I tell Amalie, "get a picture of me in front of it before someone passes me again!"

A funny thing happens, though, after my moment in first is immortalized: it doesn't end. Minutes tick by, and no one passes me. In fact, with Dallas goalie Lehtonen making save after save, I'm actually extending my lead. I've got twenty-five points, and the next-closest challenger is a few full points behind me.

People start coming by, perching themselves near our couches, milling around behind us. Underjones arrives, too, hearing that I'm doing pretty well. I guess being in first place attracts that kind of attention. What I didn't expect was the paparazzi.

No, really. Paparazzi. As the points leader, suddenly DraftKings' in-house photographers are snapping away at my face, and a full video crew films the scene around our area. It's completely unnerving. I try to act natural and pretend they're not there, but it's impossible. I'm subconsciously posing, gesticulating a little bit more than usual, sitting up a little straighter, unsure which exactly would be my "good side."

Beep and I huddle to handicap my chances. If Lehtonen can hold on for the shutout, and maybe my Dallas line scores another goal, I'll end up in the high thirties, maybe even around forty points.

"It wouldn't normally be enough to take down a tournament like this, but maybe today. Today's really low scoring," Beep says.

With the Dallas game in its final minutes, we collectively train our eyes on the screen, hopeful that Eakin, Benn, and Sharp have one more goal in them. The trio get an empty-net scoring chance—but they can't get the puck into the net. And then they're skating off the ice, with only a minute remaining. I slam my palm on the table. They're probably done for the night.

Just as the Eakin line is hitting the bench, another roar erupts from the crowd.

"Dallas scored!" Underjones exclaims, as we watch replays of the puck traveling down the ice and into the empty net.

"Not my guys," I say quickly, feeling ashen as I realize that my chance to win is gone. Doing the math, I'm going to get the points for Lehtonen's shutout, but there's no way they'll be enough. I'm around thirty-three points, and thirty-three points doesn't win big hockey tournaments. Ever.

I must look particularly glum, because Amalie rests her hand on my back.

"Hey, you're still in first place. And that's crazy. A few months ago did you ever think you could be in first place in the hockey final? Enjoy it," she says.

I put my arm around her. She's right, as usual. And hey, who knows, thirty-three points might be enough to finish top ten, and if I'm really, really lucky, maybe top five. That's a ton of money. I go out into the hall to grab another drink and check my phone. There are texts there from back home: one from Eric, and one from John Tomase.

"HOLY SHIT you're in first!!!!" reads the one from Eric, whose 2 percent stake gives him a shot at just under $2,000 if I somehow win.

The text from Tomase gives me a start, however.

"DraftKings just tweeted out your photo. Name and everything," he writes.

I pull up their Twitter account, which has 200,000 followers. Yep, there it is, a goofy picture of me smiling in my red minor-league hockey jersey, touting me as the leader, with a reference to my Twitter account—which uses my real name, @DanBarbarisi. What if someone from my old life sees the tweet and realizes what I've been up to? Strange.

I've still got a five-point lead over the peloton, the group of Draftcharts, Slewfoot, JayWilly, and JBO2727 all packed in right behind me. A single goal and assist from any one of their players will vault any of them past me, and there are a ton of minutes left. Winning is simply not realistic.

But it's impossible to stop myself from dreaming on it, even if only briefly. A giant check. A goofy belt. Being the best. Oh, and did I mention that $100,000?

Shaking my head, I push and push until those images are out of my skull. Gotta take my mind off it all. I spot Timex hanging out nearby, and ask the vaunted poker pro if he wants to go play Ping-Pong in the other room. He readily agrees, and we get the heck out of the watch room before I go insane.

Despite knowing Beep since high school—and sharing in many of his biggest wins—this is Timex's first DFS live final, and he's struck by how different a DFS final is from his usual live events.

"It's a totally different energy from a poker final. Those are grinds, intense. Railing this is actually a lot more exciting," Timex says, using the poker term for watching your friends compete. I figure it would be poor form to ask exactly how much money he has riding on me.

We volley back and forth easily as the minutes slip away, and I manage to avoid checking my phone or the leaderboard. What willpower— not even the siren song of occasional whoops or cheers from the watch room tempts me to check in. After another twenty minutes, Amalie comes in. This is it, has to be.

"Sorry—I just wanted to get away from it all," I say. "Is it over? It's over, right? I'm out of first?"

She shakes her head. "No—you're still in first. Nobody's scoring. You still have a two-point cushion, and most of the middle games are ending."

How is that possible? I've held first place at the hockey final for more than an hour. Nuts. Well, if that's the case, why not return for a little while and enjoy these last few unlikely minutes of glory? The three of us head back toward the watch room, but we're waylaid by Beep, who is sitting at a high-top table scarfing down appetizers.

"This is so, so sick," he says, referring to me, I assume, and not the food. "Every minute that you hold first, your chance of winning goes up. Like, ten minutes ago it was probably five percent. Now I bet it's something like eight percent, eight point five."

Saahil, who is standing nearby, is a little more reserved. And realistic.

"You know there's no chance, right?" he says. This is how you become the best. Brutal realism!

I nod. I do know that.

"I get it. But every minute I stay at this spot, I get closer to a top-five finish. That's real money. For me, at least," I say as I shoot him and his millions a look.

I return to my spot on the couch and study the leaderboard. The player who I figure will unseat me is JBO2727. He had been one of the few to use the same Detroit players I did, plus the inspired pick of New

Jersey's Kyle Palmieri.* He's got a ton of St. Louis players left, and with that game just getting under way, he'll probably pass me shortly. He's got high-scoring top liners Vladimir Tarasenko and Jori Lehtera playing, and goalie Brian Elliott.

I've got those players, too—along with St. Louis winger Jaden Schwartz and defenseman Kevin Shattenkirk—in my second-best lineup, which is sitting around fifteenth place right now, thanks to some strong work from my Ottawa Senators line. But I've hardly noticed what that lineup is doing. My focus is entirely on the lineup in first.

I stand in the center of the room, a few feet from Slewfoot and his crew, as we watch St. Louis's top line pelt Vancouver's goalie with shots. JBO2727's lineup creeps closer and closer to my score. At 9:21 p.m., after 1:51 atop the leaderboard, JBO2727 passes me and takes over first place. It's over. I raise my glass to him across the room, and Draftcharts comes over to give me a pat on the back.

"Good work, buddy, you gave it a hell of a run," he says.

"Oh well, at least I managed to—" I begin.

A whoop goes up from the front of the room, cutting me off. Amalie points at the main screen, jabbing her finger in the air.

"St. Louis scored. Tarasenko . . . from Schwartz. And Lehtera. Oh my God. You have all those guys. Look at the standings."

The leaderboard makes me do a double take. I'm in the top five again—with my second lineup. It leapfrogged my first and is now just behind JBO. Less than five minutes had elapsed between falling out of first and the St. Louis goal.

We spring into action, everyone in my crew suddenly looking up the ways we can win, and whom we need to be afraid of. That Dallas-Detroit group that had spent so long in first is now completely irrelevant. It's all about my St. Louis–Ottawa lineup and the five Blues I've still got in action: Tarasenko, Schwartz, Lehtera, Shattenkirk, and the goalie, Elliott.

---

* Which came to him, apparently, during a meditation session on the San Diego beaches that morning.

"JBO doesn't have Schwartz or Shattenkirk, but he does have Elliott," I tell the group. "JayWilly has the whole top line, plus Shattenkirk, but doesn't have Elliott. OldT has the same thing—Tarasenko, Schwartz, Lehtera, Shattenkirk—but not Elliott."

"So basically you need Elliott to get the shutout, and either Schwartz or Shattenkirk to score," IHaveAReputation sums up.

"And like, nothing to happen in any of the other games." Cal laughs.

Yep. That's pretty much it. A bunch of things have to go my way. But I'm alive, and with only three games still in action—St. Louis–Vancouver, Tampa-Arizona, and Boston-L.A. Two of them are nearly over. If Elliott can at least hold the shutout, I'm virtually guaranteed a top-five finish. Twenty thousand dollars.

The group of Beep, Saahil, Underjones, Cal, IHaveAReputation, and I stand shoulder to shoulder while Amalie watches the computer screens. Cal suggests I try to work out some sort of chopping arrangement with JBO, like we did between Underjones and RockenRaven at the football final—but as soon as I ask around, it turns out that JBO has gone back to his room, saying he was overwhelmed by the pressure. I can't believe anyone would do that—why wouldn't you want to be here for this? I feel frenzied, alive, on fire. I can't even think about sitting down—my eyes dart from the St. Louis game to the Tampa and Boston games, praying that the Blues will score and that nobody else will do anything. The minutes tick away. Elliott stops a few more shots, Tarasenko fires a few more of his own on goal. A half point here, a half point there.

Amalie gives me the update. "As it stands now, if Elliott holds the shutout, we'll get third."

Third. Thirty-five thousand dollars. But there's no way I can get more unless one of my guys, Shattenkirk or Schwartz, scores. And if Elliott loses the shutout—well then, I'll fall fast, maybe out of the big money entirely. I bounce up and down on the balls of my feet, coursing with energy.

"You're definitely live for first place," Saahil coolly reminds me, probably meaning to calm me down. Has he met me? It has the opposite effect, revving me up further as I watch players fly around the ice. A horn sounds through the speakers, signaling the end of the Tampa game. The players skate off, and it looks like there weren't any frightening empty-net goals, the kind that could have boosted some of the teams behind me. Great news. There's just the final few minutes of the St. Louis and Boston games left to play now, and I'm pretty much locked into a top-five spot if Elliott can keep the shutout.

I glance back at Amalie. She looks up at me wide-eyed, shaking her head in disbelief. There are at least ten people clumped around her, looking over her shoulders at our laptops. I turn my gaze back up to the giant wall screen; with a little over a minute left, Vancouver pulls its goalie in order to bring on an extra skater. The Blues fight off attacks from the Canucks, shots peppering Elliott in goal. He deftly pushes one after another away as my score rises by 0.20 with each save. But that hardly matters. There's just no way I can pass the two teams in front of me without another goal. JBO is going to win the whole thing, and either OldT or JayWilly is going to claim second. I'm in fifth now, but once the win and the shutout bonus register for Elliott, I'll end up in third, and that's fine. Third place—$35,000. It's insane to even think about it.

I never really get the chance. In an instant, everything changes.

The Canucks try another attack. The Blues fend them off and one of their defensemen gets the puck. He passes it up the ice, and another pass sends the puck on to St. Louis's young winger, the hyperaccurate sniper Jaden Schwartz, at center ice. Schwartz throws back his stick and fires at the empty, gaping goal, halfway across the arena. The puck hums through the air, hovering a few inches above the ice—and flies in, rattling around the cage. I gasp, looking up at the leaderboard as it registers the 3.5 points for the goal and jumps me into position just behind JBO, less than a point back. I'm going to get second place. Second fucking place—$60,000. It's incredible, too much to process. I throw up my arms—and then freeze. Wait a minute. Someone had passed the puck to Schwartz. Are there assists?

I run over to Amalie, as she frantically clicks and reclicks the NHL .com feed to see if any assists have been added.

"Was there an assist? Who passed it to him?" I demand.

The Blues are still celebrating out on the ice. It seems like they're celebrating forever. It feels like I'm waiting forever. Finally, they flash the goal information across the gigantic, wall-sized television screen.

GOAL: Schwartz. Assists: Stastny, Shattenkirk.

Shattenkirk.

I'm going to win the whole goddamned thing.

"SHATT-EN-KIRKKKKKKK," I bellow, in a moment of pure testosterone. It's a scene straight out of those awful Gomes brothers commercials that had blanketed the airwaves all those months before—I'm yelling, jumping up and down, wearing a jersey, about to claim a massive prize, as dudes slap me on the back and cheer all around me. It is bro-topia.

As I bounce around, the St. Louis game goes final, and the win and shutout bonuses register. My name leaps up the leaderboard, settling at 47.30 points—first place. Right below my username, Pimpbotlove, there's a number, a beautiful, perfectly emerald green number: $100,000.

Beep comes bounding over, and I wrap him in a hug.

"I can't believe it!" I shriek.

"Neither can I," he says with amazement. "But it's not over yet."

Technically, he's right. There are still seven minutes left in the Boston-L.A. game, but I'm fifteen points ahead of the next-closest challenger with anyone in that game. It would take a massive scoring surge to beat me. That tempers the euphoria slightly, but inside, I'm already beginning to celebrate.

Cameras swarm around me—several different official photographers, plus the DraftKings video crew, and other finalists with their camera phones. My attempts to look candid and natural are going pretty well as one after another of the top players comes by to offer congratulations—Draftcharts, JayWilly, and finally Slewfoot, who looks at me with a smile curling up from the corner of his mouth.

"You're the champ," he says, with an awkward laugh. "You're the best."

But the words are flat, and I think I can see the meaning behind them. It feels like he's saying, "You're an asshole. You're a Johnny-come-lately who got lucky." Which, well, I suppose I am. I can certainly understand if he's pissed. This is the biggest hockey final ever, with the first truly big prize pool. It's his sport; he's the consensus best player. This should be his coronation. Then I show up and stomp all over it.

Next comes second-place JBO, back from self-imposed exile in his room.

"You only had one guy that could have beaten me—Shattenkirk. The one thing that could have happened to beat me, did," he says, dejected. "But it's cool, man, congratulations."

Overstatement, maybe, but he's right about one thing: Shattenkirk made all the difference. The New Rochelle–Rye Brook–Boston connection came through. That gives me an idea. I scan the room until I see Boooooourns, happily wearing the autographed Shattenkirk jersey he won in the skills competition. I slink over, ready to make a deal like the used car salesman my dad always said I should be.

"If I actually hang on to win this thing, and Shattenkirk is the reason, I totally want to buy that jersey off you," I tell him.

He gives me a look that indicates I'm nuts, and says he doesn't really want to sell. Playing hard to get, eh? I know how this works—I tell him I'll find him later to discuss it further. There's only two minutes left in the Boston-L.A. game, and it would take an all-time miracle to unseat me now. This is really going to happen. I look around to find Amalie, but she's nowhere to be seen; then she appears through the doorway, bearing glasses of champagne. Perfect. The whole crew— Cal, Saahil, Underjones, IHaveAReputation, Beep—circle around me, glasses in hand, as we count down the final seconds of the last game of the night. Five, four, three, two . . .

It's over. I'm the champ. I hold my glass high up in the air, shaking my head back and forth, over and over, as the rest of the group cheers and the whole room applauds.

"I didn't see that coming, ladies and gentlemen," I say to the crew, in the understatement of the year.

Before I even have a moment to process what has happened, DraftKings head of VIP services Jon Aguiar is pulling me toward the stage, where four models stand holding two giant checks and a belt.

"Okay, JBO will go up first to claim his check, and then you'll get to the stage where you'll pose for pictures with the check and with Kalish, and we'll do an interview in front of the crowd—all good?" he says, rapid fire.

"Uh, sure—" I say, realizing quickly that I'd better get stone sober fast if I'm doing an on-camera, live interview in front of the hundreds here.

That's not all, I realize. Because I never expected to win, I hadn't considered how I'd play this—especially regarding Amalie. Even though she's soon to change jobs and move on to NHL.com as a general feature writer, this whole time she's still been a hockey beat writer at the *Boston Globe*. Now, I'd learned pretty fast while betting on the Yankee beat that the writers don't have any magic formula that helps them be good at DFS. There's no secret knowledge we're holding back, certainly not on a big, competitive beat like the Yankees or Bruins; every tidbit gets tweeted out as reporters try to out-insider one another. Besides, being good at this game is about understanding stats, correlations, and your opponents, not about knowing whether A-Rod or Patrice Bergeron is a genuinely good guy once you get to know him. Amalie never gave me any actionable info I could use that wasn't on her Twitter page; realistically she didn't have it to give.

But outsiders wouldn't understand that. I could see the headline now: "Husband of hockey reporter wins DFS hockey championship betting on team wife covers." It doesn't matter that I didn't even use any players in the Bruins game tonight. The whiff of impropriety would be there, and that would be enough. Other questions start to race through my mind—am I supposed to celebrate? Is that journalistically proper?

Hell, am I even a journalist anymore? I just won more than I'd made any year as a reporter—tonight. Am I a professional gambler now? What the heck am I?

Panic starts to overtake joy.

There's no time to write up a full pro-and-con list, however, because before I know it JBO is onstage, holding up his own $60,000 giant check, shaking Kalish's hand.* Then a model escorts me up there, too, as the crowd cheers, and they hand me the championship belt. Jesus, this thing is heavy; I sling it over my shoulder as Aguiar sticks the microphone in my face and immediately asks me to tell the crowd about my project.

"I'm a storyteller," I say, "and I got into this in order to tell the story of Daily Fantasy. Its rise, its beginnings, where it's going . . . as part of that, I wanted to really understand, and be a part of it. Quite frankly, I never expected to be any good.

"But I had a great teacher, Jay Raynor, BeepImaJeep, who has really taken me under his wing, and is one of the funniest people I've ever met," I continue, as everyone cheers for Beep, who seems genuinely touched to have been mentioned. "To have this experience is really an incredible phenomenon, and I really look forward to celebrating that for the next three hours and forty-five minutes, until San Diego closes."

Okay, good, that gets a lot of laughs. I sidestep a question about Amalie and her hockey coverage, explaining how I didn't really know anything about hockey six months ago and I spent most of my time asking her really basic questions like "What the heck is icing?" Aguiar moves on, asking what's on tap now that I've won.

"I think I'm just going to wander around my apartment in a T-shirt, shorts, and a really, really heavy belt."

That seems to appease both DraftKings and the crowd, and the gaggle of models suddenly crowds around, holding the giant $100,000

---

* On my way up to the stage, I asked Kalish, "So does *this* finally get me a sit-down interview with Jason [Robins]?" It did not.

check in front of me as we pose for pictures. Then their thin fingers lift the belt off my shoulder and two of the models fasten it around my waist—I hold up my left hand and jokingly point to my wedding ring as if to say, "Hey, ladies, I'm married, hands off," which the crowd eats up. I'm definitely better at this than Jeter.

Finally, it's time for the signature DFS moment—holding up the big check. I grab it from both sides and hoist it high in the air above my head, as confetti rains down from the ceiling and everyone cheers. God, I hope this doesn't end up in some fucking commercial.

A few painfully ill-advised belly flops in the confetti later, I walk off the stage, belt and check in hand, and it's over. Or, it's just getting started, depending on how you want to look at it.

"Now you get to choose: do you want a night out at a club, or do you want to go to dinner?" Aguiar asks.

That's the easiest decision of my day. I am not a club guy. Extraordinarily expensive sushi, however? Count me in.

There's only one problem, as Aguiar points out—Nobu is closing in less than ten minutes. Whatever. I'm the hockey champ!

"Let's make it happen," I demand, ever the greedy victor.

To his credit, he does. I make good on my promise to take Slewfoot and one of his friends, and Beep, Underjones, Aguiar, Amalie, and I enter Nobu as conquering heroes. Aguiar promptly explains to them that DraftKings just spent a half-million dollars at their hotel, and they would be staying open a little past their usual closing hours tonight.

Within minutes, appetizers arrive, and we're popping the cork on a $350 bottle of Dom Pérignon, just as I'd daydreamed earlier.

"Smells like victory," I say as we clink our glasses.

The plan after dinner is to head up to Float, the rooftop bar, for one final victory celebration. By the time we arrive, the party is in full swing—and the crowd actually applauds when we make our grand entrance. Most everyone is already there—the Slewfoot crew, the basketball pros, all the DraftKings staffers—everyone except Beep, who had headed off to the clubs. I make the rounds, toasting and doing celebratory shots with anyone who asks. But before I descend into a well-earned stupor, there's one piece of important business still outstanding.

I spot Booooourns in the corner of the bar with his wife; he's hard to miss in the white and blue Shattenkirk jersey.

"I'm serious—more so now than ever. I've got to buy that jersey off you. How can we make this happen?"

He is hesitant. So, flush with cash and determined to get my way, I make the proverbial offer he can't refuse.

"I'll tell you what: we'll look up whatever it's worth on the Internet, and whatever price comes up, I'll pay you double."

Amalie shoots me a look that I think means I'm a fool—it's definitely true that I have zero idea what the jersey might be worth. This could get very expensive, very fast. But what's a big check for if not irrational and excessive splurging?

Unsurprisingly, he agrees to my terms, and Amalie googles "Autographed Kevin Shattenkirk jersey" on her phone. The price? Four hundred and fifty dollars.

"Four-fifty. So, nine hundred dollars. Done," I say, shaking his hand. Best money I ever spent, I think, as Booooourns peels the jersey off his back and I put it on mine. For the rest of the night, I roll around San Diego in a comically oversize, autographed hockey jersey and a twenty-pound gold-and-metal belt as we go out in search of Beep, who is clubbing. I need to tell him one more time how appreciative I am. Finally, we catch up with him back at the hotel. In Slewfoot's hotel room, with those guys weighing a wee-hours trip to Tijuana, I wrap my arm around Beep's shoulder and thank him again, for everything. He looks at me like he's going to cry.

We hug, and after one final victorious round of high fives, Amalie drags me back to our room at last, exhausted and desperate for bed. Within minutes, I'm in satisfied oblivion, enjoying the blissful sleep of the wealthy and drunk.

The clock reads 7 a.m. as my eyelids crack open, crusty and gross and weighed down with too much last night on them. The first thing I do is grab for my phone and check my DraftKings account. It's all there, all real—my balance reads $116,000.

I spring into action. I'm not taking any chances that some federal investigation into DraftKings might freeze my assets or, worse, make cash disappear as it did for the online poker players who lost their money on Black Friday. I immediately request a withdrawal of $100,000 and not long after, get an email informing me that withdrawals of that size require a wire transfer. I send DraftKings my bank account information, and to their credit, within three hours the $100,000 is safely in my bank account. My take-home from last night is $70,000—the Dallas lineup ended up in fourteenth place for an extra $4,000—after I pay my three backers, Beep, IHaveAReputation, and Eric.

The rest of the day is spent on a victory tour at the San Diego Zoo—we actually run into Booooooourns there and write him the check for $900—and at another DraftKings-sponsored trip to Nobu, before flying out Monday. I'm sitting at the airport Monday morning with Amalie, Beep, and Timex, waiting on our flights back east, guessing at how much it costs to produce one of those championship belts, when my phone buzzes with a text from Saahil.

"Wow at the NY news," it says.

What New York news?

It doesn't take long to find out. Headlines blaring across the Internet announce a sudden and stunning change in the DFS landscape: FanDuel and DraftKings have both agreed to pull out of New York State. They've reached a settlement with Attorney General Schneiderman.

As part of the settlement, Schneiderman will hold off on pursuing his claims against the two companies; if the New York State legislature passes laws explicitly legalizing DFS by the end of the legislative session in June, then Schneiderman will drop all claims entirely, except those pertaining to false advertising. The sites could return to business in New York before football season.

But if they fail to get a bill passed? They'll be out of New York, probably for good, and will face a legal battle that they clearly believe is going to be a loser—or else why take the deal? They're pinning all their hopes on the New York legislature. What happens next will be Daily Fantasy's biggest and most important battle yet, with its future more uncertain than ever.

Why does this stuff always happen in airports?

13

The New York State Capitol building in Albany sits at the top of a long, sloping hill overlooking the Hudson River, not far from where Henry Hudson himself first made landfall when he and the crew of his ship, the *Half Moon,* arrived here in 1609.

The building itself cost more than the U.S. Capitol in Washington, and it presides over the city like a fortress. Inside are exhibits detailing the history of New York State, including a Hall of Governors touting the accomplishments of famous statesmen like Martin Van Buren, Theodore Roosevelt, and Franklin Roosevelt.

Imagine trying to explain to those men that Daily Fantasy Sports would take over their state capitol building in June 2016.

Yet that's exactly what's playing out, as the fate of DFS will be decided in the halls and back rooms of this impressive edifice. The companies need to get a bill passed in the state legislature to legalize DFS in New York so they can return to business in their most important state. A powerful array of special interest groups is lining up to stop them. It will all come down to a few days in June.

A lot has changed in the three months since I'd won the hockey final and the companies had agreed to pull out of New York—both for me, and for the industry. After a post-finals swoon where I blew about $10,000 in a week of awful lineups (Beep assured me this was normal), I roared back with a string of wins through the end of the hockey season and into the playoffs, well exceeding my previous highs. When baseball started up in early April, I began attacking that hard, as well. Unlike the previous season, when I was a baseball-writing expert but a DFS newbie, now I was a winning player almost from the start. Understanding at last that stacking and correlating tournament lineups are the way to go, I built smart stacks, emphasized pitching, and cashed in. While I didn't make nearly as much as I had playing hockey, I notched several $3,000–$5,000 wins, culminating in my turning $200 in qualifier entries into a spot in FanDuel's eighty-seat Playboy Mansion Baseball Final in June. That seat was worth $13,000, and the final had a top prize of $100,000, just like the hockey final. After flying out to Los Angeles in early June, I was dreaming big, and I built a long-shot, hypercontrarian Tampa Bay Rays–Washington Nationals stack that was destined to end up either near first or near last. As my friend Eric and I toured the mansion zoo, the grotto, and the bar like pros—Miss August 2015 Dominique Jane complimented my Felix the Thundercat shirt!—my lineup sputtered and sank, placing 73rd out of 80. I blame Hef.

All the while, I was experimenting with new methods. With Beep's help, I built a rudimentary projection system in Microsoft Excel, one that allowed me to predict daily lineup value before moving on to more precise analysis. I felt like Luke Skywalker in *Return of the Jedi*, when Darth Vader notes that, now that Luke has built his own lightsaber, his training is finally complete; to me, building that system was the final step to becoming a DFS Jedi. It was so basic, however, that I never really used it after building it, going back to making my assessments by hand.

And with Oreo's assistance, I learned how to multi-enter like the big, high-volume players did, using FantasyCruncher's tools to submit hundreds of lineups at once, adjusting the percentages of players I wanted used and letting it spit out all the combinations for me. I had a little bit of success doing this, but honestly, it felt dirty, and not at all fun—like using brute strength instead of finesse and skill to win. After a few days, I'd stopped completely, and never went back to it.

I'd been doing so well, I'd even had to contact a fantasy sports tax specialist, Patrick Guinan out of Philadelphia. I knew I owed the IRS massive amounts on my winnings, yet keeping track of it all was near impossible, as the companies don't send your tax forms until the calendar year is over. I arranged to send some estimated tax payments, in the hopes that the excellent, kind, wonderful, intelligent, well-dressed, and strikingly attractive people at the Internal Revenue Service wouldn't audit me. I crossed my fingers that those fine, fair souls would understand that I did my absolute best to be as honest and exact as possible.

Yet despite the successes, despite now being a finalist in two sports, ever since the hockey final it felt like a certain fatigue was setting in. DFS was taking a toll on me—on my life, on my stress level. The constant sweats were wearing me down. I'd been at this for more than a year now, playing almost every day at some level on some site, from the big two to Yahoo! or FantasyAces. Whether or not my dopamine receptors were burned out, they sure felt like it.

More than that, I just wasn't enjoying it in the same way anymore. To really be any good, it takes four, five, six hours a day, time I initially had enjoyed putting in. But a year later, those hours had started to feel a lot less like research in pursuit of a goal, and a lot more like a regular job. Maybe it was that I wasn't as good at baseball as I'd been at hockey, or simply that the newness had worn off. But the same fire to be great was no longer there.

At the industry level, DFS was experiencing the same kind of lows and highs over these past few months.

They had suffered through a revolt by the small businesses of fantasy sports, who, frustrated by the dominance of FanDuel and DraftKings, broke off from the FSTA to form their own trade association. This new Small Business Fantasy Sports Trade Association (SBFSTA) fought for the small companies and the season-long operators, those who felt like FanDuel and DraftKings had conducted a hostile takeover of their industry.

"They made a conscious effort to say that DFS is fantasy sports, and fantasy sports is DFS, and that didn't sit well with us," SBFSTA founder Alex Kaganovsky told me. He was ticked for many of the same reasons fantasy original Ron Shandler was—the FSTA and the DFS companies had used season-long fantasy as a shield in their campaign to legalize DFS, and now the little guys were rebelling, actively fighting bills that didn't include provisions to protect the smaller businesses.

There were other issues and setbacks. Both companies had stopped offering college sports DFS entirely at the request of the NCAA, and new regulations setting the minimum user age to twenty-one in Massachusetts cost them valuable college-aged customers there. Groups of sharks were already coming up with ways to fight the new regulations and circumvent entry limits, creating syndicates where multiple users work in tandem, splitting entry fees and pots. They had also pulled out of a few more small states—Hawaii and Idaho—bringing FanDuel's total to eleven no-play states, DraftKings' to ten. At the same time, a push by both companies to expand into the United Kingdom met with a decidedly lukewarm response, with bet-happy Brits simply not that interested in learning this new game. And efforts to pass legislation in some very important states—Illinois, for instance—had failed. The Illinois bill appeared to be moving well, until concerted opposition from casino companies Rush Street Gaming and the Rivers Casino, among others, derailed it—combined with a mini-scandal where members of the Illinois Black Caucus accused a DFS lobbyist of offering to trade donations for guarantees of votes. The Illinois DFS bill died days later.

Still, against all odds, the industry had regained some of its earlier momentum. After throwing millions of dollars at lobbyists across the country, the companies were coming back from the legal brink. They managed to get bills specifically legalizing DFS passed in six states—Virginia, Indiana, Tennessee, Missouri, Colorado, and Mississippi. Daily Fantasy had embraced regulation with gusto, both to avoid further legal trouble and as a means of restoring faith in the damaged industry.

"One of the things that can establish trust is that once regulators go in, and really look deep down into what we're doing, they're going to find exactly what we've been saying: this is a fun game, this is a fair game," DraftKings cofounder Paul Liberman says. "That's going to bring back trust better than we could bring it back ourselves. All these states have looked at it and made it a fair and regulated market. That's the net positive of all of this. Look at stocks—who would ever invest in stocks if the SEC wasn't regulating the shit out of it? You don't have any insight into what goes on. The only reason the stock market exists is that the SEC exists. And now we're creating that type of environment for the long term."

With their feet held to the fire for months now, both companies were making positive, proactive changes to balance the lopsided ecosystem. DraftKings built a Game Integrity and Ethics Team to seek out and quash unethical play, and actually proved it had teeth by going after players suspected of colluding to circumvent the new entry limits. FanDuel says they've banned or suspended hundreds of accounts for similar reasons. FanDuel was rebranding almost entirely, changing its focus to make its product about the fun of the games and not the money involved; the company was also creating a "bill of rights" to protect players and seemed to be genuinely trying to rebuild trust. Both companies introduced new products that are clear hybrids of daily and season-long leagues, and both companies added experience badges to identify sharks to new players—though those served only to identify who the new fish really are, as the limits for experience are low enough that almost everyone gets a high-level badge.*

More important, they thumbed their nose at the most powerful body in the land, and survived. The long-awaited congressional hearings on DFS were scheduled for mid-May in front of the U.S. House Subcommittee on Commerce, Manufacturing and Trade, which called both companies to appear. Instead, both DFS companies spurned Congress, telling the FSTA to speak in their place. Incredibly, it didn't matter; the hearing turned out to be a wholly ineffectual event, as members of Con-

---

* Any system where Saahil and I have the same-level badge probably needs a little work.

gress showed they hardly knew what DFS was, to say nothing of showing any desire to shut it down. I flew down expecting fireworks, but
the hearing was little more than an opportunity for proponents of fully
legalizing sports gambling, led by New Jersey congressman Frank Pallone, to air their opinions on gambling expansion. Ethan Haskell hardly
merited a mention.

But all this is ancillary to what really matters for DFS: New York.
When the companies agreed with Attorney General Schneiderman to
cease operations in New York in March, it was in the hope that the state
legislature would pass a bill to explicitly legalize DFS in the next few
months. If they got that, they could return to business in the state by
football season. If they didn't, they'd be in a world of trouble.

New York is, for so, so many reasons, the most important state for
DFS. It's the second-largest market behind California, with a half-million
DFS players, and also the most public battleground, after Schneider
man's aggressive campaign against the game's very existence in the fall.
It's the home of FanDuel, and of the sports leagues—the NBA, MLB,
and NHL—that had partnered with these companies. MLB execs had
made some pointed comments about wanting to see the results of DFS
legislation efforts in the state before resolving whether to continue their
engagement with DFS. It sounded a lot like baseball might pull out of its
deal with DraftKings if New York decided not to legalize Daily Fantasy.

More than that, other states with similar laws look at New York as the
trendsetter. Whatever New York decides to do will set the tone, as Eccles
explained to me in the early days of June. If the companies can't get DFS
back in New York this year, the effects could be catastrophic.

"There's a revenue impact, but much more important is the direction
of travel impact," Eccles said. "Other states would go, okay, New York
was the one who was most aggressive—if they are now willing to pass a
law, we should go in that direction. Also, financial institutions are here.
Payment processors are here, the leagues are here. New York matters."

For those reasons, I'd started following the legislative process in New
York in early April. The sides were already beginning to take shape: the

FSTA, DraftKings, FanDuel, and their hired-gun lobbyists would push hard to get the bills passed, while parts of the New York casino industry would likely come out in opposition.

To get the lay of the land, I contacted Long Island assemblyman Dean Murray, an outspoken supporter of DFS—and recreational player—who had introduced a bill to legalize DFS back in the fall, when Schneiderman first began his attacks on FanDuel and DraftKings. Murray became a household name in DFS circles after a mildly infamous twenty-minute on-air debate with New York radio host Mike Francesca over the difference between the layman's definition of gambling—where DFS certainly qualifies—and the legal definition of gambling, where it may not. Murray is a charismatic former radio reporter who now owns a Long Island advertising agency, and the fifty-one-year-old Republican resented Schneiderman's attempts to crack down on what he saw as a fun and relatively harmless pastime. He wanted to make it legal. But while the issue was tied up in the courts, the legislature was largely sidelined. Once the companies agreed to cease operations in New York, it became a legislative issue once again.

"When the AG, FanDuel, DraftKings, and then Yahoo! made the agreement that they would cease operations for now, that threw the ball into our court completely, and that's when we said, okay, let's do this now. And I think we're very close, to be honest with you. I think it's going to get done," Murray told me in mid-April.

But in the nearly two months since, little progress had been made. Several different DFS bills had been introduced, but the New York State Senate and Assembly hadn't been able to reach a compromise on their differing versions, to say nothing of Governor Andrew Cuomo. And powerful interests were now marshaling in opposition.

One of the state's most connected and influential groups had come out strongly against the DFS bills: the New York Gaming Association (NYGA), a coalition of nine "racinos"—horse racing tracks that offer video slot machines and electronic versions of blackjack and poker. One of them, the Empire City Casino at Yonkers Raceway, was near where I grew up. Even though my buddies and I loved real casinos, we never went to these. They're an odd mix between old-time racetrack and modern casino, but they lack even the seamy, tired glamour of Connecticut's Foxwoods or Mohegan Sun; something about piles of used horse-betting slips and the impersonality of video blackjack confers a second-class citizenry that is hard to overcome. The racinos are hopeful that someday, New York State will fully legalize gambling, and they'll be in perfect position to cash in, building themselves into local versions of those Connecticut full-service palaces. Until then, they support anything that expands gambling for brick-and-mortar casino operations in New York and oppose anything that threatens it by existing outside the casino structure—DFS, for instance.

The NYGA insisted that DFS be tied to brick-and-mortar casinos, which they knew to be a poison pill from the start; offering DFS through a casino, on-site only, runs counter to the entire tech-heavy structure of what DraftKings and FanDuel had developed. The DFS companies could never, and would never, accept it.

"The industry believes [fantasy sports] is another form of gambling," NYGA president James Featherstonhaugh told the *Buffalo News* in early June. "If it's going to be done successfully—provide employment and support education [funding]—you need to have a limited number of facilities and a high tax rate."

All that uncertainty left everyone's eyes on Albany as the state legislature entered the final week of its legislative year. The session was scheduled to end at midnight on June 16. If the legislature passed a bill legalizing DFS by that date, the companies would return to business in New York soon after. If they failed, there would be dramatic fallout that would reshape—and could potentially destroy—the entire industry.

Some of that was on display early in the week, at the FSTA's Summer Conference in Times Square, held in mid-June, right smack in the banned DFS state of New York. This was the companion to the conference I had attended in the winter in Dallas, where Mark Cuban had spoken and proclaimed that DFS was going to survive and then grow. There were no such proclamations here. Only bad news.

Days before the conference, Eccles had warned state officials that if New York didn't approve DFS, his New York–based company would have no choice but to move its headquarters elsewhere. Clearly politicking, but also probably true. But it was the news that broke in the first minutes of the FSTA conference that really ramped up interest, and concern, over DFS: that FanDuel and DraftKings were in merger talks. Now, unlike many others at FSTA, I knew that the companies had discussed mergers before, starting in the winter of 2014–15, but the terms had never been right. FanDuel wanted it to be an acquisition, DraftKings wanted to be a (relatively) equal partner in a merger. Both said no.

But since then, everything has changed, and a merger makes sense now, in a way it never had before.

DraftKings had grown to equal FanDuel in size. Legal and regulatory fees are crushing the two companies, no one wants another advertising war, and both companies are hurting for available cash, thanks to their significant commitments. At the same time, working together on legal and regulatory efforts has fostered a new era of detente between the two DFS powers, and in that environment, the subject of a merger arose again. In March 2016, while in Richmond, Virginia, to witness the first major DFS bill being signed into law, Eccles and Robins met and began to seriously discuss the possibility. Later, Eccles traveled to Boston, sat down with Robins and his team, and the two realized that they and their companies had more in common than they'd thought, if only the two executives could put aside their past differences. A true thaw began, and the founders and their companies began to see each other as embattled brothers, rather than mortal enemies.

I spot Eccles at the conference, and he sidesteps my questions on the merger chances, while making it clear that yes, a merger is a real possibility in the not-too-distant future. I hear that the question of who would actually run a joint company, to say nothing of what it would be called, hadn't been dealt with, and for now, nothing immediate comes of the talks.

Meanwhile, up in Albany, things are starting to move. On Tuesday, June 14, former NFL quarterbacks Jim Kelly and Vinny Testaverde are on hand at the state capitol, pressing the flesh with legislators as paid boosters for fantasy sports. The starstruck legislators fawned over them, posing for pictures. I can't know if that made a difference, but the next day, as I pack up to get on the road to Albany, news comes down that the governor is on board with the final version of a DFS bill; once DFS revenues were earmarked for education, Governor Cuomo's office agreed to back it.

They still have to get it past the casino opposition, which is firming up. But I've got more important things to think about as I drive up to Albany—like, how to enter my lineups? Being stranded in New York for several days, I'd been DFS-free, and actually had started to miss it. Some of the pros would do whatever it took to enter their lineups—JeffElJefe had been taking an Uber across the Hudson River to Hoboken and entering his teams from a New Jersey coffee shop. I wasn't quite willing to go that far, but since I'm on the road now anyway . . . I plot a course that will take me through the tiniest sliver of Greenwich, Connecticut, on the way north. Once I see the "Welcome to Connecticut" sign, I pull into the first (very impressive) driveway I find, enter $600 worth of lineups, and am back on the road to Albany before the butler knew I did it.

Hours later, I see Albany rising out of the Hudson Valley with an impressiveness that belies its size, boasting the skyline of a much larger city, thanks to all that state government money. At the ground level, it's somewhat less impressive. It's got all the bleakness of Hartford, yet none of the charm of Providence, placing it somewhere toward the bottom of the northeastern state capitals rankings.

But it does have that Capitol. As I park my car on State Street, the broad old Mohawk trail that leads up to the Capitol itself, I take in the grand old structure. Majestic places like these have always captivated me. They are focal points, places where people come to change their worlds. Perhaps we'll see the fate of DFS decided inside those walls in the next few days. But time is getting short. There's only thirty-six hours left until the end of the legislative session, unless the legislature votes to extend the deadline. Passing through the metal detectors, I climb up the Great Western Staircase toward the Assembly chambers, where the body is in session, legislators tackling the many outstanding bills on the docket before DFS. There's an ethics reform package, a drug bill, a bill changing Airbnb regulations—I have no idea when DFS itself is going to come up, if ever.

Fortunately, I know a few people in the building. Standing outside the house chambers is a small army of DFS lobbyists, waiting to corral legislators on their way in and out of the chambers. The lobbyists will take any chance to get some face time, enabling them to argue for their bill and explain why DFS should be legal.

Among them is Derek Hein, a friendly (I guess they have to be?) DraftKings lobbyist I'd met at the FSTA's winter conference. Since then the midwesterner has been flying to and fro working on DFS legislative efforts, claiming successes in Colorado, Missouri, Tennessee, and Indiana. His track record led DraftKings to call him in for this last push. He gives me an update—the bill is looking good, and they'd made dramatic strides that day, but the casinos are fighting this hard, and it's going to be a race against the clock to bring it to the floor for a vote before the session ends.

"I think we're getting there. The big thing was putting the money towards education. That swung a lot of people. Now we've just got to get it to a vote," Hein says as he brings me over to an alcove outside the Assembly chambers, where lobbyists and media congregate to wait for legislators to emerge.

I sit down with the DFS lobbyists, who are going over lists of legislators, trying to check off which ones they've talked to, who still needs some cajoling, who is proving intractable.

Peering out onto the Assembly floor, I see pro-DFS assemblyman Murray sitting at his desk looking rather bored as his colleagues drone on about some bill or another. I shoot him a text to see if he'll come out to chat a bit, and before long, he bounds through the door.

"Hey, the hockey king!" he says, eagerly shaking my hand. Murray is cue-ball bald, with big ears, glasses, and a wide smile. Murray catches me up on the latest, saying that now that the governor is on board, things should move along.

Murray figures that the reason Governor Cuomo is backing the bill, even though he's a Democrat, is that Cuomo is looking to stymie Schneiderman, who has been making noises about challenging Cuomo in the 2018 gubernatorial primary. Fighting DFS was Schneiderman's crusade; thwarting that, and bringing the games back to New York, could be a nice feather in Cuomo's cap, Murray muses.

"It makes him look good," Murray says. "But also, with all the rumors about Schneiderman challenging him, this is his way to stick it to Schneiderman—he can say to the three million New Yorkers who play this, 'Hey, who wanted to take it away, and who wanted to keep it here? Oh, and by the way, I just got us a few million dollars for education.'"

At this point, Murray says, the biggest issue is needing to wait out a seventy-two-hour period from the time the latest DFS bill was introduced on Monday, before it can be taken up on the floor. Since it's only Wednesday now, that means DFS won't be heard until either after midnight Thursday, or on Friday if the legislature chooses to stay in session another day.

"So I should get a hotel room for Thursday night, too, is what you're saying," I groan.

He grins, and nods. I frown.

Every news reporter worth their salt wants to say they've covered a statehouse. News reporters traditionally came up through the ranks, covering town politics, then city, then usually state. Those heavy hitters you see on TV or in the biggest national publications covering the White House almost always traveled this route, though changes in media have started to undo that path in recent years. Now reporters come up through the campaign trail, covering the fight of politics and not the process of legislation.

I was never a full-time statehouse reporter, but I spent enough time in them during my stints at the *Providence Journal* and *Boston Globe*. The one thing I'd been around state government enough to know? It's boring. Mind-numbingly so. Albany proves no different. The legislature is moving slowly, in a way that insults traditional icons of plodding like tortoises and molasses.

So slowly, in fact, that it becomes a foregone conclusion that the legislature will need to return on Friday for another full day of sessions. In the meantime, lobbyists on both sides have been working the DFS issue hard; it's one of the perhaps three most contentious outstanding subjects in Albany, and both sides are claiming progress. It's becoming clear that in the lower house, the Assembly, where Murray and Mount Vernon Democrat J. Gary Pretlow operate, DFS is going to pass by a wide margin. The problem is in the Senate, where rumors are circulating that DFS might not even make it to the floor for a vote before the Senate adjourns, regardless of what happens in the Assembly.

"What's the difference between the two houses? Why would it be so good in one and so weak in the other?" I ask Griffin Finan, DraftKings' top on-staff lobbyist.

"The lobbyists they hired are better over there," Finan says with a shrug.

Meanwhile, DraftKings and FanDuel are doing everything they can to pressure legislators. Through their get-out-the-vote proxy organization "Fantasy Sports for All," the companies set a goal of getting more than one hundred thousand calls and emails to New York legislators before a vote takes place. By midday Friday, they're within range of that number, overwhelming legislators who can't understand how such a seemingly niche activity could generate so much attention.

One caller tells Representative John Ceretto's office, "Don't come home if you don't pass this," the stunned Niagara Falls Democrat reports.

The companies are also targeting their casino opponents, trying to pick off weak links. One of the staunchest New York DFS opponents is Batavia Downs, a racino in rural western New York. While I'm sitting on the Capitol steps, an odd email announcement arrives from FanDuel, trumpeting a deal to host future events at . . . Batavia Downs. Huh? It turns out that FanDuel reached a $300,000 marketing agreement with Batavia, and that caused the racino to switch sides and support the DFS bill, according to ESPN. I can't wait for the 2019 FanDuel Fantasy Baseball final, live from scenic Batavia, New York.

All that momentum and those backroom dealings help push DFS to the Assembly floor, and after two-plus days of wandering the halls and skimming exhibits about the long and storied history of the state of New York, I sit down at 2 p.m. Friday, among throngs of lobbyists and media, as they call the DFS bill at last.

Pretlow, chairman of the Assembly's racing and wagering committee and a DFS backer, stands first to introduce the bill, explaining that they've circumvented New York's restrictive prohibitions on gambling expansion by adding language stipulating that DFS is a game of skill.

"We came to the conclusion that fantasy sports is not gambling," Pretlow says.

But just as that hasn't passed the smell test with the general public, it isn't good enough for a number of legislators, who rise to speak against the bill.

First and loudest is a mad-scientist-looking older man with round glasses, a brown mustache, and poofy white hair flying in all directions. First name Andy, last name Goodell. Yes, that Goodell. The NFL commissioner's dorky cousin, a western New York legislator, comes out strongly opposed to DFS.

"In my mind this is clearly gambling. It's sports gambling," Goodell says, making the easy comparison to poker. "There's certainly a high degree of skill in poker, and we all agree that's gambling."

Goodell, a lawyer, has done his homework. He recognizes that the political will to pass DFS exists; yet he raises real issues as to whether the legislature can unilaterally legalize it without a constitutional amendment—any expansion of gambling, he says, skill or not, requires a change at that level, which could mean a long, drawn-out referendum process that could take years.

"The [state] constitution doesn't say gambling that has a bit of skill, it says any kind of gambling," Goodell says.

Pretlow argues that because the legislature defines DFS as specifically not gambling, it means it isn't subject to those constitutional provisions. That may not eventually be enough to appease the courts, but for now it lets the floor debate proceed.

That brings Murray up to defend his beloved pastime, and with legions of DFSers watching and cheering him on via Twitter, Murray delivers an impassioned defense of the bill and of DFS in general. Responding to the casinos' fears that allowing DFS would cost brick-and-mortar gambling jobs, Murray shoots back, "People have been playing fantasy sports for ten years. This only came up when the commercials started running."

And as to the gambling comparisons, he offers this: "In my opinion, DFS is nothing more than day trading for sports fans."

That inspires other lawmakers to get out of their seats and defend day traders as distinct from recreational bettors, and the back-and-forth continues. It's notable, really, for how lightheartedly everyone is approaching this debate. After months of hearing Schneiderman and Company rip DFS as a grand criminal conspiracy, the New York legislators seem to treat the whole issue like a lark. Every other line is a reference to a fumble, a Hail Mary, a touchdown—all prompting chuckles from both sides of the aisle.

"I would argue there's a flag on the play," quips Long Island representative Mike Fitzpatrick as he rises to speak in opposition. After the pols spent the previous two hours talking about the impact of heroin addiction on New Yorkers, who could blame them for having a little fun? Or perhaps it's the predetermined nature of these deliberations that lends it such levity. Everyone knows it's going to pass. Even though Pret-

low and Murray are nearly alone in their vocal support of the bill, and
the majority of speakers have come out strongly against it—including
one woman who proclaims DFS "totally chance"—the bill sails through,
passing 91–22, green Y's lighting up the voting board in the chamber
like DraftKings winning numbers. The lobbyists, DFS players, and companies exult, everyone shaking hands and slapping backs. Yet this was
the easy one; the Senate was always going to be the harder route, and
there is no indication that Republican leadership has even taken up the
bill in private yet. The clock is running, and there's still a long way to go.

————————

With time to kill, I sit on a stairwell underneath the portrait of founding father George Clinton, the state's first chief executive, in the Hall
of Governors. It's been hours since there's been any news. Republican
leadership has been conferencing in private, leaving us to wait out in
the halls and wonder what's going on inside, the odds of DFS surviving
falling with every passing minute.

At last, just after 9 p.m., the Republican meeting breaks up. John
Bonacic, the Senate Republican guiding the bill along, emerges and
promises that he has the votes to pass the bill. Digging a little deeper, I
learn that he had taken the rare step of crossing the aisle, appealing to
Senate Democrats, and the bipartisan coalition he's built should mean
enough votes to ensure a majority for DFS. The way things work in Albany, legislators almost never bring a bill up for a floor vote if they don't
believe it's going to pass; they think it shows that the majority is weak.
This rare show of Republican-Democrat cooperation means that DFS
is now going to come to the floor, so ipso facto, DFS is going to pass. It
still has to be brought out of the Rules Committee for the actual vote,
but as Friday night wears on and midnight nears, the signs are all good.
The session can go past midnight if needed—DFS just needs to pass by
the time the Senate closes tonight. Theoretically, this means sometime
before dawn.

It's early Saturday, 12:04 a.m., by the time the Rules Committee moves the bill forward. As the Senate reconvenes at last, observers—and there are a surprising number of them, even after midnight—stream into the galleries to see what the Senate will do with DFS and the few other straggler bills still remaining on the agenda.

I settle into my seat, overlooking the semicircle of senatorial desks on the floor below. It has the same basic look as the U.S. Congress, just smaller and more informal. A few senators I recognize are walking about, including the bill's sponsor, Bonacic. At seventy-four, he probably should be in bed by now. Instead, the bronzed, swaggering senator, who represents part of Orange County, works the room in a tan suit complemented by an orange tie and matching pocket square. It makes me want a Creamsicle.

Immediately to my left are the double-digit members of the casino lobby. Their leader, NYGA president James Featherstonhaugh, sits in the second row of the gallery, arms crossed. He doesn't look altogether unhappy as the Senate president bangs the gavel and resumes the session. He actually seems a little pleased, quietly smug. I would have thought that someone who was about to lose such a massive campaign would look a little more . . . ticked off? Maybe I'm reading too much into it.

The session begins, with the clerk reading off a series of inconsequential bills. Murray and Pretlow have come over from the Assembly and are standing on the Senate floor. That must be a good sign. Hopefully it'll all finish up soon.

I glance over at the casino lobbyists, and they're still sitting quietly. Wait, are they still all there? It looks like some of them have left. The group seems smaller now. Then, no mistaking it, a few more rise quietly and stride purposefully out of the room. Others begin checking their phones. Maybe something is up? But no, the Senate is proceeding as normal.

Until it isn't.

Republican deputy majority leader John DeFrancisco suddenly rises and asks for a recess. A recess? They've only been in session for ten minutes! What the hell? The senators themselves look confused. Scanning the room, I see Bonacic, Pretlow, and Murray all disappear into the back areas, followed by members of the Democratic leadership. Something is wrong.

Almost on cue, my phone buzzes. It's a text from Cal.

"It's in trouble," it reads.

I shoot out a few texts of my own and hear much the same, but I can't get details. I venture out into the halls, trying to see any faces I recognize. I hear that Pretlow was spotted down the hallway in a heated debate with a few members of the casino lobbying gang.

Contacting sources, I'm told that the casino lobby promised something—I still don't know what—and it prompted a group of Democrats to pull their votes. The DFS majority is gone. And without a guaranteed majority, it isn't even going to come to the floor.

The bill is dying.

Heading back inside the Senate chambers, I see some of the DFS lobbyists and ask what's happening. They shrug meekly, saying only that we'll see. Bonacic and Murray are nowhere to be found, and the clock is now nearing 1 a.m. The regular reporters covering the Capitol tweet that the delay has something to do with DFS, but it's impossible to tell what.

Slumping in my seat, I tap my foot incessantly as the minutes tick away. The Assembly has been at ease for close to an hour and shows no signs of returning. Texts keep popping in from DFS players around the country, asking if I know what's going on—they're all live-streaming the hearing, close to four hundred of them, in what is either a victory for civic government or a testament to the obsessive nature of gamblers. Even Amalie texts to tell me she's watching the live feed. I have nothing to offer any of them.

Then, gradually, legislators begin to trickle, and then stream, back into the chambers. Bonacic and Murray reappear downstairs. With 1:30 a.m. nearing, the legislature has come back to life. But to what end?

The gavel bangs, restarting the session. DFS is still on the docket, though only after a mind-numbing procession of hotel tax bills can be addressed. One vote, another vote, everyone fidgeting in their seats as these boring procedural bills are dealt with.

After another excruciating half hour, the clerk calls the bill at last, S8153. Everyone leans forward in their seats, legislators and lobbyists and observers all, as Bonacic straightens himself up to speak in favor of the bill.

"Football season is around the corner," Bonacic says, and they need to get a bill passed now. The bill, he promises, represents "a three-way agreement with both houses and the governor."

Well, it had at one point, I knew that. But is that agreement still binding?

He is brief—it's late, now after 2 a.m., and everyone wants to move fast. Only one person rises to speak in opposition: Democrat Liz Krueger. She's well known as a vocal opponent of gambling—and a colorful one. When an online poker bill came before the Senate earlier in the session, the veteran Manhattan legislator decried it as creating "junkies on our computers" and turning players into "living zombies."

Apparently she burned her best material in the poker fight, because at 2:10 a.m. Saturday, all she can muster is a tribute to everyone's favorite waterfowl.

"If it walks like a duck, swims like a duck, and quacks like a duck, it's a duck," she says. "This is just another gambling bill."

Her point made, she sits, and the clerk calls the roll.

I hold my breath. This is it. New York, and the future of DFS, all come down to this moment. I've been through some serious sweats this past year, but never anything like this.

After what seems like an eternity passes in silence, the clerk speaks again.

"Forty-five in favor, seventeen opposed. The bill passes," he says.

Daily Fantasy Sports is coming back to New York.

Everyone looks around, in shock. The casino lobbyists immediately stand and exit en masse. I see Murray slide through the back door of the chambers. The Senate immediately moves on to other business.

I rush to gather my belongings and pack up, hoping to find people to explain what the hell just happened.

I'm later told that what unfolded that night was politics, in its purest form. After the casino lobbyists had made their big promise and turned that group of Democratic votes, it was clear that the DFS supporters didn't have enough backing to pass the bill. A few Republicans with casinos in their district were always going to vote against it. And a few others disagreed on moral—that is, this is straight gambling—grounds. So the Republicans had enough votes to merit bringing it to the floor for debate, but not enough to ensure passage once there. Usually that means a dead bill, because Republican leadership doesn't want to look weak by bringing up bills that don't eventually pass.

But Bonacic, Murray, et al made the argument that with the session ending, there's virtually no business left for the Republicans to look weak on. They demanded that the bill be brought to the floor, majority or no, and put before a full vote. If the Democrats wanted to vote the bill down, they could. But before they did, they were all reminded that one very important date falls smack in the middle of football season: Election Day.

The legislature was already blown away by the level of response the DFS issue had generated. If the DFS Republicans had to, they would make sure that every senator who voted against the bill would have that issue brought up every day of football season, through Election Day. New York's three million fantasy players and half-million DFS players would be constantly reminded who had gone against them. So vote against it if you want, they were told—but remember that nothing happens in a vacuum.

And with that, they took it to the floor.

On my way out of the building, I track down Dean Murray, who had returned to the Assembly side to continue working even at this late hour. He's elated over the passage of the bill, and also seemingly exhausted. The DFS battle will go down as one of the toughest, if not the toughest, of his time in the legislature.

"This was the hardest I've ever seen lobbyists fight against something, since I've been here—and I've been through the gay marriage vote," Murray says.

Around the DFS world, the celebration is already under way. As I throw my stuff into the backseat of my Audi A5 and head off into the night on my way back to Boston, I see on my phone that FanDuel and DraftKings have already released triumphant statements touting their victory. Cal texts me a picture of the round of celebratory shots he and the RotoGrinders crew are about to take in Nashville. Twitter is alive with GIFs and Crying Jordan faces put onto DFS enemies like Schneiderman and Liz Krueger. When ESPN's David Purdum and I talk about the ramifications later, he sums it up with aplomb: "I think the New York decision was the most important, impactful, influential ruling that the fantasy sports industry has ever received."

DFS is still not out of the woods. There will almost certainly be legal challenges to this law and probably several others nationwide, by foes in the entrenched casino industry and beyond. Other states will still probably fall away, though they'll get a few others back. California is in flux, Illinois is in the courts, and who knows if these new regulations even comply with federal law? Merger talk continues to percolate, and I doubt this victory will do anything to change that. Still, with New York solidified, DFS will probably continue to grow, slowly, but consistently. I can't see the industry ever regaining the momentum it had before the 2015 football season—partially because that market was overheated, but more so because in its desperate hunger for growth and expansion, it lost the trust factor, the newness factor, the "anyone can win" excitement of an unexplored venture. DFS will never be viewed the way it was before Haskell, when the whole thing seemed like a crazy, fun, uncharted enterprise that really would let average fans leverage their sports knowledge into a little walking-around money.

That said, it's in a far, far better place than it was when I first discovered it. The measures the companies have taken—under pressure, to be sure—to level the playing field are good ones, and I believe they're working, both to reestablish that trust and to dull the edge enjoyed by the best players. There will be more improvements made now that the companies realize they're on notice. For the long-term survival of DFS, if not for the companies' coffers, all this scrutiny has been a good thing. Shine a little light, expose what needs to be changed. Move forward.

Maybe it's Stockholm syndrome, but it's remarkable how my view of the pros has changed over time. I don't think most are bad guys. Sharks, yes. But basically smart kids who have found a way to make either their math knowledge or their sports knowledge, or both, pay off. There are a few true weirdos, and a few bad apples who really are predatory, or cheaters. But most aren't. They're playing by the rules, leveraging the (too great) advantage the companies gave them. Beep, Underjones, JeffElJefe, Oreo—hell, even Saahil, whom I resented with a passion at the start of this—have all grown on me, a lot.

Yet hurtling through the night toward the Massachusetts border, I can't help but feel tired, worn down, and I don't think it's only from the legislative slog or the hour of the night. To this point, I've entered a total of $244,000 worth of buy-ins across the various sites, with just over $130,000 in pretax profit, about a third of that owed to Beep and my other backers. Is this the time to get out? There's that old gambling saying: Quit while you're ahead. And its partner: The house always wins in the end. Well, there's no house here, but Saahil and crew are probably going to start taking back some of those winnings of mine if I give them too many chances, especially with hockey season so far away. It's probably smart to stop now.

My headlights flash upon a familiar sign: "Welcome to Massachusetts." My adopted home. After a few miles, another placard comes into view, advertising a rest stop in the town of Stockbridge. I turn the wheel and pull into the rest area, with its gas pumps and twenty-four-hour McDonald's. The drive-thru is closed. If I'm going to get enough caffeine to keep me awake for the drive home, I'll need to go inside. The entire place is deserted, save for the one unfortunate counter guy pulling the overnight shift.

"Large fries, please. And a Coke," I tell him.

The fryolator isn't even on, and he has to start it up. So I stand and wait, leaning up against the counter, nothing to do. Well, there is something. I'm in Massachusetts. It's all legal here. And it's a Saturday . . . there are going to be early baseball games. Before I know it, I'm pulling out my phone, opening the DraftKings app, and looking up the afternoon slate. I'm scrolling down to the $300 contest. There are spots available, a good number of them. I feel that familiar excitement coursing through me as my finger hovers over the button to enter the contest.

Maybe it's dumb to keep playing. Maybe it's a sign that I can't let go. But I've worked hard to earn my place in the DFS food chain. And I'm still hungry.

I click "enter," grab my fries, and push open the door into the warm night air. There's a long drive ahead, and I've got lineups to build.

EPILOGUE

On November 18, 2016, DraftKings and FanDuel officially agreed to a deal that had once seemed impossible but now was merely inevitable: a merger.

The rivals, who had only a year earlier been recklessly trying to defeat each other, were now confronted by a depressing truth. They had squandered so much cash, made so many outsized commitments, and gotten themselves in so many legal entanglements that the best way to survive now was to combine.

The warning signs had been there for months. Despite their legislative success in New York, business was poor in the first months of the NFL season. The casual players who had signed up in 2015 during the ad blitz didn't return in 2016, perhaps due to a lack of trust. The New York victory had ensured that DFS would survive. It didn't mean it would suddenly restore public faith in the industry and spur it to grow as it had before the Haskell scandal.

Rumblings surfaced, first in the *New York Times*, that the companies weren't paying their bills, something I confirmed with an employee of one of DraftKings' Boston-area contractors. FanDuel laid off sixty employees, primarily in marketing. Then, in October, both companies reached an agreement with Attorney General Schneiderman's office, paying $6 million each to settle claims of deceptive advertising, and allegations that they targeted individuals "with a propensity for gambling and addiction." A source said they requested to make the payments in installments. It was all a far cry from the days of valuations close to $2 billion.

With that bit of ugly business settled, and cash reserves dwindling, the companies agreed to combine forces, setting aside years of mistrust and hatred in the name of survival. Jason Robins would lead the unified company as CEO, Nigel Eccles would serve as chairman of the board, and the company would be co-headquartered in Boston and New York following a 50/50 merger. Both sites would remain intact, serving customers independently as DraftKings and FanDuel until the merger is final sometime late in 2017. Now that they were one, there would be no need for costly ad campaigns, or wasteful sponsorship deals, or pricey overlay wars. They could combine staff, and shed employees who came on board when all believed DFS was going to expand indefinitely, those sacrificial lambs cast aside as victims of industry-wide hubris.

Together, the combined company will control more than 90 percent of the Daily Fantasy space, a fact sure to bring the attention of federal regulators with antitrust questions. The companies expect to counter that by arguing that they are actually part of the much larger total fantasy market, as they expand their offerings to include more season-long content to supplement their Daily Fantasy core, positioning themselves alongside ESPN and Yahoo!

Regardless, this move promises a way forward for the embattled companies, another step toward that still-faraway goal of consistent profitability, and a path toward IPO rewards for the investors who had put so much into these companies and gotten little return to this point. Eccles and Robins have even buried the hatchet and play nice in public. Robins told Yahoo! that FanDuel deserves all the credit for building DFS, and Eccles responded that perhaps his company should have taken some of the risks that DraftKings took—that "on a lot of occasions, we were pretty wrong for resisting."

Peace, it seems, in our time.

The players, of course, keep grinding through all the merger talk, largely unconcerned by whose name is on the building.

Al_Smizzle's Daily Fantasy Boot Camps didn't survive the scandal-plagued year, closing up shop in 2016. But his status as an elite player certainly did. Smizzle won DraftKings' Week 2 Millionaire Maker contest in September 2016, becoming the first major pro to take down the $1 million first prize. His winning, as a DraftKings-connected-and-sponsored pro, raised questions from Deadspin and others, but the controversy soon blew over. In the style of the original Rotisserie league champions from the inaugural 1980 season, who celebrated their win with Yoo-hoo, Smizzle raised a glass of chocolate milk to toast his victory.

CSURAM got married, after staging an epic bachelor party at the famous Chateau Marmont in Los Angeles. The wedding was lovely, Jonathan Bales said though most of the male attendees were consumed with the real money prop bets they had placed on various outcomes: from whether Peter or his bride would cry, to the number of mentions of Jesus, to the big one, the length of the best man's speech. It ran eight minutes, twenty seconds. Bales guessed too low and lost.

JeffElJefe joined TommyG, as the brash pro started a well-received tout service, FantasyGuruElite.com. That put Jeff in direct competition with his pal DraftCheat, who became a prized voice for another budding tout service, FanVice.

Oreo, worried both that the rush of DFS wasn't enough for him anymore and that the value is disappearing, said he was considering starting a high-end escort service using contacts he made through a new friend—an exotic dancer—believing there may be both excitement and value in the system.

Underjones ditched his office in Hoboken and started working from New York the moment the governor signed the DFS bill into law. After an underwhelming MLB season—perhaps owing to the logistical issues—he got back into the swing of it in NFL, and resumed his winning ways.

Saahil decided he was spending too much time in his apartment, watching DFS. So he rented another apartment in the same building and turned it into an office, with a huge multiscreen command center for watching sports from around the world. Now he "commutes" down several floors each day. Perhaps motivated by my success—if a yutz like me could do it, obviously it isn't that tough—he also jumped into hockey DFS in a major way.

Beep found himself at a crossroads, knowing that he had accomplished much in DFS, but feeling like he was no longer learning and growing, and that he wanted to do something else with his life after five years of constant grinding. Casting about for a new passion, he explored multiple areas, from building his board game to becoming a professional e-sports player to consider running an e-sports team.

John Tomase never went back to playing DFS.

Amalie left her job at the *Boston Globe* and moved to the NHL to write feature stories. With my newly expert hockey knowledge, there was suddenly a lot of hockey talk in our lives. A lot. Not long after the DFS NHL final, Amalie went to St. Louis to cover a Blues-Bruins game. There she met Kevin Shattenkirk himself, and told the defenseman the tale of our mutual connections and how his last-minute assist won me the hockey final. He laughed at the whole thing, before asking the obvious, all-important question: "Where's my cut?" Shattenkirk's framed autographed jersey from the final now hangs in my office.

As for me? I quit DFS cold turkey for the few months from baseball's All-Star break through the beginning of football season. It felt freeing to not have it constantly tugging at me. When NFL season showed up, I hardly noticed, playing on the first week and sporadically thereafter. But when hockey arrived again—well, it was hard to stay away. I found myself looking at the contests. And gazing at the prize pools. And before long, entering.

The first full night of the season, I won the main DraftKings NHL contest, for $10,000. You can't have a problem if you're good, right?

Right?

ACKNOWLEDGMENTS

Newspapering can be a very solitary pursuit: work your sources, produce your story, move on to the next one, with hardly any impact, assistance, or interest from anyone around you. Writing a book proved to be—at least for me—an entirely different experience. *Dueling with Kings* wouldn't have happened without the assistance, understanding, and effort of dozens of people.

My agent, Jane von Mehren of Zachary Shuster Harmsworth, was the first one to believe in me, to tell me that I could actually be an author worthy of writing a book. I also owe her greatly for holding my hand through this process, and remaining calm as our subject matter offered new challenges daily—which I know wasn't easy.

Everyone at Touchstone and at Simon & Schuster believed in this project from the beginning, even when it was clear no one knew where DFS was going. My editor, Matthew Benjamin, trusted me to be able to follow the story and adjust to whatever twists and turns came along the way, and that's a big, big leap. I don't know why they had such faith, but they did, and I'll be forever grateful.

Thanks to all my colleagues at *The Wall Street Journal*, both for their excellent co-workerness over the years, and for supporting this project from the very start, especially Sam Walker, Jason Gay, Brian Costa, Geoff Foster, and my replacement on the Yankee beat, Jared Diamond.

Thanks as well to the AP's Phil Marcelo, who helped me get in touch with some of the people I needed in the DFS world.

A hearty cheers to my friends—and road family—from my two past baseball beats, including but not limited to Mark Feinsand, John Tomase, Bryan Hoch, Ian Browne, Chad Jennings, Wally Matthews, Jason Mastrodonato, and Joe McDonald. Tomase, of course, gets a special thanks for introducing me to this whole crazy thing. And a shout-out to the entire RBP—who probably all saw these hijinks coming decades ago.

My great friend Eric Siwy proved to be both a smart bettor (for backing me) and a surprisingly good editor. Maybe there's a future in that if architecture doesn't work out. Ditto for my mother, Barbara Goodstein; my sister, Rachel Barbarisi; and her husband, John McKenna; and my in-laws, Midge and Ross Benjamin. As trusted readers, all helped me to remember that this can be a very foreign land to those who don't live in it full time, and that means it's smart to err on the side of explaining too much.

In the world of DFS, Jay Raynor, Mike Zheng, Cal Spears, Jeff Collins, Al Zeidenfeld, and Saahil Sud deserve special thanks for letting me into their world, and trusting me with their stories. Jay has become a real friend through this process, and not just because I made him a bunch of money. This book couldn't have happened without him, and because of his curiosity and smarts I know he will be successful in whatever he chooses to do in life.

Finally, the fullest thanks go to my wife, Amalie, without whom this book never would have happened, and for multiple reasons. She is the best partner, editor, rock, supporter, monkey trainer, live final assistant, and yes, character a guy could hope for. In *Dueling with Kings*, I know I failed badly in one respect: I didn't adequately capture how lovely Amalie really is.

GLOSSARY

ACTION: The amount of money a user has in play on a given slate, day, or week.

BANKROLL: The amount of money one has set aside to play DFS.

BUMHUNTING: The practice of targeting inferior players in head-to-head matchups.

BUY-IN: The cost to enter a contest.

CASH GAME: A game type with flat payouts where roughly 50 percent of entrants win; types include double-ups, 50/50s, and head-to-heads.

CHALK: The most obvious, widely selected players on a given slate. (Al_Smizzle's term)

CONTRARIAN: Actively choosing players who one thinks will have low ownership; also, picking players whose outcomes are negatively correlated with the outcomes for highly owned players.

DONKEY: A poor player, one who makes dumb moves.

EXPOSURE: The amount one has invested in a certain player. If one has Peyton Manning in three-quarters of his lineups, he has 75 percent exposure to Manning.

FADE: To avoid picking (and thus root against) a certain player or team.

FISH: A new, inexperienced, or poor DFS player, easily gobbled up by the sharks.

GPP: Guaranteed Prize Pool; a tournament where the site awards the same prize regardless of the number of entrants.

GRINDER: A consistent, regular player, one who grinds out action daily.

HEAD-TO-HEAD: A winner-take-all contest against only one other player.

HEDGE: To reduce upside while reducing risk, as when one sells or swaps action.

LATE SWAP: A feature on DraftKings allowing users to swap out players whose games have not yet begun, even if the first games on the slate have already started. FanDuel does not allow late swaps.

LIVE FINAL: A tournament featuring large prize pools, usually conducted by bringing finalists together for one big sweat.

MULTI-ENTRY: For one user to enter multiple lineups in the same contest.

OVERLAY: The difference between the number of buy-ins in a GPP and the total GPP; the site must pay the difference, and loses money on the contest.

PRO: A professional Daily Fantasy Sports player.

QUALIFIER: A contest where the prize is entry into a larger contest, usually a live final.

RAKE: The percentage the site takes of each entry fee; usually somewhere around 10 percent.

REG: A regular player, but not a pro.

SCRIPT: A purpose-built computer program that offers functionality beyond what the site originally provided, like an add-on that allows a user to alter multiple lineups at once.

SHARK: A high-level player, one always looking for an edge. Sometimes used negatively, sometimes not.

SHARP: Another term for a high-level gambler. A smart player.

SLATE: A set of games grouped together for DFS contest purposes. Slates can be as small as two games, or bigger than fifteen, and cover an afternoon, or multiple days.

STACKING: The strategy of drafting multiple players from the same team into one lineup, to achieve maximum correlation. Useful in tournaments.

SWEAT: To watch your players as they perform, usually in a situation where a big win is realistic.

TILT: To make bad, emotional decisions as a result of negative outcomes in a contest.

TOURNAMENT: A contest with a small number of winners (usually 20 percent) and significant prizes for the top finishers.

TRAIN: The same lineup entered multiple times in a multi-entry contest.

UNREGISTERING: Pulling your lineup out of a contest before it begins, often so as not to get matched against another shark.

WHALE: An extremely heavy-volume player—one who eats up action like baleen. Has a bigger bankroll than a shark, and will take action more freely.

ABOUT THE AUTHOR

Daniel Barbarisi is a longtime sports and news journalist at the *Wall Street Journal*, *Boston Globe*, and *Providence Journal*, and has appeared on hundreds of radio and TV programs over the course of his fifteen year career. Most recently he was on staff at the *Wall Street Journal*, serving as the Yankees beat reporter. He holds an undergraduate degree from Tufts University and a master's degree from Brown University. He and his wife reside in Boston. *Dueling with Kings* is his first book.